London, Radical Culture, and the Making of the Dickensian Aesthetic

London, Radical Culture, and the Making of the Dickensian Aesthetic

∞

Sambudha Sen

The Ohio State University Press / Columbus

Copyright © 2012 by The Ohio State University.
All rights reserved.

Library of Congress Cataloging-in-Publication Data

Sen, Sambudha.
  London, radical culture, and the making of the Dickensian aesthetic / Sambudha Sen.
     p. cm.
  Includes bibliographical references and index.
  ISBN 978-0-8142-1192-2 (cloth : alk. paper)—ISBN 978-0-8142-9293-8 (cd)
  1. English fiction—19th century—History and criticism. 2. Dickens, Charles, 1812–1870—Criticism and interpretation. 3. Thackeray, William Makepeace, 1811–1863—Criticism and interpretation. 4. Literature and society—Great Britain—History—19th century. 5. Radicalism—Great Britain—History—19th century. I. Title.
  PR861.S46 2012
  823'.809—dc23
                          2012007257

Paper (ISBN: 978-0-8142-5685-5)
Cover design by Greg Betza
Text design by Juliet Williams
Type set in Adobe Sabon

CONTENTS

List of Illustrations		vii
Acknowledgments		ix
INTRODUCTION		1
CHAPTER 1	Dickens, Thackeray, and "The Language of Radicalism"	13
CHAPTER 2	The Aesthetics and Politics of Caricature: *Bleak House, Little Dorrit,* and *Vanity Fair* in Relation to "Radical Expression"	36
CHAPTER 3	Re-Visioning the City: The Making of an Urban Aesthetic from Hogarth to the Stereoscope	65
CHAPTER 4	Novelizing the City: *Bleak House, Vanity Fair,* and the Hybridizing Challenge	94
CHAPTER 5	Radical Culture, the City, and the Problem of Selfhood: *Great Expectations* and *Pendennis*	116
CHAPTER 6	Working with Fragments: *Our Mutual Friend* as a Reflection on the Popular Aesthetic	141
Notes		163
Bibliography		177
Index		184

ILLUSTRATIONS

1. George Cruikshank, frontispiece to *The Political House That Jack Built* (1819)   5
2. George Cruikshank, *Coriolanus Addressing the Plebeians* (1820)   28
3. George Cruikshank, from *The Queen's Matrimonial Ladder* (1820)   29
4. William Hogarth, "The Industrious 'Prentice Lord-Mayor of London," Plate 12 of Series *Industry and Idleness* (1747)   69
5. William Hogarth, "The Fellow 'Prentices at their Looms," Plate 1 of Series *Industry and Idleness* (1747)   70
6. William Hogarth, "The Idle 'Prentice Executed at Tyburn," Plate 11 of *Industry and Idleness* (1747)   72
7. William Hogarth, "The Idle 'Prentice at Play in the Church Yard, during Divine Service," Plate 3 of *Industry and Idleness* (1747)   77
8. I. R and G. Cruikshank, frontispiece to Pierce Egan, *Life in London* (1821)   80
9. William Hogarth, *Gin Lane* (1751)   97

ACKNOWLEDGMENTS

THIS BOOK, which is about Charles Dickens and the popular print and visual culture of nineteenth-century Britain, has been written almost entirely in India. My location in Delhi turned out to be very helpful not because it enabled me to sustain some shopworn postcolonial perspective but because it provided a context that helped to explain, in ways London no longer can, some of the central concerns of the Dickensian aesthetic: the fabrication of a language of opposition in a society characterized by deep disparities and the expressive possibilities of an internally fractured cityscape. For their interest in my engagement with these problems, their many illuminating suggestions, and also for their skepticism and the many, quite brilliant jokes that they improvised about "pedagogues" and "mugpots," I want to thank the following Delhiites: Abhibsha Chakraborty, Arotrika Das, Arindam Sengupta, Ashok Bhattacharya, Baidik Bhattacharya, Deabashish Chaterjee, Debolina Dey, Maitrayee Roychoudhury, Nivedita Basu, Prasanta Chakravarty, Shilpi Malhotra, Swagat Sen, and Teja Varma.

I also thank A. N. Kaul, Pradip Datta, Shirshendu Chakrabarti, Sumit Sarkar, Tanika Sarkar, and Udaya Kumar, all of whom were or continue to be associated with the University of Delhi where I work. When I look back on the ten years or more that it took me to write this book, I am struck by how dependent I was, at every stage, on the interest each one of them showed in my work. I am very grateful to them for the many tough, specific questions that they asked and for their willingness to take my project for what it was rather than judge it by the protocols of this or that academic trend. I want to thank A. N. Kaul again for giving me the benefit of his legendary abilities as a teacher and for instilling in me the conviction that has kept me going—that there is no research problem in this world that cannot be confronted with an idea. From the others I learned several general but vital lessons: that, for example, it may be necessary to work with a range of sub- or nonliterary material while attempting to track the genealogy of a literary effect or that the worth of a piece of academic writing may lie not in its display of scholarship but in the power of its explanations. I am particularly grateful to Udaya for the selfless commitment and hard work with which he single-handedly transformed the institutional space where we all work into a site where ideas such as those outlined above could emerge.

A book such as this could never have been written if I had not gained access to material housed in libraries in Britain and the United States. I am extremely grateful to Clare Hall, Cambridge, The Huntington Library, Pasadena, The Rockefeller Foundation, and The Leverhulme Trust for generous fellowships that enabled me to spend extended periods of time in the Cambridge University and the Huntington libraries. I am very grateful to the library staff at Cambridge University Library and the Huntington for the courtesy and cooperation that I invariably received from them. I am still trying to figure out why I was transported to the Villa Serbelloni with no responsibility except to soak in its many splendors, write, and spend the evenings drinking with some remarkable men and women, and I thank the Rockefeller Foundation for the absurdly high level of happiness that they provided for me through the course of writing one of my chapters. Thanks also to the Leverhulme Foundation for a generous fellowship that enabled me to spend an extended period of time at the Anglia Ruskin University in Cambridge. It was the availability of uninterrupted writing time and free access to the Cambridge University Library that enabled me to finally put my book together. The English Department at Anglia Ruskin turned out to be a warm, welcoming, and intellectually vibrant place, and I want particularly to thank Rowly Wymer for helping me fit into the Anglia community with innumerable, thoughtful gestures, Rebecca Stott for lending me her office, and the two Johns, Gardner and White, for their friendship which, as the three of us know, will last through the rest of our lives.

This book, together with the research opportunities that facilitated its writing, would have merely remained pleasant fantasies if I did not have the long-term support of two remarkable people: Andrew Miller and Catherine Gallagher. I first got to know Andrew about twelve years ago when he sent me his response to an essay full of typographical, spelling, and formatting errors that I'd submitted to *Victorian Studies*. In his three-page editor's response Andrew summarized the readers' comments, cautioned me about the technical errors that I was making, and gave me several specific and very serious suggestions about how I could take my work forward. Andrew's letter turned out to be the beginning of an incredibly generous relationship that we sustain to this day. His comments on sections of this book and finally on the book as a whole helped me address several problems ranging from the specific and local to those related to the book's structure and argument. Andrew's continuing interest in the work of a person whom he had never met and who did not have any claim on his time represents for me that utopian impulse that has never really faded in academia. I want him to know that it was his commitment to keeping in touch with people working far away from the centers dedicated to the study of Victorian culture that kept this work going.

I cannot adequately express my gratitude to Cathy Gallagher for the many ways in which she has supported my work through the last fifteen years. As will become evident, this book works all the time with conceptual categories that Gallagher developed in her books and essays. What may not be obvious is the extent to which her responses to my work helped to shape it. She led me to several readings that turned out to be seminal and transformed the arguments that I was making. Her own comments—razor sharp in their ability to open up conceptual flaws—have been, by far, the most important influence on this work, for it is around those comments that the vital organizing knots of this book have been tied. Of course, I alone am responsible for any shortcomings from which this book is bound to suffer, but readers should know that without Cathy's help there would be no book.

I thank Sandy Crooms for the firm but always cheerful way in which she handled this manuscript in its early, unformed stages and even more for the outstanding external readings that she organized for the complete manuscript. The comments of my anonymous external readers were enormously helpful, and I hope that they will read this book if only to see how much they have contributed to its final version. Thanks also to Rimli Borooah and Maggie Diehl for giving this work the benefit of their considerable copyediting skills at differing points of its evolution from a manuscript to a book.

This book uses material from the following essays that have been published previously: "Radical Satire and Respectability: Comic Imagination in Hone, Jerrold and Dickens," in *The Working-Class Intellectual in Eighteenth- and Nineteenth-Century Britain,* ed. Aruna Krishnamurthy (Farnham: Ashgate, 2009), Copyright © 2009; "Hogarth, Egan, Dickens, and the Making of an Urban Aesthetic," *Representations* 103, no. 1 (Summer 2008), © 2008 by the Regents of the University of California; and *"Bleak House, Vanity Fair,* and the Making of an Urban Aesthetic," *Nineteenth-Century*

Literature 54, no. 4 (March 2000): 480–502, © 2000 by the Regents of the University of California. I thank the University of California Press and Ashgate for permission to reprint.

The other figures that appear in this book gained a great deal from the professional skills of my nephew, Anshuman Sen, who produced high-resolution digital images from the frayed, old prints that I gave him. Other members of my family helped in the writing of this book simply by being who they are—individuals who respect other people's individuality. My eighty-seven-year-old father, who remains independent yet deeply connected to anything concerning me, has been a great source of strength over many years. My mother, whose bright and far-reaching optimism sustained me through many difficult periods, would, if she were here, have been proud of this book. So, I hope, will Polu and Milu—my scientifically minded children—who never let their skepticism over my activities get in the way of helping me out in a million specific ways. And I was really lucky to have met Nivedita when I was eighteen because without her friendship, support, and tolerance I would have sunk long ago.

INTRODUCTION

IN 1859, many years after he had established himself as the preeminent novelist of his age, Charles Dickens launched what would, for long afterwards, be considered the definitive edition of his novels. The novels that appeared as part of the Charles Dickens Edition were designed for posterity. Each reissued work took the form of a single, freestanding hardbound volume. Every volume, moreover, was embossed with gold lettering and carried a facsimile of Dickens's signature inscribed across its red cover. Clearly Dickens was projecting his books into the future as stable, unified, and autonomous "classics," authenticated by their author's personal stamp.[1]

As it happens, the Dickensian novel has held its status as a classic long after the publication of the Charles Dickens Edition. In the twenty-first century, it enjoys all the prestige attendant on its longevity, and it is presented to modern readers as a unique and unified whole, to be read and enjoyed in its own right without the distracting influence of any extraneous material. Yet the ideas of unity and permanence were utterly alien to the format with which *Pickwick Papers* changed the dynamics of the nineteenth-century book market and which remained Dickens's preferred mode of publishing until late in his career. Kathleen Tillotson and John Butt provide a clear description of the magazine-like monthly numbers with which Dickens and his publishers cut through the stranglehold that the three-decker novel and circulating libraries exercised over the production and dissemination of novels: "each monthly 'part' or number consisted of three or four chapters, covering thirty-two pages of print, with two plates, and several pages of advertisements. It was issued in green paper covers and was published at a shilling, nominally on the first day, actually on the last day, of each month."[2] The emergence of the part issue—"the moment of Pickwick," as N. N. Feltes has called it[3]—was part of a sales strategy that would work very successfully for Dickens and his publishers. But the salability of the Dickensian part issue was inseparable from the *form*—part novel fragment, part illustrations, and part advertisements—in which it was sold. The hybridity and open-endedness of the part issue should not be mistaken for simple and removable side effects of the monthly number's publication conditions. On the contrary, the three segments of the part issue were often well coordinated, and they worked with a common set of expressive strategies to unfold as parts of a single field. Thus, as Richard Altick has shown, companies and individuals who advertised in the part issue often chose products that would synchronize with themes, events, or locations that may have appeared in a particular number.[4] Indeed, Gerard Curtis has argued that advertisements were "part of the original reading process of the serial, an integral part of its framing device and of its effects." To give Curtis's own example, the advertisement for the Dakin Tea Company that appeared with the monthly numbers of *Bleak House* drew the viewer into a narrative of sociability based on tea drinking by using a set of visual techniques that were identical to those used by the cover design of the part issue, pictorially anticipating for the reader the story that was about to unfold.[5]

It would seem, then, that the transformation of Dickens's novels into single-volume, internally integrated "classics" obscured not only the economic underpinnings of novel writing in nineteenth-century England but also the movement of expressive strategies across the disparate but contiguous discourses that constituted the original Dickensian part issue. The latter dynamic, indeed, energized the workings of a much larger entity—the nineteenth-century market for print and visual entertainment—and its hybridizing effects on the products of this market will prove essential for our understanding of the Dickensian aesthetic.

The market in which Dickens found his feet as a writer was characterized by its propensity to not just promote incessant movement of expressive resources across genres and media but also to destabilize demarcations between popular and high art. As Martin Meisel puts it:

> After a period from the Restoration forward, of comparative cultural stratification, there was a considerable mingling and enlarging of audiences, in the early nineteenth-century, accompanied by an explosion, technologically

induced, of print and picture. The popular audience of print and picture consumers, reaching all the way from the palace to the city streets, came into its own in the nineteenth-century and found entrepreneurs to provide for it, by the penny and the pound.[6]

One way in which to gauge the extent to which the print market loosened both the social demarcations between the consuming public and generic distinctions between different cultural products is by tracking the transformations experienced by William Hogarth's prints through the course of their extraordinarily long afterlife that extended well into the nineteenth century.

When Hogarth decided, in 1732, to "publish" a series of four pictures depicting a harlot's declining career in London and to sell multiple, mechanically reproduced copies to a group of subscribers,[7] he was consciously probing the print market for expressive and commercial opportunities that it might offer. But even he could not have anticipated the kind of afterlife that his prints were destined to enjoy. Produced in multiple copies, focusing often on the varied, everyday life of the city, Hogarth's prints were, in any case, designed to circulate among a socially varied group of consumers.[8] Moreover, the increasing popular appeal of Hogarth's pictorial stories through the later eighteenth and the first half of the nineteenth centuries caused the artist's ideas, plot patterns, and modes of characterization to proliferate across a range of disparate genres. The continuing popularity of *Industry and Idleness* (1747), for example, meant that nineteenth-century melodramas, pantomimes, and novels regularly absorbed and reactivated its plot patterns, characters, and, above all, its techniques of unfolding the city. About ninety years after the publication of *Industry and Idleness,* the author and illustrator of the best-selling *Jack Shepherd* (1839) declared that they had worked from Hogarth's picture series in the attempt to produce what the author described as a "sort of Hogarthian novel."[9] Moreover, *Jack Shepherd* was itself adapted several times for the stage, and the claim made in a playbill of one of the adaptations demonstrates the enormous expressive possibilities that opened up for popular modes of articulation as they moved from one genre or medium to another. This advertisement claimed that *Jack Shepherd* would offer its viewers a panoramic version of Hogarth's London, that is, it would unfurl across the large, three-dimensional space of the stage the London that Hogarth had inscribed in *Industry and Idleness*.[10]

The history of transformations experienced by Hogarth's pictures throws into relief a basic feature of the nineteenth-century market for print and visual commodities: its propensity to encourage, not generic autonomy, but a process of hybridization. This hybridizing process is very clearly exemplified in two texts that are representative of early nineteenth-century popular print culture and that will, moreover, figure prominently through the early chapters of this book.

The first, Pierce Egan's *Life in London* (1822), is marked in a physical sense by the incessant intersection of genres and media that the print market promoted: its typography is full of attention-grabbing capitalizations and italics, its colored plates depicting sensational city scenes are very much part of its expressive repertoire, and it even contains the full music score for a popular song. In these circumstances it is not at all surprising that in his meandering, loud, and energetic invocation, Pierce Egan ranges across virtually the entire breadth of a stratified cultural field: he hopes to imbibe some of the properly literary talent which animated a "FIELDING, a GOLDSMITH, a SMOLLET, a STERNE, in their portraitures of 'Life,'" but also to incorporate, within his book, some of the audience-gathering techniques perfected by "Cribb, admired hero of the stage" and "HONE the king of parodists!"[11] Again, William Hone, who is brought together in Egan's equalizing discourse with Fielding, was able, in *The Political House That Jack Built* (1819), to dredge out of radical pamphleteering a recipe for an instant bestseller and, in this way, to open up a large market for comic political journalism, precisely by hitching the popular appeal of antiruling class graphic satire to the radical "nursery rhyme." Hone self-consciously emphasized the hybrid nature of the form that he saw himself as pioneering: the frontispiece of his best-selling radical pamphlet (fig. 1) depicts its two primary producers, Cruikshank and Hone himself, sitting on opposite sides of a table engaged precisely in the act of bringing together the effects of language and of drawing in a single text.

In what ways did the market's propensity to move expressive strategies across diverse forms and media affect the practice of novel writing? Ainsworth Harrison publicly declared that *Jack Shepherd* drew much more on Hogarth's picture series than on some properly literary tradition of novel writing. But the hybridizing trajectory within the nineteenth-century novel that Ainsworth's work represented unfolded against the resistance of several writers and critics who were convinced that the influence of techniques that had originated in graphic caricature or the city sketches could only degrade the novel as a form.

One of the most interesting examples of such resistance is to be found in the work of William Makepeace Thackeray, interesting because Thackeray sought to insulate his novel writing from the corrupting influence of subliterary forms even as he earned his livelihood from the "low" parodies, squibs, and caricatures that he contributed to various magazines.

FIGURE 1. George Cruikshank, frontispiece to *The Political House That Jack Built* (1819) Hone and Cruikshank, being the vignette to "Facetiae and Miscellanies," 1828.

Thackeray's dependence on magazine work was especially acute during the early and most difficult phase of his career, when he kept himself financially afloat by producing various comic pieces for *Punch*—a magazine whose very name connected it to the sort of slapstick comedy that Thackeray would find unsuitable for serious novels. But even after his dependence on comic journalism decreased, he defended the more commercially oriented and ephemeral forms of writing on the grounds that authors had the right to sell their wares in the market like other tradesmen. Indeed, in contrast to Dickens, who, in his public pronouncements, often subsumed the economic exchange that was taking place between author and reader within a rhetorically produced sociability,[12] Thackeray frankly described the professional writer as someone who was driven not by the "irresistible afflatus of genius" but by the need to exchange his "literary artifact" for money.[13]

Thackeray's frequent use of the word "trade" to describe the exchange that took place between writer and reader, and his defense of "fugitive literature" against "the big book interest,"[14] should not, however, be understood as a simple, objective attempt to "undercut," as Peter Shillingsburg has suggested, "both the social snobbery and the mystical trappings of *artist* which some writers cultivated."[15] Rather, these positions express only one side of Thackeray's deeply divided relationship with the print market. Thackeray may have believed that the print market was a fair regulating mechanism for the *economic* exchange that took place between an author and reader. But coexisting with his defense of writing as trade and his defense of those who produced "fugitive" literature in order to earn a living are the private anxieties about his own magazine writings that he expressed so often to his mother and to his friends. For example, in an 1841 letter to his mother, Thackeray confessed that he had not let anyone know that he was writing for *Punch* because, although it offered a "good pay ... and an unrestrained opportunity for laughing," it was a "very low paper." Moreover, Thackeray's "odious magazine work" not only compromised his social status but also demanded the kind of literary drudgery that was sure to "kill any writer."[16] The presence of the "writer" behind the "quill driver," of William Makepeace Thackeray,[17] whose artistic instincts cry out for expression in an unsympathetic print market, behind Michael Angelo Titmarsh, who floods this market with parodies and caricatures, would suggest a relationship with the print market so divided that Thackeray could sustain it only by formally splitting his authorial personality.

Thackeray self-consciously separated his novel writing from the kind of work that he did for *Punch* because he believed that the extravagant effects of comic entertainment were fundamentally incompatible with the aesthetic goals of the novel as a work of "Art." It was from this perspective that he sought to distinguish his own mode of novel writing from that of Dickens:

> I quarrel with his art in many respects: which I don't think represents nature duly; for instance Micawber appears to me an exaggeration of a man, as his name is of a name. It is delightful and makes me laugh: but it is no more real than my friend Punch is: and in so far I protest against him . . . holding that the Art of Novels *is* to represent Nature: to convey as strongly as possible the sentiment of reality . . . in a drawing-room drama a coat is a coat and a poker a poker; and not an embroidered tunic, nor a great red-hot instrument like the Pantomime weapon.[18]

In this well-known passage Thackeray formulates an opposition that will remain important through much of this book: he posits against the popular appeal of Dickens's entertainment-oriented effects his own commitment to convey "the sentiment of reality." Moreover, although in a maneuver that would enjoy a long afterlife, Thackeray conflates realism with "Nature," he was always aware—as the many comments he made in his letters, prefaces, and even in his novels testify—that the realistic mode of novel writing itself worked with a very specific set of representational conventions. Without necessarily imputing aesthetic superiority to one or the other author, this book will often invoke the representational conventions that Thackeray identifies with the "Art" of novels in order to throw into relief a very different but equally powerful set of expressive strategies with which Dickens worked.

Implicit in the passage from Thackeray quoted above is a second criticism of Dickens's mode of novel writing that has to do with the problem not so much of realism as of autonomy. Thackeray was not, of course, the first to argue that Dickens had degraded "the Art of Novels" by opening his own fiction to the influence of extraliterary forms such as pantomimes or satiric, political journalism. Indeed, as Kathryn Chittick has shown, the highbrow press refused, until after *Oliver Twist,* to even describe Dickens as a novelist.[19] Rather, the customary classification of Dickens's early writing as magazine pieces or as periodical sketches inserted them in a promiscuous discursive field bereft of firm generic contours where expressive modes from a host of genres could have free play.

It is not surprising, therefore, that Dickens's early reviewers echoed Thackeray in commenting (most often derisively) on the heterogeneous, subliterary expressive modes on which Dickens's novels depended to achieve their most characteristic effects. The *Spectator,* striking a familiar note, compared the topical satire that insinuated itself so often in Dickens's fiction to the "passing hits of a pantomime,"[20] while the *Edinburgh Review* commented that in *Pickwick Papers, Nicholas Nickleby,* and *Oliver Twist* Dickens had "called in the aid of the pencil, and [had] been contented to share his success with the caricaturist."[21] Many years later, after Dickens had established himself as a major if not the preeminent novelist of his period, the quarterly press continued to remind the public of the generic promiscuity that Dickens's schooling in the lower levels of print culture had encouraged in his novels. The Circumlocution Office passages in *Little Dorrit, Blackwood's Magazine* complained, "betrayed a total want of art" and was "as inartificial as if [Dickens] had cut half-a-dozen leading articles out of an Opposition newspaper, and stuck them in anyhow, anywhere."[22]

As the phrasing by *Blackwood's* suggests, the quarterly press often tended to constitute as "irregular" or "desultory"[23] a mode of novel writing that was based on the constant interaction with various, often extraliterary genres. However, Mikhail Bakhtin's idea that "the most intense and productive life of culture takes place on the boundaries of its individual areas and not in places where these areas have become enclosed in their own specificity" might counterpoise against this emphasis on the formal integrity of the novel.[24] From this perspective, the Dickensian novel could be conceptualized as a discursive formation which was characterized by a certain formal indeterminacy and semantic open-endedness and which was always capable of reactivating within itself expressive resources from the numerous popular genres and media that circulated in the nineteenth-century market for print and visual entertainment.

This book will be overwhelmingly concerned with what Dickens's novels gained from two sub- or nonliterary representational traditions that flourished in the nineteenth-century market for print and visual entertainment. The first of these, which I will, following James Epstein, call "radical expression,"[25] designates the literary and visual satire that entered the discursive domain through the work of such writers and artists as Thomas Paine, William Hone, William Cobbett, and George Cruikshank, and that continued to be an important presence in the print market of the late 1830s, despite the fragmentation of the radical journalistic tradition itself. As young men making their careers in the print market of the 1830s, Thackeray and Dickens would have access to the satiric techniques that developed in the radical journalistic tradition, irrespective of whether they shared the political goals of Hone or Paine. In these circumstances, it is rather surprising that few among the several literary critics and historians who write on the popular radical satire of the early nineteenth century have attempted to connect this satire with the work of Dickens.[26]

The one exception (apart from an article of mine that appeared in the *English Literary History*[27]) has been Sally Ledger's recent *Dickens and the Popular Radical Imagination* (2007). Ledger breaks from the influential view that associated Dickens with the middle-class radical politics of the 1840s and 1850s.[28] Instead, she connects the populist orientation that so often underpinned Dickens's political pronouncements to the "language of radicalism" fabricated by an earlier generation of radical publicists in their endeavor to bring the masses excluded from the processes of an unreformed parliament into the political domain.[29]

The many specific connections Ledger makes between Dickens and writers like Cobbett and Hone is crucial to the argument that this book develops. My criticism of Ledger's work, though, is that the "Popular" in her title brings together, in a relationship of unmediated continuity, political practices and literary effects, the political mobilization that Hone and Cobbett hoped to sustain through their pamphlets and Dickens's novelization of "radical expression."[30] Thus, Ledger repeatedly argues that Hone and Dickens were part of a unified, continuous, "truly disruptive" political tradition and that Cobbett and Dickens shared a "similarly instrumentalist" view of writing.[31] But Hone's mobilizing pamphlets and Dickens's entertainment-oriented novels worked in very different domains and were likely, therefore, to produce very different kinds of political effects. The bloody circumstance out of which *The Political House That Jack Built* had emerged and the prosecution that always threatened the radical publicists suggest that these publicists were also political organizers capable of confronting the state with serious mass protests. Dickens's political satires, on the other hand, were not conceptualized as instruments for organizing the masses or for precipitating direct, bloody confrontations. Rather, the Dickensian novel was addressed to a respectable, predominantly middle-class audience, and it achieved its political effects gradually and indirectly in some corner of the mind of the reader who read Dickens in her leisure time for pleasure rather than for political education.

It would seem, therefore, that rather than embedding Dickens in any stable political project, popular radical writing and graphic satire worked their effects deep within the internal dynamics of his fiction. In order to uncover these effects, I will need to address not this or that political goal that Dickens may have shared with Hone or Cobbett but rather the ways in which radical expression helped to produce Dickens's *method* as a novelist.

What were the series of displacements that transformed "the language of radicalism" from a powerful instrument of political mobilization to a socially acceptable, relatively nonthreatening mode of political entertainment? What exact visual and linguistic forms of radical expression were available to writers such as Thackeray and Dickens when they began their careers as writers? What possibilities did "radical expression" hold out for the novel form, for example, for its modes of characterization? In what ways did these modes relate to the increasingly normative protocols of realism? These questions will lie at the heart of this book's engagement with the first of the two subliterary traditions that, it argues, helped to produce the Dickensian aesthetic.

A second tradition of representation that developed in the domain of popular rather than literary culture and that proved vital to the making of the Dickensian novel were the visualizations of London stretching all the way from Hogarth's *Industry and Idleness* and the early nineteenth-century city sketches to the images produced, through the first half of the nineteenth century, by such technologically advanced forms as the panorama and the stereoscope.

These visual representations of London sustain, in varying ways, a common tension between, on the one hand, the attempt to grasp the city as a whole, to map and make accessible its far-flung locations and, on the other hand, to bring together these geographically and socially disparate locations in tense, discontinuous relationships. In Hogarth's inaugural exposition, this tension probes, breaches, redraws, but also seeks to fortify the boundary between such interiors as the home or the workplace and the chaotic, dangerous life of the streets. Moreover, even as London became more organized through the course of the nineteenth century, the city sketch and the panorama sharpened their techniques of mapping the city, of probing into its hidden nooks and crannies, and of encouraging juxtapositions between these and the more respectable parts of the metropolis. By the mid-nineteenth century, the unstable diversity of the city—its propensity to fragment, but also to generate unexpected convergences—could be made to unfold across three- (rather than two-) dimensional space in the technologically sophisticated operations of the stereoscope.

Throughout his career Dickens engaged very seriously with, and often wrote about, Hogarth's images of London as well as the expressive possibilities offered by the panorama and the stereoscope. These writings suggest that techniques originating in Hogarth's prints or in the operations of the stereoscope not only influenced his representation of the metropolis but also produced a basic organizational orientation of the Dickensian aesthetic.

This orientation, inseparable from the synchronicity of the visual modes, relates to the unusual way in which time and space are arranged in Dickens's novels. Thus, unlike realistic novels such as Thackeray's—which are often driven by the transforming effects of time, especially on characters, rather than by dramatic shifts in social space—Dickens follows the visual forms discussed above by working with the social and spatial diversity of the city and with the tense juxtapositions that these make possible. The space-driven urban aesthetic that Dickens inherited from the visual forms would have a determining influence on such vital features of the Dickensian novel as plotting and characterization.

THIS BOOK will frequently refer to William Makepeace Thackeray's *Vanity Fair, Pendennis,* and, to a lesser extent, *The Newcomes.* I should clarify, though, that this is not really a comparative work on Dickens and Thackeray. It neglects several features of Thackeray's fiction including those that may be thought of as nuanced elaborations of issues that interested Dickens as well. For example, I don't really engage with the way credit works in *Vanity Fair* to produce unexpected social intersections or with the internal depth that Thackeray manages to give to the world of the aristocracy even while exposing this world as moribund and parasitic. Moreover, a nuanced comparison between the ways in which Thackeray and Dickens responded to the aristocracy would require, for example, researching the relative similarity of positions that they took on the aristocracy's domination of the bureaucracy. I have not engaged with these problems because Thackeray's relevance to this book is inseparable from and limited to the effects that his self-conscious rejection of the resources of print and visual entertainment had on his novel writing and to the light that this sheds on the distinctiveness of the aesthetic choices that Dickens made.

Unfortunately, this orientation may draw my book inadvertently into that long-established tradition of scholarship that locks the two greatest male novelists of Victorian England in a rigid binary relationship. This tradition, moreover, has often used the Dickens–Thackeray opposition to privilege one author at the expense of the other. I have no interest in constituting Thackeray as Dickens's discredited other. Both Dickens and Thackeray found in the novel form the means of elaborating perspectives on, for example, the aristocracy that were underpinned by as many similarities as differences. Moreover, it bears reiteration that this book does not engage with various features of Thackeray's writing that it would need to bring into play if it were a properly comparative study of Thackeray and Dickens.

Rather than comprehensively comparing the fiction of Thackeray and Dickens or embedding them hierarchically in some putative scale of literary value, my concern is primarily with the making of the Dickensian aesthetic. Thackeray becomes part of that concern because nineteenth-century critics regularly held up his novels as examples of that realism that Dickens never managed to achieve. Thus, if I juxtapose Dickens's caricaturized representation of Tite Barnacle against Thackeray's psychologically complex portraiture of Pitt Crawley, it is not in order to assert the superiority of the one over the other but to show that each character came out of a specific set of aesthetic choices that, working within a set of constraints, became capable of producing specific effects. The purpose of this book will have been served if it is able to demonstrate that the expressive resources of various popular subliterary forms that came together in Dickens's work produced a novelistic aesthetic whose methods were different from those encoded in what Thackeray described as the "Art of Novels" but which were capable of producing effects just as powerful as anything achieved in the great realistic tradition of the English novel.

CHAPTER 1

Dickens, Thackeray, and "The Language of Radicalism"

IN A LETTER to Mrs. Brookfield, written a few months before he resigned from *Punch,* Thackeray declared that he found it impossible to "pull in the same boat" with a "savage little Robespierre" like Douglas Jerrold.[1] Thackeray's outburst is significant for what it reveals not only about his overt political opinions but also about his relationship with certain techniques of representation that my "Introduction," following James Epstein, described as "radical expression," and that Thackeray associated above all with Jerrold.

When Thackeray first joined *Punch,* Jerrold dominated the journal and sought to sustain, within an expanding print market, the sort of radical political satire that had gained such popularity through the late eighteenth and early nineteenth centuries. In these circumstances, Thackeray himself had little option but to provide for the magazine the parodies and caricatures that fed "the quickening and widening of interest in public matters and public men, brought about by the agitation which had preceded the passing of the Reform Bill of 1832 and continued after its enactment."[2] Yet he was also deeply conscious of the artistic limitations of journalistic sarcasm, although he publicly defended his early political satire as a legitimate means of earning his livelihood. These limitations were evident for Thackeray, above all, in the way that the radical journalists represented the elite. Indeed, one way in which to chart more precisely Thackeray's responses to this problem is by focusing on the silences as well as the emphases that underlie the two long essays he wrote on artists whose work not only overlapped with his early career but also represented the elite from the differing social standpoints that Thackeray associated with journalism, on the one hand, and "literature," on the other. In the first of these—a two-part essay on Cruikshank—Thackeray creates around the figure of the illustrator a powerful sense of nostalgia for a much-loved world full of fantastic prints and illustrations that Thackeray's aging generation was losing. In this way, Thackeray touches on the transforming effects of time—a problem that he was to explore with great sophistication in his fiction—but he also commits himself to a certain sympathy for even the kind of political caricature that had seemed to embarrass him in his letters to friends such as Edward Fitzgerald:

> Knight's, in Sweetings's Alley; Fairburn's, in a court off Ludgate Hill; Hone's, in Fleet Street—bright, enchanted palaces, which George Cruikshank used to people with grinning, fantastical imps and merry, harmless sprites,—where are they? . . . Slop, the atrocious Castlereagh, the sainted Caroline (in tight pelisse, with feathers in her head), the "Dandy of Sixty" who used to glance at us from Hone's friendly windows—where are they?[3]

This well-known description is so sympathetic that even radical historians have quoted it as a historically accurate account of the milieu in which political prints of the early nineteenth century were produced and disseminated.[4] Thackeray's representation, however, also seeks to smoothen and render as easily negotiable the disjunction between the middle- and upper-class readers for whom he was writing and the plebeian milieu for which Cruikshank produced his political caricatures. More specifically, in Thackeray's nostalgic recollection of what he projects as a lost world, the militant artisanal communities that gathered around the works of Cruikshank and Hone become "grinning, good natured mechanics,"[5] and Cruikshank's brutal caricatures of the most powerful politicians of the Regency "merry, harmless sprites." This means that Thackeray's representation erases not only the confrontationist context in which Cruikshank's political prints were produced but also the representational modes by which this confrontation with the political elite was expressed.

If Thackeray felt it necessary to evade any analysis of a central feature of Cruikshank's political caricature—its propensity to represent the political elite from the point of view of the excluded—it was because he believed that Cruikshank's social location made it impossible for him to produce artistically viable images of the upper classes. Indeed, in a second essay on his colleague John Leech, Thackeray sharply criticizes James Gillray and, by implication, the brutal caricatural technique which Cruikshank was to bring into the domain of radical journalism precisely on the grounds that the "garret . . . or a tavern parlour" could never emerge as valid observation points for the representation of "public characters." On the other hand, as a "social painter" who belonged to "the world which he depict[ed] and native to the manners which he portray[ed]," Leech was properly positioned to delineate realistically the details of what Thackeray, addressing his upper- and middle-class readers, describes as "your house and mine."[6]

Thackeray's privileging of Leech over Gillray and, by extension, over Cruikshank is important for my purposes because it has implications for the distinction that Thackeray made between journalism and literature, and it looks forward ultimately to Thackeray's own movement away from "magazinery" to what he saw as the more properly literary vocation of novel writing. More specifically, Thackeray's comments on Leech, taken in conjunction with his increasingly contemptuous attitude toward the sort of radical satire that appeared in the early numbers of *Punch*,[7] may be seen as part of an ongoing polemic in which Thackeray pits a novelistic aesthetic, based on closely observed, realistic delineations of the social and political elite, against a popular tradition of political representation that developed continuously from Paine to Jerrold and that was predicated on, as Thackeray sarcastically remarked, looking "up at the rich and the great with a fierce, a sarcastic aspect, and a threatening posture."[8]

The language of radical satire, which Thackeray believed to be incapable of producing that nuanced realism that he associated with literature, was an integral aspect of Dickens's staple writing. Indeed, in an article entitled "Modern Novelists: Charles Dickens," the *Westminster Review* argued that Dickens's authorial tone was inextricably bound up with those high-pitched political debates of the reform years which had sustained Jerrold's strident sarcasm as well, and "Modern Novelists" concluded with a suggestion that Thackeray would presumably endorse: that by seeking to cater to the tastes of the overpoliticized masses Dickens had perverted "the novel from a work of art to a platform for argument and discussion."[9]

The *Westminster Review* is right not only in situating Dickens's early career in the lower rungs of the market for print entertainment but also in suggesting that Dickens (unlike Thackeray) absorbed the language of radical politics into the expressive system of his novels. However, the *Westminster Review*'s condescension toward those forms of novel writing that do not qualify as "work(s) of art" obstructs what might have been a more productive and historically informed inquiry into the relationship between "literature" and what it vaguely describes as a "highly popular treatment of politics."[10] Indeed, it is possible to demonstrate that the "reactivation" of radical expressive modes in Dickens's fiction was not the first or only example of the interaction between literature and popular politics,[11] and that early radical publicists such as William Hone and Thomas Wooler would certainly have contested the separation that Thackeray and the *Westminster Review* seek to effect between the popular radical writing and what could be properly described as literary. Just now, though, my focus will be on the uninterrupted process of displacements and reactivations by which radical expressive modes became uprooted from the mobilizing texts that had originally sustained them, but continued to lead an active, if reified, existence in the entertainment-oriented Dickensian novel.

One way in which to track this movement is by focusing on what Iain McCalman has called "the Rabelaisian" strands that coexisted within radical journalism with the more austere, rationalist modes characteristic of Paine and Carlile.[12] It was the extensive use that journalists like Hone, Wooler, and Davison made of literary devices such as exaggeration, parody, caricature, rhyme, and meter that made the language of subversion not so much solemn as entertaining and salable.

A very good example of a mobilizing text that might, at the same time, be seen as a landmark in literary entertainment was William Hone's *The Political House That Jack Built*. *The Political House* was very much an exercise in political mobilization, provoked as it was by the Peterloo massacre. On the other hand, it was also cast as a parodic political nursery rhyme. This allowed Hone to combine colloquialisms, parodic reaccentuations, and the familiar rhythms of nursery rhymes to achieve a mode of political articulation whose most productive afterlife was to unfold in the pages of *Punch* and in the novels of Dickens rather than in a newspaper like *Northern Star* or a book such as *On Liberty*. Moreover, *The Political House* was, in a very basic sense, coproduced by Cruikshank, and the combination of Cruikshank's etchings and Hone's letterpress not only inaugurated a format that would prove very successful in the market for print entertainment but also set into motion an interactive relationship between visual and linguistic satire—a process that was to affect the Dickensian aesthetic in significant ways. Above all, *The Political House* did not just anticipate a recipe for a best seller—it turned out itself to be an instant best seller. First published in 1819, *The Political House* sold 100,000 copies even at the relatively high price of one shilling.

The very high sales achieved by a radical pamphlet such as *The Political House* suggests that the demarcation made by one of the greatest historians of the popular press between "the journalism of a community or a movement" and "market journalism" based on more efficient production and distribution and incomparably higher levels of capitalization was, in fact, never absolute.[13] It is true, of course, that the commercial press irrevocably broke up the community of radical readers in the process of creating a larger, more diffuse, entertainment-seeking audience and, indeed, the movement of radical satire from the mobilizing pamphlet to the Dickensian novel also implied the uprooting of this satire from real political struggles. On the other hand, it is equally true that radical journalism contributed very significantly to the shaping of the nineteenth-century market for print entertainment. Indeed, the radical journalists themselves often emphasized this. Thus, Hone himself was to claim that the illustrated pamphlets that he produced during the 1820s had "created a new era in the history of publication":

> By showing what engraving on wood could effect in a popular way, and exciting a taste for art in the more humble ranks of life, they created a new era in the history of publication . . . They are parents to the present cheap literature, which extends to a sale of at least four hundred thousand copies every week . . . Besides this . . . my little pieces acquainted every rank of society, in the most remote corner of the British dominions, with the powers of Mr. George Cruikshank, whose genius had been wasted on mere caricature till it was embodied in my ideas and feelings.[14]

Hone's anxious egoism is characteristic of many plebeian writers seeking to assert, to a hostile middle-class audience, their contribution to the making of culture, and it should not obscure the substantive point that he was making: that he and other radical journalists (whom Hone characteristically does not acknowledge) had generated formats, expressive resources, modes of articulation which, once they began circulating in the print market, would attract large sections of proreform middle-class readers. In other words, Hone seems to be reflecting, from the hindsight of a decade, on the history of displacements and reactivations by which such imaginative modes of political expression as caricature would move from militant artisanal politics into an expanding economy of print entertainment that would service ever increasing numbers of middle-class consumers. What Hone does not comment on in this passage is that radical expression in the 1830s and '40s would inevitably have to contend with the demands of respectability. In fact, this tension between radicalism and respectability is visible across an entire sequence of works, from the journals produced by those radical writers who survived the 1830s[15] through to the early numbers of *Punch*.

The tension between radicalism and respectability that runs through the early numbers of *Punch* has conventionally been attributed to the prolonged personal antagonism between Jerrold and Thackeray.[16] But while Jerrold's work did, in fact, prove to be an important conduit by which the expressive strategies that had developed in the work of Hone or Cobbett would move to Dickens's fiction, it is possible to relate the radical slant in *Punch* not just to Jerrold's personal influence but also to certain preexisting traditions of representation or, to adapt Roger Chartier's more precise formulation, to a "preknowledge" that readers of *Punch* would have of certain conventions through which political satire was most effectively articulated. In "Texts, Printings, Readings" Chartier argues:

> people read books with previously gained knowledge that was easily evoked in the act of reading. This knowledge was gained from the recurrence of coded forms, from the repetition of themes, and from the books' images . . . This "preknowledge," as it were, was mobilized to produce comprehension not necessarily in conformity with that desired by the producer of the text or the maker of the text . . .[17]

Certainly many *Punch* readers worked with the "preknowledge" they had of the literary forms or artistic tropes that underpinned radical expression and that the most recent source of this were the radical newspapers and magazines. Hone's pamphlets, which had continued to circulate in their original as well as modified forms throughout the 1820s and '30s, had generated many conventions of representation that were to remain part of the standard repertoire of political satirists throughout the first half of the nineteenth century. Clearly, therefore, *Punch* was depending on the "comprehension" that radical representational conventions would produce among its readers, when it deployed the nursery rhyme as a vehicle for political satire or used the allegory of the "political house" or the political menagerie as a site from which it could launch its satiric commentaries on politics and politicians.[18] On the other hand, however, *Punch* was also refashioning these radical tropes so that they would not offend the sensibilities of the increasing number of middle-class readers that the magazine was gathering around itself.[19] For example, *Punch* followed the parodies of Hone in using the nursery rhyme form as the vehicle for its antiaristocratic satire in a mock primer that it devised for Queen Victoria's children. But *Punch* not only maintained a consistently respectable tone due to the royal nursery; it also used this respectability to contain any excess in content that might offend middle-class tastes.[20] This maneuver by which *Punch* sought both to exploit the expressive possibilities of radical satire and at the same time to contain these possibilities is evident again in the way that it dealt with a second radical trope: the political menagerie. Here again, *Punch* was following the lead of a pamphlet by Cruikshank and Hone in its use of zoomorphism as a means of political demystification.[21] Significantly, however, the element that disappears in the movement from the woodcuts of Cruikshank in *The Political Showman* (1821) to the visual satire of *Punch* is the violence that Baudelaire associated with early English caricature.[22] Thus, unlike Cruikshank's deeply disconcerting representations of the Lord Chancellor as a crocodile, the Duke of Wellington as a scorpion, and the king himself as a water scorpion, the creatures who inhabit an etching like Richard Doyle's "The Opening of Parliamentary Pie" (1847) have the bodies of birds but faces that are untouched by the venomous distortions of the caricaturist.[23]

The respectablizing trajectory that diffused the more brutal effects of radical satire for the increasing number of middle-class readers that *Punch* was beginning to attract would alter the basic character of the magazine after the 1840s, shifting its focus from the political to the social. Moreover, Thackeray rode this trajectory, and his movement from the caricatures and parodies that he half-reluctantly produced for the early numbers of *Punch* to the more nuanced social observations of *The Book of Snobs* looked forward to a novelistic aesthetic that would be fundamentally hostile to the methods of the radical publicists. On the other hand, Dickens produced no graphic caricatures and only the occasional political doggerel,[24] and he was never a full-time employee of *Punch*. Nevertheless, the Dickensian novel was deeply implicated in the process out of which *Punch* had emerged: the redeployment of radical expressive resources for the production of a certain kind of political satire that would attract a very large, entertainment-seeking, and socially diverse group of consumers. This should call attention to the politically restrictive influence that the print market—and especially the powerful middle-class consumers within this market—exercised on Dickens's fiction. But it should also help to conceptualize the early numbers of *Punch* and especially the work of Douglas Jerrold as the conduit through which certain strands of radical expression found a continuing, if reified, existence in the novels of Dickens. It is on these strands and on the transformations that they experienced while moving from Hone to Dickens that I will now focus.

The first and most basic of these strands would be what Gareth Stedman Jones called "the language of radicalism" and Kevin Gilmartin later termed "a style of political opposition."[25] One important strategic orientation of the radical "style" would be to constitute as a community all those who were debarred from the processes of an unreformed parliament. Thus, Paine often used the "present tense and the pronoun 'we'" to underline the experience of political exclusion that he shared with his readers and, in this way, to generate, as Olivia Smith has argued, "the illusion that he and [they] share the activity of constructing an argument."[26] Moreover, as William Hone demonstrated during his 1817 trial for blasphemy, Paine's discursively constituted community could be transformed into a material force capable of exerting real pressure on decisions taken traditionally only by those who wielded power. During his extended trial, Hone used his knowledge of how parody worked in English literature to demonstrate, with great wit and irreverence, that the court could not convict him for blasphemy without at the same time convicting some of England's greatest writers, artists, and politicians. Indeed, during the process of defending himself, Hone demonstrated how some of the most characteristic resources of radical expression—laughter, parody, and irreverence—could be used to transform the public domain of the court into a site of political mobilization. After successfully mobilizing the very large audience who had gathered in the court into the kind of community designated by Paine's "we," Hone pitted this community not only against his notoriously intolerant and conservative judge but also against the much larger problem of censorship.[27] In the 1810s and '20s, however, mobilizing activities of publicists like Hone were very far from being painless. The "radical style" may have produced politically conscious communities capable of confronting the government, but it also attracted very severe penal retributions from an intolerant and insecure state.

In contrast, Douglas Jerrold, whose work may be said to represent the more improvisational and imaginative forms of the "radical style" during the 1840s, made his name writing for a magazine whose commercial success was based on its ability, on the one hand, to avoid anything that might attract legal or punitive action and, on the other, to sustain the interest of a large, subscribing readership. Therefore, Jerrold's propensity to position himself among the plebeians while commenting sarcastically on, for example, the Duke of Wellington's moral exhortations to the poor,[28] was certainly indicative of the greater rights of expression that the radical journalists had fought for and won, and of the state's increasing capacity to accommodate dissent. But Jerrold's tone and position would also suggest that the radical division between "us" and "them" could now be used freely in relation to the large, politically diffuse, socially disparate reading audience that *Punch* was gathering around itself. In this sense, Jerrold's essays operated within the economy of print entertainment, although they seem, in terms of their tone and orientation, to continue the radical journalistic tradition of the 1820s. More specifically, their significance lay not so much in their continuing ability to sustain radical movements as in their role in redistributing radical expressive energies within the many popular forms that emerged out of the print market of the early nineteenth century. Indeed, Jerrold—as so many of his contemporaries realized—had as much in common with Dickens as with Cobbett.[29] In fact, it is possible to see in Dickens's frequent use of "us" a novelistic site capable of sustaining the point of view of the excluded, the completion of a process by which the language of radicalism transformed itself from an instrument of political mobilization to a powerful expressive resource within the Victorian period's dominant form of print entertainment: the novel itself.

> There was a dinner party given in the Harley Street establishment, while Little Dorrit was stitching at her father's new shirts by his side that night; and there were magnates from the Court and magnates from the Lords, magnates from the Bench and magnates from the Bar, Bishop magnates, Treasury magnates . . . all the magnates who keep us going and sometimes trip us up.[30]

Unlike the journalism even of someone like Jerrold who directed his attack against a specific, real-life political adversary, the subjects of Dickens's discourse—the people to which it refers—have become fictional "nobodies";[31] mere simulacra that would, at best, absorb and diffuse the antagonism that Dickens's readers might have felt toward real-life politicians and bureaucrats. However, the movement from Paine's "we" to Dickens's "us" suggests not only dissipation but also continuity; not only the fictionalization of politics but also the politicization of fiction. In this sense, it is important to pick up in Dickens's "us" "the stylistic aura" of "the language of radicalism,"[32] to be alert to the effects that the discursive strategies of the radical style were to have on Dickens's representation of those great objects of the radical discourse: the processes and people associated with power. Did this discursive confrontation with the establishment imply that Dickens had appropriated for the novel form at least some of the radical publicist's capacity for political mobilization? The answer, as will become evident later, is that despite major transformations in effectiveness and context, the language of radicalism did not entirely lose its mobilizing charge as it moved from Lord Ellenborough's court, where William Hone had defended his right to parody the ten commandments, to the virtual space of novels like *Bleak House* and *Little Dorrit*.

But what were the exact expressive improvisations and rhetorical strategies that drove the language of radicalism? The question is important because it has not really been addressed in the only exhaustive account of Dickens's artistic debt to the radical literature of the 1820s. Instead, Sally Ledger's *Dickens and the Popular Radical Imagination* subsumes within the general category of satire, the complicated and even contradictory ways in which radical writers and artists, in fact, engaged with the discourses of power.

As something that was committed to cutting through the consecrating symbolism of power with, as James Epstein said of Paine's writing, "an irreverence that proved fundamental to [its] development,"[33] the popular radical language was, indeed, in general, satiric. But it is also important to take into account the differences within radical modes of articulation caused by a tension lodged at the heart of the radical demystificatory project: that between the suspicion about the mystifying functions of icons, emblems, and metaphors and the riot of figures, analogies, and metaphors into which the radical discourse itself so often burst.

The suspicion that icons and emblems, metaphors and figures were vehicles of mystification was integral to English dissident thought since at least the beginnings of Protestantism, and it lies at the very heart of Tom Paine's *The Rights of Man* (1791)—the document that, in a very real sense, inaugurated the radical journalistic tradition. Paine recognized immediately that Burke's representation of the French Revolution achieved its most far-reaching effects through what W. T. J. Mitchell was later to call its rhetorical "extremism and excess."[34] Against Burke's "pathless wilderness of rhapsodies" Paine generates a discourse based on "facts," "principles," and "data" within which the signifier would always be accountable to the signified, and the metaphor would be exposed as a "fraud" that enveloped its object in a mist of illusory connotations: "But, after all, what is the metaphor called a Crown, or rather what is Monarchy? . . . Does the virtue consist in the metaphor, or in the man? Does the goldsmith that makes the crown, make the virtue also? Doth it operate like Fortunatus's wishing-cap, or the Harlequin's wooden sword? Doth it make a man a conjuror?"

Paine's deep suspicion of symbolic consecration as a means of sustaining "Mystery," "craft," "fiction," "superstition," and, ultimately, "the puppet show of state and aristocracy"[35] was to remain a very powerful strand in radical thinking until as late as Dickens's condemnation of the ceremonial unfolding of Chancery practice as "barbarous usages that the world has passed by."[36] Yet it is also true that many radical writers habitually deployed metaphors to counter symbolic consecration. They complicated Paine's dream of a transparent language where the signifier would be completely accountable to the signified by engaging symbolically in what E. P. Thompson calls "the contest for symbolic authority"[37]—not just by stripping the consecrated object of its mystifying imagery but also by associating it with a new set of images; refiguring it as degraded or ridiculous.

The counterimagistic, allegorical techniques that developed within radical journalism enjoyed a particularly rich afterlife in the pages of those journals that operated during the 1830s and '40s at the intersection of the profit-driven demands of an expanding print market and a continuing reform movement. Such journals found in allegorical displacements the means of articulating their proreform political concerns without attracting the censorship or taxation that a sharper focus on particular persons or events may have attracted.[38] The allegorical mode, moreover, was capable of endless expressive improvisations and, in this sense, of keeping together a politically conscious but also entertainment-seeking audience. In the following extract from an early contribution that Douglas Jerrold made to *Punch*, the Harlequin's ability to effect magical transformations is not contemptuously dismissed but made to drive an elaborately improvised and entertaining story about the Woky Poky Indians:

> A throne changed into an armchair! Why, no one, save a Hampden or a harlequin, would think of such a trick. Besides if a throne were once turned into a chair—if such transformations were once begun, who could answer where it would end?
>
> Once upon a time the Woky Poky Indians worshipped the Blue Monkey. Now, the said Blue Monkey had bands of gold about his head, a pearl as big as a swan's egg in each ear, and a diamond that, if sold, would have kept the Indians and their families for half a century dangling from his royal nose—great was the adoration paid to the Blue Monkey. Now it came to pass that some thieves (republicans) despoiled the Blue Monkey of his gold, his pearls, and his diamonds, leaving the said Monkey in his wooden poverty and nakedness. What followed? Why not a single Indian bent his knee to the god—the gems were stolen, and with them the sacred odour of the idol; therefore every dark skin raised his tomahawk and, splitting the Blue Monkey into logs, the Indians made a fire of them, and cooked the goat's flesh by their flames, and their embers, yams and bread.[39]

Jerrold's parable resonates at many levels against the extract from *The Rights of Man* quoted above. Both are centrally concerned with reducing to their basic material status the consecrating symbols that legitimize the arbitrary exercise of power. Moreover, both pick on the fantastic powers that the Harlequin enjoys on stage to describe the transformations that metaphors are capable of bringing about in the commoner's perception of the unfolding of state power. For Paine, however, the (thankfully unrealizable) power of the Harlequin's bat has the potential to raise dangerous illusions; like the metaphor it is capable of overlaying the metal headgear that the goldsmith designs for the king with a bogus "virtue" that it does not in itself have. On the other hand, in Jerrold's essay the transformatory power of the Harlequin's bat (and of the metaphor) destroys the majestic aura of the throne by refiguring it as a wooden armchair. Indeed, like the pantomime itself, Jerrold's technique *thrives* on transformations. Thus, Jerrold not only weaves around the object of demystification a range of counterimages but also rewrites the sanctifying protocols that surround the king (the blue monkey god) as an extended comic ritual that ends in an act of radical desacralization.

Jerrold's political parable exemplifies, at a fairly elaborate level, the working of that familiar impulse toward literary improvisation that writers such as Hone and Wooler had sustained. This impulse, moreover, would enjoy a long afterlife in the relatively alien terrain of the Dickensian novel. Equally, however, the hyperboles, parodies, and allegories that drove the improvisational trajectory within radical writing would expose it to the charge of inaccuracy: a charge which would remain active all the way from the *Quarterly Review*'s sneering reference to Hone as "a poor illiterate creature,"[40] to James Fitzjames Stephen's accusation that Dickens's propensity to exaggerate and caricaturize led to seriously distorted pictures of England's public institutions. What the proestablishment press could not neutralize, on the other hand, was the radical style's ability—exemplified in Jerrold's piece—to destabilize the very discursive protocols on which official pronouncements based their legitimacy. Indeed, at its most creative, "the language of radicalism" engaged not only with the arguments made by an established politician or social thinker but also with the educated modes of writing that insidiously vested these arguments with a value that they may not, in fact, have possessed. A very good example would be the following (fairly typical) attack that Cobbett unleashes against Malthus:

> The laws of nature [are] written in our passions, desires and propensities . . . Yes, say you: but nature has *other laws,* and amongst these are, that man shall live by *food,* and that if he cannot obtain food, he shall *starve.* Agreed, and if there be a man in England who cannot find, *in the whole country* . . . [a] shop, house, mill, barn . . . sufficient [food] to keep him alive, *then* I allow, that the laws of nature condemn him to die. . . .

"Oh!" you will, with Parsonlike bawl, exclaim, "but he must not commit *robbery* or *larceny!*" Robbery or larceny! What do you mean by that? Does the law of nature say anything about robbery or larceny? . . . So you will quit the law of nature now will you? (italics in the original)[41]

The aggression that drives Cobbett's writing is directed at Malthus's argument but also at what Raymond Williams has called, in a great but somewhat neglected essay, "the composed, quiet, and connected prose of the formally educated traditions,"[42] and especially at the monopoly that this prose exercised in the production of public opinion. Put another way, Cobbett's strategy is to throw into sharp relief a vital and naturalized function of the educated style: its ability to discredit and marginalize modes of articulation that do not or are not able to confirm to its protocols. Thus, Cobbett invades Malthus's measured prose with all the accumulated resentment of those shut out from knowledge production by the discursive barriers of formal education. Rather than constructing a logical counterargument in the clear, unencumbered prose style that Paine would have approved, Cobbett draws on the colloquialisms, exaggerations, and hyperboles of popular radicalism to destabilize the legitimizing mechanisms of Malthus's prose: its formal elegance, its rhetorically constructed illusion of logic, the truth effects that it achieves by the selective deployment of formal knowledge. What Cobbett creatively produces, thus, is a whole hybrid style within which Malthus's ideas—ripped out of the authorizing context of the scholarly treatise—are rearticulated in colloquial language, and the dignifying inflections of Malthus's official mode of address, entangled in a tone of absolute contempt, reduced to a "Parsonlike bawl."

The techniques of satiric overwriting popularized by Cobbett and Jerrold proliferated in the market for print entertainment where Dickens and Thackeray found their feet as writers. The two novelists, however, responded in very different ways to the expressive resources made available by the language of radicalism. These differences had significant effects not only on the internal aesthetics of Dickens's and Thackeray's novels but also on the way that these novels were received.

Thackeray was, of course, adept at working with radical expressive modes, as the many antiaristocratic and antimonarchial caricatures and parodies that he contributed to *Punch* testify. However, Thackeray also argued that the satiric displacements that drove his magazine work were incompatible with the realism that ought to underlie what he described as the "Art of Novels." Indeed, in the well-known 1849 letter, quoted earlier, Thackeray follows Paine in invoking the conventions of the pantomime to describe the distorting effects of embellishments, exaggerations, and magical transformation on certain kinds of novel writing. Specifically, he criticizes the Dickensian mode for habitually turning "a coat" into "an embroidered tunic" and the poker into "a great red-hot instrument like the Pantomime weapon."

For Thackeray then, the Painite suspicion of rhetorical embellishments moves from the domain of the political to that of the literary and is, indeed, made the basis of a system of novel writing that Thackeray associates with "Nature" and "the sentiment of reality." It is not surprising, then, that Thackeray's properly realistic representations of the elite, no matter how critical, would be based on the orchestration of details that he felt could be available to only those with direct access to the world of the upper classes. Moreover, Thackeray's realism would demand that conversations among the socially sophisticated or the speech that a politician might make in parliament be naturalized, integrated seamlessly into the ebb and flow of their everyday lives, rather than be held up for public scrutiny.

In sharp contrast, Dickens self-consciously defamiliarized the language of power, representing it not as it really was but as it appeared to those excluded from its processes. Thus, Dickens worked with techniques that may be associated with Cobbett's writing—repetition, magnification, exaggeration, parody—to expose and also to ridicule the ways in which languages of power drew upon their internal resources, on the socially sophisticated nuance or on the rhetoric of formality, to constitute themselves into those "practical metalanguage[s]" which, as Pierre Bourdieu argues, disguise semantic arbitrariness with an awe-inspiring formal rigor.[43] The radical aesthetic that Dickens fabricated involved absorbing and redeploying, within the expressive system of the novel, those techniques of rewriting that Thackeray felt were appropriate for journalistic satire rather than literature. This would transform the novel's representation of the languages of power: the sophisticated language that circulated in what Mrs. Merdle calls "Society" and the ceremonial discourses that came out of such institutions of the state as the law court or parliament. The activation of radical resources within Dickens's novels would have consequences on the way the nineteenth-century critical establishment would receive these novels.

Radical publicists were adept at working with not just linguistic but also visual satire. The groundwork for the popular political cartoon may have been laid by the ultraconservative James Gillray, whose horrific images of the revolutionaries in France both laid out the expressive parameters within which graphic satire would develop and demonstrated the effectiveness of political cartooning as a means of political mobilization. But by the first decade of the nineteenth century, radical publicists were using the political cartoon so effectively in their demystificatory project that it was recognized as, in the words of one of their most powerful adversaries, "a deadly weapon."[44] It is exactly this political efficacy of the radical print that is dramatized in *Coriolanus Addressing the Plebeians* (1820) (fig. 2). Here, Cruikshank depicts King George as Coriolanus, seemingly standing firm against Cobbett, Carlile, Hunt, Wooler, and the rest. But among these radical plebeians two figures stand out. One is, in Jonathan Bate's summary, "William Hone holding two clubs, one marked 'PARODY' and the other 'MAN IN THE MOON-HOUSE THAT JACK BUILT,' and the other is George Cruikshank holding a folio marked 'Caricature.'"[45]

The confrontation that Cruikshank was dramatizing should be taken seriously. A few months before the publication of *Coriolanus,* Cruikshank had demonstrated for a very large, predominantly plebeian audience how opposition to an act or policy of the government could be inscribed in the images of state dignitaries. In a devastating sequence of caricatures that he produced for Hone's pamphlets Cruikshank expressed the popular anger with the Peterloo massacre and with the king's marital behavior by portraying King George himself as a "dandy of sixty"—grossly overdressed, overweight, ridiculous in his attempts to appear young and later, in E. P. Thompson's summary, "blind drunk in his throne surrounded by broken bottles in front of a screen decorated with satyrs and large breasted trollops" (fig. 3).[46] Moreover, Cruikshank's *Coriolanus* is concerned with more than caricature's innate capacity to degrade its subject, or the increasingly public nature of the discursive space within which it was now operating. It is also a self-conscious celebration of the collaboration between caricature and the language of radicalism.

As it happens, Hone, whose satiric fabrications in language are, in *Coriolanus,* shown to complement Cruikshank's caricatures, commented at length in a later work on the relationship between the caricaturist's unalterable lines and the more abstract conjurations of language. Referring to a "sketch" of a parish beadle that he had just delineated in prose, Hone acknowledges that the beadle's "corporeal lineaments are 'borrowed' (with permission) from a new caricature, if it be given so low a name by one of the authors of 'Odes and Addresses to the Great.'"[47] Interestingly, however, Hone's interest in this particular caricature seems inseparable from its movement away both from the definitiveness which was associated in Romantic theories of representation (as W. T. J. Mitchell has shown)[48] with the visual arts and from the easily recognizable subjects of political caricature. Dissociated from the particularizing compulsions (and energies) of an existence in

FIGURE 2. George Cruikshank, *Coriolanus Addressing the Plebeians* (1820)

FIGURE 3. George Cruikshank, from *The Queen's Matrimonial Ladder* (1820)

the theatre of live politics, Hone's caricature exemplifies a mode of satiric articulation that is "broad and comprehensive," being directed, not at a person, but at a "class." One might argue, indeed, that Hone's "universal parish beadle" hovers on the edge of what Catherine Gallagher has called "the figure's alluring fictionality which stimulates our desire to witness palpable human fabrications 'appear as independent beings endowed with life.'"[49] Hone himself thinks of his beadle not as mere "caricatura" but rather as "a graphic satire of character"[50]—an imaginary entity which, freed from the fixity of the line drawing as well as the stable referents of real life, strives for those more speculative, abstract effects of literature. Hone's collaborations with visual caricature—from the improvisations in language with which he complemented Cruikshank's devastating portraits of King George during the period 1819–21 to the caricature that he raised in his *Everlasting Calendar of Popular Entertainments* (1827) to a "graphic satire of character"—mark in an unexpectedly clear fashion the process by which the radical caricaturist's capacity to inscribe popular resentments in the very physical image of a state official or dignitary passed into language. Here it remained a potential expressive resource even for discourses that were generated not by the pressures of active real-life politics, but by the demand for satiric, entertaining fiction. Indeed, Hone considers radical graphic caricature in relation not only to real political events or people but also to the novelistic problem of characterization.

As young entrants to the print market of the 1830s, Thackeray and Dickens inevitably encountered both visual and linguistic caricatures of the beadle, bureaucrat, or the Member of Parliament, but they related to these in very different ways. Thackeray's relationship with the demystifying techniques of radical portraiture was far more paradoxical than that of Dickens: he produced graphic caricatures of monarchs that seem almost like continuations of Cruikshank's portraits, but he was also committed to a mode of novel writing that would replace the mobilizing, collective orientation of radical portraiture with the psychological complexity, the dense internal detailing, in short the depth of the lifelike character. Thus, as in so much of his other magazine work, Thackeray found himself pushed by the demands for antiestablishment satire in the print market of the 1830s into producing a print like "Rex, Ludovicus, Ludovicus Rex" (1840) where the king, stripped of his royal regalia, is imaged as a physically pathetic specimen of humanity. On the other hand, the movement from "Rex" to, say, the younger Sir Pitt Crawley in *Vanity Fair* is precisely a movement away from a mode of articulation based on extraindividualistic public concerns to one that seeks to unfold a sharply individualized consciousness across time and in relation to that taken-for-granted, almost unnoticeable orchestration of details that would, in fact, be available only to those with access to the internal world of an aristocratic Whig politician.

How did the techniques of radical graphic satire affect Dickens's characterization? One way to begin answering this question is by engaging with Alex Woloch's seminal work on characterization and especially with the ways in which this might help in the understanding of the different, almost opposed, ways in which Dickens and Thackeray articulate the relationship between the inner lives of characters and the external social domain. Thackeray's move in the direction of realistic characterization had been predicated on a shift in emphasis from those external signifiers—the king's regalia, for example—that gave the figure its social or political identity, to the ways in which the social unfolds within what Alex Woloch has called "the interior life of a singular consciousness." On the other hand, Dickens's protagonists, as Woloch himself demonstrates with great insight, are typically constituted as weak subjects. They are "epistemologically and psychologically *passive*," subordinate to that which they observe. Indeed, in Dickens's fiction "the distribution of energy" is often so strongly weighted in favor of the scene and against the viewer, that it "overwhelm[s] contemplation or understanding itself." The fourth chapter of this book will be more centrally concerned with the extremely interesting connection that Woloch makes between the Dickensian protagonist's inability to sustain a full inner self and the frenetic, always changing cityscape where he or she so often operates. More relevant for my immediate purposes, however, is Woloch's argument that the weak subject's inability to sustain continuous inner contemplation results in his converting "seeing *into* 'sights,' processes into substances." For Woloch this reflex is, in fact, symptomatic of Dickens's own method that "consistently replaces incomplete vision with distorted visibility, hardening a social process into a substantive physical phenomenon." Woloch argues that this incessant transformation of "incomplete *seeing* into eccentric or obscure *sights*" may be one of the reasons for the overwhelming presence of minor, caricaturized characters in Dickens's fiction.[51]

The significance of Woloch's work on Dickens's characterization lies in that it simultaneously explains the weak subjective life of Dickens's protagonists and the incessant proliferation in his novels of caricaturized minor characters. It is important, however, to think through the problem of observation that is so central to Woloch's explanation, in relation not only to the subjectivity of the observer or to the conditions in which observations occur but also to a set of more historically determined and collective ways of seeing. *Sketches by Boz,* for example, assumes a certain agreement—especially on political matters—between the point of view of Boz and those who read what he observes and describes. Thus, the opening lines of "A Parliamentary Sketch" invoke a certain taken-for-granted skepticism about parliament and politicians that Boz shares with his readers and that will determine every subsequent observation that he makes: "We hope our readers will not be alarmed at this rather ominous title. We assure them that we are not about to become political, neither have we the slightest intention of being more prosy than usual—if we can help it."[52]

The "we" in this sentence represents an observer very different from Pickwick or Pip, who are always liable, as Woloch shows, to be overwhelmed by the frenetic action of the world outside. More specifically, Boz here is constituted not as a weak subject but as a figure who has subsumed his individuality under the collective identity that he shares with his readers. For this reason, the caricaturized portraits of parliamentarians that Boz will present have to be understood not as products of "incomplete seeing," but rather as ways of embodying that skepticism about politicians that is inherent in Boz's observing position and is indeed encoded in the sentence with which he opens "A Parliamentary Sketch."

Boz's situation and observations in "A Parliamentary Sketch" point to the limits of any explanation of Dickens's caricaturization that is based entirely on the internal dynamics of his novels: on the relationship between the protagonist and the external world that surrounds him and, at a deeper level, on the ways that these novels absorb and replicate within their character systems the historically constituted hierarchies of the social world outside. One way to address this limitation is by focusing on a discursive process to which Thackeray and Dickens related in differing ways: the movement of expressive resources across divergent genres and media. Thus, even Thackeray, who sought self-consciously to insulate his serious writing from the influence of low forms like graphic caricature, found it impossible to write about George IV without getting inundated by the visual details that Cruikshank had set into circulation:

> But this George, what was he? I look through all his life, and recognize but a bow and a grin. I try and take him to pieces, and find silk stockings, padding, stays, a coat with frogs, and a fur collar, a star and blue ribbon, a pocket-handkerchief prodigiously scented . . . and a huge black stock, underwaistcoats, and more underwaistcoats and then nothing.[53]

What Thackeray seems to focus on is the pervasive influence that Cruikshank's caricaturizing tropes exercised over every subsequent attempt at representing George IV. Thackeray, who was committed to delineating characters in all their psychological complexity, would certainly find this influence restrictive. But Cruikshank's satiric visual vocabulary—the "schemata" (in the parlance of art criticism) that he set into circulation[54]—could also be thought of as a "cultural legacy," "a total repertoire of potentialities" available as much to subsequent novelists as to artists.[55] From this perspective, the following caricature of a "doctor of civil law" in *Sketches by Boz* seems to have been produced not by the weak observing subject, as Woloch may have argued, but by Dickens's redeployment within the novel of techniques of articulating public figures that radical visual satire had pioneered:

> There was one individual who amused us mightily. This was one of the bewigged gentlemen in red robes, who was straddling before the fire in the centre of the Court, in the attitude of a brazen Colossus, to the complete exclusion of everybody else. He had gathered his robes behind, in much the same manner as a slovenly woman would her petticoats on a very dirty day, in order that he might feel the full warmth of the fire . . . We shall never be able to lay any credit as a physiognomist again, for, after a careful scrutiny of this gentleman's countenance, we had come to the conclusion that it bespoke of nothing but conceit and silliness, when our friend with the silver staff whispered in our ear that he was no other than a doctor of civil law, and heaven knows what besides. (87–88)

Replicating within the symbolic system of language precisely those visual details of dress, body, and posture with which graphic caricaturists achieve their effects, this portrait exemplifies what William Hone had described as "a graphic satire of character." Moreover, Boz's mode of representation is inseparable from an observing position that comes very close to what the radical journalist Wooler would describe as that of the "crowd": "While [folly] struts in the robe of office, it is unconscious of the ridiculous appearance which it offers to the crowd. It would render laughter high treason if possible. . . ."[56]

Similarly, it is by positioning himself among those unable to comprehend the protocols of courts that Boz is able not only to cut through the hierarchizing operations of officialdom but also to privilege a petitioner's disgusted response to the petty domination exercised by some nameless official over an intimate and detailed knowledge of that official's everyday life. In this sense, this early sketch might help clarify the whole sequence of caricaturized figures who appear in Dickens's fiction, from Bumble to Tite Barnacle, not as products of Dickens's unique comic genius or as figures flattened by the dynamic character systems that Woloch describes, but rather as displacements within a certain form of entertainment-oriented fictionalizing, of a strand of radical satire oriented toward building around its irreverent representations of those who wielded political power a community of the excluded.

In their confrontation with the persons and processes associated with state power, the radical caricaturists deployed not only the disfiguring techniques discussed above but also that profusion of allegorical detail, which, as Baudelaire suggested, was integral to the work of the English caricaturists.[57] The "art of the rebus and of the primitive ideographic script" had,[58] of course, always found expression in the insignia of the aristocracy and in the emblems of the state, but it had also developed, through the early modern period, as a burlesque of official heraldry. Moreover, although the radical discourse itself sustained a considerable iconography which served as targets for conservative satirists, a great deal of its expressive energies was generated by the recognition that emblems, insignia, and symbols were never merely "the trimmings of political culture, but often went to the heart of what was ultimately at issue: how power at all levels of the state and civil society was to be defined and exercised."[59]

Radical publicists disrupted the state's consecrating symbols in many ways: from burlesquing the general's cocked hat or the judge's wig in their caricatures of these dignitaries of the state to generating full-blown counteremblematic reworkings of official protocols. The important thing, though, is to locate traces of the counteremblematic techniques of radical satire in the *language* of popular radicalism after this had moved from the mobilizing texts of the 1820s to the print market of the '30s. At this level, too, the work of Douglas Jerrold proves to be invaluable. Thus, an essay like "The Order of Poverty" (1846) not only addresses itself directly to the problem of what it sees as the arbitrary consecrating function of heraldry but also self-consciously reactivates, within the symbolic system of language, some of graphic satire's most effective modes of demystification.

One obvious example of such reactivation is Jerrold's use of juxtaposition as a means of demystification. Thus, Jerrold habitually uses the synchronic possibilities of pictorial representation to generate disconcerting juxtapositions—for example, to set off against the prestige that a royal decoration confers the actual achievements of those who receive such decorations. Moreover, the metonymic extensions through which counteremblematic graphic satire attains its most characteristic effects are not only replicated but, in fact, find freer if more diffused expression in Jerrold's prose. Liberated completely from the boundedness of the physical image, and from even a minimal commitment to visible similarity as the basis of association, Jerrold can find in the radical indeterminacy of the linguistic signifier the means of effecting drastic and unexpected transformations on the object of his satire. Thus, it is not the visible imagery of the "Order of the Thistle" but its very antiquity that serves as the basis of Jerrold's destabilizing counterdiscourse. If the "Order of the Thistle" is very old it can, by a metonymic extension, be said to be as "old as asses" and then be made to sustain the full-blown counterimage of an asinine "nobility" that "browses" on thistles. This kind of radical refiguring of traditional imagery generates unlimited expressive possibilities in Jerrold's prose: the idea of the "order" itself proliferates into many parodic orders—for example, the Order of the Golden Calf whose knights have discarded armor and helmet for "the magic mail of impenetrable Bank-paper."[60] Again, since the counteremblematic imagery that Jerrold fabricates in language exploits but is no longer tied to the synchronicity of the picture frame, it becomes capable of sustaining not just a wider range of comic improvisations, but also sequence and, ultimately—as Jerrold's parable of the Woky Poky Indians testifies—narrative itself.

The movement of the emblematic techniques of visual satire into the domain of literary print culture had important implications for the Dickensian aesthetic. It enabled a novel like *Bleak House* not only to generate a counteremblematic discourse against the ceremonious unfolding of the Chancery proceedings but also to sustain, within the spatially unconstrained novel form, a narrative based on the metonymic extensions of visual caricature. It was this new set of expressive possibilities that came to the novel from visual satire that was to produce the single most inventive episode in *Bleak House*: the symbolic death of Krook—the grotesque mirror image of the Lord Chancellor himself—by spontaneous combustion.

CHAPTER 2

The Aesthetics and Politics of Caricature

Bleak House, Little Dorrit, and *Vanity Fair*
in Relation to "Radical Expression"

IN CHAPTER 30 of *Pendennis,* Archer, a pillar of the "Corporation of the Goosequill," boasts of his encounter in the palace anteroom with the Lord Chamberlain, who walked in "holding the royal tea cup and saucer in his hand" (vol. 1, 313). This vignette is significant because in it Archer's claim about providing an insider's account of activities in the palace anteroom is satirized but also constituted as part of a process by which the world of *Pendennis* is itself partially produced. On the one hand, Archer is exposed satirically, from the point of view of the skeptical outsider, as a lackey of aristocratic politicians whose birth invests them with arbitrary power. On the other hand, however, Archer ferrets out a form of news that is shown to be not only in great demand in the world of Thackeray's novels but also vital to the way that Thackeray himself represents this world. Thus, *Pendennis* is full of people hungry for inside information on the social and political affairs of the elite. It is this constituency that Finucane, the subeditor of the *Pall Mall Gazette,* services by never allowing "a death or a dinner party of the aristocracy [to] pass without having the event recorded in the columns of his journal" (vol. 1, 356). Indeed, it would hardly be possible for Thackeray himself to represent the details of aristocratic life that circulate so incessantly in the world of his novels without acquiring some knowledge of those details.

Thackeray's representation of Archer's boast both as the object of his satire and as symptomatic of his method corresponds to a flexibility of authorial position that he always managed to sustain. At one level, thus, Thackeray represents the aristocratic public figures from the satiric point of view of those subjected to their arbitrary governance. In "Going to See a Man Hanged" (1840), for example, aristocratic members of parliament are reduced to faceless and nameless abstractions who are engaged perpetually in "shouting, yelling, crowing, hear-hearing, pooh-poohing, making speeches of three columns, and gaining 'great Conservative triumphs,' or 'signal successes of the Reform cause.'" Yet even in this essay, which belongs to the radical *Punch* phase of his career, Thackeray gestures toward a different kind of social allegiance when he apologizes to his (presumably middle-class) readers for the "unconscionable republican tirade" that he has just unleashed against members of parliament.[1] Of course, Thackeray's apology is ironic, but he always thought of irony as a response that was finer, more nuanced, and based on a more detailed knowledge of its object than the one-sided and uninformed sarcasm that he associated with radicals such as his *Punch* colleague Douglas Jerrold.

The flexibility that underlies Thackeray's self-positioning in relation to the social domains that he describes is often consciously discussed as part of an author's responsibilities, as he moves from his journalistic pieces to his novels. For example, the comradeship that the narrator of *Vanity Fair* is able to claim with his predominantly middle-class audience is based on their common exclusion from those "august portals . . . guarded by grooms of the chamber with flaming silver forks with which they prong all those who have not the right of the *entrée*."[2] But Thackeray also uses the outsider's status that his readers and he share to whet the former's curiosity about what really goes on in the drawing rooms of the gentry. For this reason, Thackeray considers it his responsibility as an author to acquire the social knowledge that will enable him to delineate aristocratic life with the accuracy of an insider. In a demystifying, metatextual gesture in *Vanity Fair* that would become increasingly rare with the progress of realism as a mode of novel writing, Thackeray exposes, as in an X-ray plate, the hidden authorial diligence that sustains the apparently spontaneous unfolding of upper-class life:

> With regard to the world of female fashion and its customs, the present writer, of course, can only speak at second hand. A man can no more penetrate or understand those mysteries than he can know what the ladies talk about when they go upstairs after dinner. It is only by inquiry and perseverance that one sometimes gets hints of those secrets; and by a similar

diligence every person who treads the Pall Mall pavement, and frequents the clubs of this metropolis, knows, either through his own experience or through some acquaintance with whom he plays at billiards or shares the joint, something about the genteel world of London, and how, as there are men (such as Rawdon Crawley, whose position we mentioned before) who cut a good figure to the eyes of the ignorant world and to the apprentices in the Park, who behold them consorting with the most notorious dandies there, so there are ladies, who may be called men's women, being welcomed entirely by all the gentlemen, and cut or slighted by all their wives. (357)

In contrast to Thackeray's ability to move between two authorial positions, Dickens, in *Little Dorrit*, entrenches himself firmly outside the charmed circle of the elite. Dickens's "us," in the description of Mr. Merdle's glittering dinner that I have already quoted, may not denote the already mobilized and confrontationist community encoded in Paine's "we" or Cobbett's "us,"[3] but it is the "stylistic aura" of precisely these collective pronouns that determines Dickens's[4] representation of Merdle's guests as not individuals but personifications of institutional power: "magnates from the Court and magnates from the City, magnates from the Commons and magnates from the Lords, magnates from the bench and magnates from the bar, Bishop magnates, Treasury magnates, Horse Guard magnates, Admiralty magnates."

The differing authorial positions that Dickens and Thackeray adopted in relation to the inner world of the political elite produced larger divergences in the ways in which they represented the aristocracy-dominated domain of parliamentary politics. To understand these differences and more specifically the ways in which Dickens's radical heritage pushed him in a direction that was different from Thackeray's realistic method, one could, to begin with, focus on the relationship between their novels and the discourses spawned by an unreformed parliament. Here the two contemporaries would have had to necessarily engage with the legacy of the radical journalists, since these journalists had all along been at the forefront of the long and complex struggle for the right to print and publicize parliamentary proceedings.[5] Moreover, as Kevin Gilmartin has shown, "radical interventions in parliamentary representation extended well beyond . . . printed reports of debates": they commented critically on or parodied every form of political speech, whether delivered in election campaigns or inside parliament. Satirizing the discursive modes that legitimized the parliamentary system, shifting the arena of political discussion from "the parliament and parliamentary classes" to "popular counter authorities,"[6] the radical journalists consolidated a politically aware audience that was capable, in the words of *Fraser's Magazine*, of judging "men in high station" with "keen and scrutinising minuteness."[7] As Olivia Smith puts it:

> Tom Paine's hope and Dougald Stewart's fear that the loss of mystery would diminish the supremacy of the upper classes were in part fulfilled. The radical press scrutinized the government's behavior and attacked traditional practices by which the government protected itself. Cabinet ministers, especially Sidmouth, Canning and Castlereagh, were exposed and reviled as was the Prince Regent . . . For several years from 1819–22, writers and readers released themselves from previous constraints. They were incessantly, aggressively, willfully and hilariously rude. The manacles had broken and the people laughed and laughed.[8]

Thackeray's relationship with the "popular counter authorities" was complex. In "Going to See a Man Hanged" he may have drawn on the mocking idioms of the newly politicized masses while reducing parliamentary debates to mere "shouting, yelling, crowing, hear-hearing, pooh-poohing," but he also argued that the "the language of radicalism" was inseparable from rabble-rousing and was, in this sense, uninformed and unreasonable. In *The Newcomes,* "radical expression" energizes nothing more significant than the outpourings of the "brawling tap orator,"[9] and far from uncovering for a large all-class audience the interests that lie hidden beneath the elevated rhetoric of parliamentary debating, it is confined, in *Pendennis,* to the shabby quadrangle in inner London "hidden from the outer world" where "Ballad-singers come and chant in . . . deadly guttural tones, satirical songs against the Whig administration, against the bishops and dignified clergy, against the German relatives of an august royal family; Punch sets up his theatre sure of an audience, and occasionally of a halfpenny, from the swarming occupants of the houses . . ." (vol. 2, 34).

In *Pendennis,* Thackeray himself claims far greater knowledge of the nuances of parliamentary speeches than what is expressed by the street musicians in their "deadly guttural tones." But this claim is sustainable only because Thackeray tracks Pen's emerging career as a future parliamentarian from within that very Oxbridge club whose members had been shown, in "Going to See a Man Hanged," to reduce parliamentary debating to mere noise. The insider's knowledge that informs Thackeray's delineation of young Oxbridge men training for a parliamentary career does not necessarily make him less critical of parliamentary activity than writers who focused on the exclusionary mechanisms of an aristocracy-dominated parliament. However, in *Pendennis* speeches made in parliament are inevitably integrated into the discursive universe of the elite. These speeches, indeed, do not even operate in a domain that can properly be described as political. Rather, they represent a set of skills that guarantee, to adept practitioners, very wide social visibility. For the Major, Pen's entry into parliament is important chiefly because it will enable him to display the full range of his "oratory" and, in this way, earn for him "a name that his sons shall be proud of" (vol. 2, 220). Displaced from the domain of politics itself, parliamentary debating—or rather Pen's skill in this activity—re-enters an elite public sphere as a sign within the system of signs by which social status is calibrated in the world of Thackeray's fiction.

A very different orientation drives Dickens's representation of parliamentary debates. The well-known Circumlocution Office passages in *Little Dorrit,* for example, are based on an approach that refuses to take what Major Pendennis admiringly calls "oratory" at face value:

> It is true how not to do it was the great study and object of all public departments and professional politicians all around the Circumlocution Office. It is true that every new premier and every new government, coming in because they had upheld a certain thing as necessary to be done, were no sooner come in than they applied their utmost faculties to discovering How Not to Do It. It is true that from the moment that a general election was over, every returned man who had been raving on hustings because it hadn't been done . . . began to device How it was not to be done. It is true that the debates of both houses of Parliament the whole session through, tended to be the protracted deliberation, How not to do it. It is true that the royal speech at the opening of such sessions virtually said, My lords and gentleman you have a considerable stroke of work to do, and you will please to retire to your respective chambers, and discuss How not to do it . . . All this is true, but the Circumlocution Office went beyond it. (145–46)[10]

What connects this passage to the language of radicalism is not so much its content as its *style.* One way in which to throw into relief Dickens's stylistic debt to the radical journalists is by comparing this passage with, say, John Stuart Mill's rigorous and well-informed argument against reactionary oppositions to the idea of a competitive examination as the basis for filling positions in the civil services. Mill's mode of presenting his argument bears all the marks of a logical, educated mind accustomed to intervening in the processes of decision making:

Another objection is that if appointments are given to talent, the Public Offices will be filled with low people, without the breeding or the feelings of gentlemen. If, as this objection supposes, the sons of gentlemen cannot be expected to have as much ability and instruction as the sons of low people, it would make a strong case for social changes of a more extensive character. . . . If, with advantages and opportunities so vastly superior, the youth of higher classes have not honour enough, or energy enough, or public spirit enough, to make themselves as well qualified as others for the station which they desire to maintain, they are not fit for that station, and cannot too soon step out of it and give place to better people.[11]

As is well known, the satire against the Barnacles in *Little Dorrit*, too, drew upon and fueled the agitation against an aristocracy-dominated administration whose incompetence had recently been exposed by the Crimean War.[12] So Dickens would agree completely with the content of the argument that Mill makes about the importance of building a merit-based administrative cadre. But Mill's *tone* is that of an insider: it is determined by the assumption that a logical argument can influence the decision made by a governmental committee. The Circumlocution Office passage, on the other hand, is positioned very differently in relation to the domain within which the discourses of power circulate. A measure of this difference is Dickens's lack of interest in the specificities of the debate on administrative reform and, indeed, his refusal to take the debate on its own terms. Rather, the tone of the Circumlocution Office passages suggests a radical lack of trust in discourses that emerge from the domain of governmental decision making, and the propensity to treat such discourses as obfuscations rather than attempts to reform. Accordingly, like Cobbett who invades Malthus's learned prose with the colloquial skepticism of those debarred from the processes of formal education, Dickens seizes upon the legitimizing conventions of parliamentary debating—its ceremonious modes of address and its lofty-sounding rhetoric—and juxtaposes these against what, from his position amidst the excluded, appears to be the essential underlying function of the bureaucracy, which is, "How not to do it." In this way Dickens fabricates a hybridized style in which the utterances of the king, the prime minister, and professional politician become entangled in a tone of absolute disbelief and contempt; in which the ceremonial phrasing and leisurely cadences of parliamentary rhetoric are met not with logic or reason but with, to adapt the terms used by Richard Terdiman in his analysis of Daumier's caricature, a "specifically *counter-discursive oppositional*" mode that "signifies the assertion of difference in the strongest possible terms" (italics in the original).[13]

The generative effects of the radical style on Dickens's novelization of the languages of power unfold across not only the political field but also the social. Olivia Smith has argued convincingly that one of the achievements of the radical writers was that they successfully challenged the upper-class use of "refined" language as an instrument of domination and that a great deal of radical writing such as Cobbett's *Grammar* were, among other things, attempts at exposing the equivocations of a "refined" language based, in Cobbett's angry words, on "sound instead of sense."[14] The impact of such perspectives on Dickens's relationship with language—with language as both mode and object of representation—is clear, considering how much he deviated from the aesthetic norms that would, through the course of the nineteenth-century, become consecrated as realism.

These norms unfold, in their most evolved form, in the realistic yet critical delineations of high-society conversations that appear so often in the work of Leo Tolstoy. Tolstoy regularly used high-society conversations to expose the snobbishness and hypocrisy with which he associated the elite. However, his representations of these conversations were invariably nuanced: he registered, with an insider's knowledge, the accents and inflections of aristocratic speech, and he distinguished between the speech patterns of individual speakers. This insider's observing position—which in *Vanity Fair* had been acquired by self-conscious authorial diligence—becomes so naturalized in War and Peace that it is not even noticed. It is, nevertheless, the essential precondition for Tolstoy's "spontaneous," apparently unmediated unfolding of, for example, a dinner party at the aristocratic Anna Pavlovna's home in *War and Peace:*[15]

> Anna Pavlovna's drawing room was gradually filling. The cream of Petersburg arrived, people differing widely in age and character but alike in that they all belonged to the same class of society. Prince Vasili's daughter, the beautiful Helene, came to take her father to the ambassador's party. She was wearing a ball dress and her maid of honour's badge. Then there was the youthful little Princess Bolkonsky, known as *la femme la plus seduisante de Petersbourgh* . . . Prince Vassily's son Prince Hippolyte arrived with Mortemart, whom he introduced. The Abbe Morio and many others also came.[16]

Tolstoy's language here is not, of course, merely a transparency. Beneath its apparently spontaneous uncovering of reality is the surreptitious orchestration of connotations by which the reader's mind is directed to a level of signification beyond what the passage literally reveals.[17] Thus, to give a particularly relevant example, the spontaneous way in which the author breaks into French suggests that the sophisticated men and women who troop into Anna Pavlovna's drawing room are completely at home in that language. Moreover, this detail feeds into a larger theme in the novel as a whole: the Frenchified elite's cultural alienation from the Russian-speaking masses. Interestingly, however, the French words appear as part of the natural flow of sentences—simply as details that seem to blend discreetly with innumerable other details that work together to simulate, discursively, a glittering, aristocratic drawing room.

In a comparable piece in the *Political Register,* Cobbett, too, denounces the elite's use of a language that is incomprehensible to ordinary people—a position with which Tolstoy would almost certainly sympathize. However, in the very process of incorporating a Latin phrase within his text, Cobbett reveals his *distance* from the world of the elite of which Tolstoy's realistic prose offers an insider's view:

> If this be the meaning of "*Uti Possidetis,*" why not give that meaning in our own language at once? Do those who make use of such phrases, which the stupidest wretch on earth might learn as well as they, in a few hours; nay which a parrot would learn, which a high-dutch bird-catcher would teach a bull-finch or a tom-tit, in the space of a month; and do they think, in good earnest, that this relic of the mummery of monkery, this playing off upon us of a few galipot words, will make us believe that they are *learned*?[18]

For Cobbett, writing from the point of view of those marginalized in a culture where "civilisation was largely a linguistic concept,"[19] "*Uti Possidetis*" cannot be allowed to lose itself among other words in the sentence. On the contrary, ripped out of the semantic system to which it originally belonged, it is *displayed* as an alien element in the everyday language in which Cobbett and his audience speak to each other. It is held up for public examination, mocked, exposed as a sham whose lack of substance is disguised under its incomprehensibility.

Cobbett's insight about language as a marker of educational or social status produced certain expressive strategies that proved crucial to the radical aesthetic that was developing in the Dickensian novel. More surprising, though, is the use Thackeray, too, makes of sharp Cobbett-like juxtapositions between two linguistic registers to mark internal differences within what would appear to be a homogeneous social domain:

> Mr. Crawley said a long grace and Sir Pitt said Amen, and the great silver dish-covers were removed.
> "What have we for dinner, Betsy?" said the Baronet.
> "Mutton broth, I believe, Sir Pitt," answered Lady Crawley.
> "*Mouton aux navets,*" added the Butler gravely . . . "and the soup is *potage de mouton a l'ecossaise* . . ."
> "Mutton's mutton," said the Baronet, "and a devilish good thing. What *ship* was it, Horrocks, and when did you kill?"
> "One of the black-faced Scotch, Sir Pitt; we killed on Thursday . . ."
> "Will you have some *potage,* Miss ah—Miss Blunt?" said Mr. Crawley.
> "Capital Scotch broth, my dear," said Sir Pitt, "though they call it by a French name."
> "I believe it is the custom, sir, in decent society," said Mr. Crawley haughtily, "to call the dish as I have called it . . ." (68)

This representation of a conversation between a baronet and his upwardly mobile son is inseparable from the protean social identity that Thackeray consistently adopts in *Vanity Fair* and that enables him, in this instance, to move between the inner domain of a minor landed family and the sensibilities of his predominantly middle-class readers. Thus, the stylized debate that Thackeray generates on the language appropriate for a dinner table conversation immediately opens up a certain critical distance between him and his characters. This distance, indeed, not only helps to synchronize Thackeray's own perspective with that of his predominantly middle-class readers but also pushes the mode of his description in the direction of satire. However, although cast as a series of sharp, satiric exchanges, the conversation between father and son is embedded in an environment which, in the density and specificity of its detailing, unfolds as a realistic representation of the world of the minor aristocracy. As an integral part of this world, the older Crawley cannot, in any sense, share Cobbett's outsider's position even though he may follow Cobbett in *confronting* his son's Frenchified English. For this reason, the older Pitt's intervention cannot be part of a radical demystificatory project oriented toward exposing how refined speech functions as a means of social domination. Rather than working as an instrument by which Thackeray might satirize the conversation that circulates in high society, Pitt's unrefined speech (together with his crude, often decadent habits) sustain the provincial strand within what Thackeray delineates as a single but amazingly varied family.

Dickens's approach to the language of upper classes is different. Specifically, Dickens follows the radical writers in representing the language of the elite as the materialization of a dominating semiotic rather than using it as a medium that will register the differences in accents or inflections in ways that different characters speak. But *Little Dorrit* also draws on the expressive possibilities available to the novel form to register the excluding effects of upper-class language, at the affective rather than exclusively at the political or social levels. Thus, the radical skepticism about gentlemanly language continues to unfurl powerfully in *Little Dorrit* and its effects are clearly visible when, for example, Mrs. General begins instructing Amy about the linguistic adjustments she needs to make in order to converse successfully in high society. Mrs. General insists that Amy must call Mr. Dorrit "papa" instead of "father"—"Father is rather vulgar, my dear. The word Papa, besides, gives a very pretty form to the lips" (359). As a professional instructor in gentlemanly etiquette, Mrs. General teaches Amy how to activate the metalingustic function of words as "signs of wealth intended to be evaluated and appreciated."[20] However, by doing this she also drains a crucial word in Amy's vocabulary of a whole history of love, suffering, self-sacrifice, and heroic resourcefulness in which it is saturated and, in this way, confirms the radical criticism of upper-class language as something that was based on form rather than content, on "sound," as Cobbett put it, instead of "sense."

Dickens's propensity to abstract the word "papa" from the naturalizing context of a drawing room conversation and to hold up to the light of day its hidden metalinguistic function as a sign of class is symptomatic of a larger representational strategy. Thus, within the system of which Mrs. General is the center, not only the word but virtually everything else—dress, posture, demeanor, the body itself—are, to quote Bourdieu again, deployed as part of "an *expressive style,* which being perceived and appreciated with reference to the universe of . . . practically competing styles, takes on a social value and a symbolic efficacy" [italics in original.][21] Mrs. General's white gloves have an expressive function, over and above their utilitarian one: they are brought into play to signify her disapproval of anything that is not "perfectly proper, placid and pleasant" and, in this sense, her good breeding (530). Similarly Mrs. Merdle instructs her husband of the social advantages of a *"degage"* posture, while she herself allows her person to be radically reduced so that it might function more efficiently as a one-dimensional social signifier. Her imposing presence in "Society" is predicated on her ability to make her bejeweled bosom represent her entire existence. This part of Mrs. Merdle's anatomy, Dickens tells us:

> was not a bosom to repose upon, but it was a capital bosom to hang jewels upon. Mr. Merdle wanted something to hang jewels upon, and he bought

it for the purpose. Storr and Mortimer might have married on the same speculation.

Like all his speculations, it was sound and successful. The jewels showed to the richest advantage. The bosom moving in Society with the jewels displayed upon it, attracted general admiration . . . (293)

This chapter has been concerned so far with showing how, in *Little Dorrit,* Dickens draws on radical strategies and presents both the conventions of parliamentary debating as well as the nuanced social languages of the elite not as they really are but rather as modes of domination that can be met only with the counterassault of parodic or satiric rewriting. However, Dickens's representation of Mrs. Merdle as a "bosom moving in Society with the jewels displayed upon it," rather than as a well-rounded, physically proportionate figure, points to another set of techniques that may have passed into his novels from the radical journalistic tradition. These techniques are most clearly exemplified in the *visual* caricatures of King George IV and his ministers with which George Cruikshank transformed the ways in which common people might relate to the highest state dignitaries. In what precise ways did the techniques of radical caricature influence the fiction of Dickens?

Here again, the doubleness of Thackeray's relationship with graphic satire serves to highlight the much more direct way in which this visual strand within "radical expression" energized the Dickensian aesthetic. Thackeray was a practicing cartoonist and he helped, as we've seen, to carry techniques of representation developed by older radical caricaturists into the pages of *Punch.* Yet, although cartoons do circulate in the world of Thackeray's fiction, these are integrated into a social universe that has nothing in common with the milieu that produced radical caricature. Thus, the young Clive in *The Newcomes* certainly does not see himself as furthering some radical demystificatory project when he produces a caricature of the "huge red-haired Scotch student, Mr. Sandy M'Collop." Rather, like Pen's book reviews or even his oratory, Clive's caricature is constituted as yet another social resource—something that helps to enhance his social prestige as he finds his way through the rivalries and alliances incessantly generated within the peer group that he inhabits:

> Clive was pronounced an "out and outer," "a swell and no mistake," and complimented, with scarce no dissentient voice . . . Besides, he drew very well,—there could be no doubt about that. Caricatures of the students, of course, were passing constantly among them, and in revenge for one which

a huge red-haired Scotch student, Mr. Sandy M'Collop had made of John James, Clive perpetrated a picture of Sandy which set the whole room in a roar. (vol. 2, 183)

Similarly, in *Vanity Fair,* Becky's performed caricatures of Miss Crawley's guests function as powerful signifiers within the self-enclosed discursive sphere that registers as news or gossip the affairs of the elite and, in this way, incessantly calibrates the exact position of individual members in an always changing hierarchy:

> When the parties were over, and the carriages had rolled away, the insatiable Miss Crawley would say, "Come to my dressing room, Becky, and let us abuse the company,"—which, between them, the pair of friends did perfectly. Old Sir Huddleston wheezed a great deal at the dinner; Sir Giles Wapshot had a particularly noisy manner of imbibing his soup, and her ladyship a wink of the left eye; all of which Becky caricatured to admiration, as well as the particulars of the night's conversation—the politics, the war, the quarter sessions, the famous run with the H.H., and those heavy and dreary themes about which country gentlemen converse. As for the Misses Wapshot's toilettes and Lady Fuddlestone's famous yellow hat, Miss Sharp tore them to tatters, to the infinite amusement of her audience. (94)

We could say, thus, that rather than *producing* characters, such as "The Dandy of Sixty" in Hone's *The Political House* or Thackeray's own "Ludovicous Rex," the art of caricature is constituted in Thackeray's fiction as a special talent that certain characters possess and deploy, often very skillfully, in appropriate social situations. In this sense, the caricatures and cartoons that circulate in *The Newcomes* or *Vanity Fair* function as details that, together with innumerable other details, sustain the nuanced realism with which Thackeray delineates his characters as well as the world they inhabit. It is not surprising, then, that Thackeray seems to self-consciously distance his novel writing from the methods employed by the radical caricaturists. Thus, the clue he offers in *The Newcomes* to his own approach to characterization is a mode of line drawing very different from that practiced by the caricaturist:

> And now let the artist, if he has succeeded in drawing Clive to his liking, cut a fresh pencil, and give us a likeness of Ethel. She is seventeen years old; rather taller than the majority of women; of a countenance somewhat grave and haughty, but on occasion brightening with humour or beaming

with kindliness and affection. Too quick to detect affectation or insincerity in others, too impatient of dullness or pomposity, she is more sarcastic now than she became when after years of suffering had softened her nature. Truth looks out of her bright eyes, and rises up armed, and flashes scorn or denial, perhaps too readily, when she encounters flattery, or meanness, or imposture. (252)

Clearly, Thackeray's unfolding of Ethel's character will not have much in common with a form of line drawing that works with distortions, exaggerations, or allegorical improvisations. Rather, the sketch that Thackeray proposes to his imaginary artist strives not only to achieve an exact physical "likeness" of its subject but also to make this subject's features expressive of a complex, mobile, always changing inner life.

Thackeray's sympathy for his imaginary artist's mode of sketching reveals something about the way in which he was likely to handle that primary object of radical caricature: the public character. Thus, in contrast to what happens in "Ludovicous Rex," the dislike that energizes Thackeray's delineation of the younger Pitt in *Vanity Fair* is never allowed to push the baronet's figure into the direction of caricature. More specifically, in his depiction of the baronet, Thackeray never severs the relationship between what Alex Woloch has incisively described as "thought and social being," between "character as social being" and "character as inner quality."[22] Thus, Thackeray never uses the distortions or emblematic improvisations of graphic satire to reduce Pitt to an abstraction for snobbishness. Pitt's snobbishness does, of course, operate powerfully as a marker of his aristocratic status, but it is also inextricable from what is presented as his inner life, developed carefully in relation to a dense network of referential systems that weave together as a seamless whole the details of his (mediocre) diplomatic career, his reading habits, his acquaintances among Whig politicians, and the crumbling landscape of his paternal estate. Thackeray's ability to produce highly individualized characters out of a set of precise and socially identifiable details prompted many contemporaries to set off against his characterization,[23] Dickens's "satiric, comic portraitures" that could never be said to come "within the strict bounds of the real."[24]

The Victorian critical establishment's propensity to privilege Thackeray's characters over those of Dickens was based on a conviction that may be said to lie at the heart of the bourgeois liberal imagination: that novels should always aspire to produce "the free standing individual, defined through his or her interior consciousness." However, the untrammeled unfolding of the individual subject privileged by the liberal imagination found itself impeded by that other great phenomenon of the nineteenth century: democracy. As Alex Woloch puts it:

> [The realist novel] also registers the competing pull of inequality and democracy within the nineteenth century bourgeois imagination. In my reading of the realist aesthetic, a dialectical literary form is generated out of the relationship between inequality and democracy. The realist novel is infused with the sense that any character is a potential hero, but simultaneously enchanted with the free standing individual, defined through his or her interior consciousness. In the paradigmatic character-structure of the realist novel, any character *can* be a protagonist, but only one character is; just as increasing political equality, and a maturing logic of human rights, develop amid acute economic and social stratification. On the one hand, the asymmetric structure of realistic characterization—which rounds out one or several characters while flattening, and distorting, a manifold assortment of characters—reflects the actual structure of inequitable distribution. On the other hand, the *claims* of minor characters on the reader's attention—and the resultant tension between characters and their function—are generated by the democratic impulse that forms a horizon of nineteenth century politics.[25]

The importance of Woloch's intervention is that it moves the problem of characterization away from the individual abilities of the author and reconstitutes it in relation not only to history but also to the internal exigencies of the text. It seems to me, however, that Woloch does not take far enough the implications of his own insights into the ways in which democracy might affect characterization and especially the novel's representation of those who, like Pitt Crawley, wield power. This shortfall is the more surprising since power relations are absolutely central to Woloch's account of characterization: minor characters, he argues, are often flattened—deprived of their inner lives—not because of some artistic failure on the part of their authors, but because they are pushed into this position by the demands of the main characters. Even weak Dickensian protagonists such as Pip help to perpetuate this process. Pip's expansive life as a gentleman is prepared for by the diminishing of other lives. The commands that Pip's tailor keeps hurling at his assistant even as he obsequiously services the now-rich Pip are suggestive, Woloch argues, of "the protagonist's social elevation . . . and Trabb's boy's social subordination." On the other hand, as Woloch himself demonstrates, the democratic impulse that forms the horizon of nineteenth-century politics also disables the smooth assimilation of Trabb's boy into the service economy from which he might self-effacingly help to sustain Pip's career as a gentleman. Thus, Trabb's boy "escapes" Pip's domination and behaves like several other minor characters in Dickens's fiction who emerge as "symbolic elaborations of or psychological foils for the protagonist's interiority *and* as competing centers of interest and agency that radically contextualize the protagonist."[26]

It seems to me, however, that the "agency" that Woloch associates with Trabb's boy extends well beyond drawing attention to the inequitable distribution of authorial energy that reduces him to an instrument in the full development of the hero's character. Instead of suffering the erasure reserved for minor characters, when the gentlemanly Pip adopts a serene and unconscious attitude toward him, Trabb's boy hits back with a devastating caricature of Pip:

> Suddenly the knees of Trabb's boy smote together, his hair uprose, his cap fell off, he trembled violently in every limb, staggered out into the road, and crying to the populace "Hold me! I'm so frightened!" feigned to be in such a paroxysm of terror and contrition, occasioned by the dignity of my appearance.[27]

What accounts for the massive excess of energy that enables Trabb's boy to overturn the very mode in which the liberal humanist tradition of characterization casts the figure of its protagonist? The answer has to be that the very marginal position into which Trabb's boy is pushed has a generative potential that Woloch does not sufficiently account for. More specifically, Trabb's boy is pushed into that experience of exclusion that provoked the satiric distortions of the radical caricaturists in their representations of politicians, society ladies, or dandies. Thus, this moving caricature of Pip works with such external signs as facial expressions or gestures or dress, not with the aim of producing a psychologically complex, sharply individualized subject, but rather of activating within the object of its representation a set of features that would immediately be recognized by large groups of people as those by which social superiority is attained and asserted.

We could say, therefore, that Trabb's boy's representation of Pip suggests alternatives to conceptualizing Dickens's grotesque public figures either as failed attempts at realistic characterization or as minor characters flattened by the pressure of the protagonist's expansive unfolding. More specifically, the caricaturized image of Pip that Trabb's boy produces, using a set of satiric verbal tags and exaggerated gestures, points to the usefulness of connecting Dickens's caricaturization to radical visual satire rather than to any properly literary tradition of novel writing. Thus, in the following portrait of Tite Barnacle in *Little Dorrit,* Dickens seems quite self-consciously to absorb and rearticulate within the expressive system of the novel that combination of emblematic satire and the more recent art of political caricaturization that Cruikshank, for example, had effected in his well-known cartoon of Lord Eldon's square face flanked by two hanging bags that signified both his judge's wig and his (presumably ill-gotten) wealth:[28]

> He wound and wound folds of white cravat around his neck, as he wound and wound folds of tape and paper round the neck of the country. His wristbands and collar were oppressive, his voice and manner were oppressive. He had a large watch chain and a bunch of seals, a coat buttoned up to inconvenience, a waistcoat buttoned up to inconvenience, an unwrinkled pair of trousers and a stiff pair of boots. He was altogether splendid, massive, overpowering, and impracticable. (152)

Clearly there is no attempt here to naturalize the character of Tite Barnacle, to delineate, from a position of proximity, the details of the environment he inhabits or the inner workings of his consciousness. Rather, the portrait of Tite Barnacle embodies the *response* of the excluded and is, in this sense, constituted as a counterdiscourse to the realistic insider's representation: it refuses to enter into the naturalizing context in which Tite Barnacle might actually have lived—into his humanity—but, on the contrary, treats him as an abstraction, an emblem for an aristocracy-dominated bureaucracy that chokes its public dealings with masses of procedure that, at the same time, it dignifies. Following Cruikshank and Hone, Dickens finds in the "grotesque stylisation of traditional caricature," to quote Terdiman again, the "mechanism that might preserve within the space of their representation the *difference* from its social object" (italics in the original).[29]

In an essay devoted largely to the English caricaturists, Baudelaire argued that the prints of Rowlandson, Cruikshank, and Seymour communicated not only with their distortions, exaggeration, and violence but also with their profusion of allusive and allegorical detail.[30] This allegorical strand within radical visual satire often targeted those emblems and insignia that sanctified the operations of the state but could also operate as markers of social distinction.

As it happens, Thackeray's fiction itself demonstrates very effectively the seamless ways in which crests and emblems intertwine with the world of the aristocracy and naturalize the aristocracy's claim to social superiority. In *Vanity Fair* and *Pendennis,* these easily recognizable signs of status help to make visible the world through which they circulate: they appear on letterheads, cutlery, and the breast pockets of gentlemen; they publicize grief and bedeck resplendent family coaches. Ever the ironist, Becky Sharp in *Vanity Fair* may make fun of the "pair of French epaulets, a Cross of the Legion of Honour, and the hilt of a sword" (311) that she presents to Mrs. Crawley in an attempt to reconcile her to her estranged nephew Rawdon Crawley, but Becky's very gesture suggests just how inextricably ceremonial insignia are woven into the texture of the aristocracy's everyday life. In Thackeray's mature fiction, in fact, emblems work with other details—of dress, accents, postures, gestures, reading habits, interior decoration, and circulating gossip—as part of a signifying system to both produce and socially circumscribe that stable, internally consistent, realistically delineated world of the elite that so many characters in *Vanity Fair* inhabit.

However, as Thackeray himself knew, emblems and seals did not necessarily have to be incorporated within the expressive economy of realism and deployed, in all their integrity, as part of those densely detailed and internally consistent scenes so characteristic of his novel writing. Thus, in "The History of the Next French Revolution" (1844)—a squib that he contributed to *Punch*—Thackeray follows the lead of his enemy Douglas Jerrold and extends, within the domain of language, the techniques that developed in popular visual political caricature: he ejects the emblem from the processes of the real world and, through a series of associations unsustainable within the expressive system of realism, generates discursive improvisations that shatter the connotations of dignity and power inseparable from the ceremonial symbols of the state. For example, a soldier in "The History of the Next French Revolution" attempts to persuade the king to give him a bottle of wine instead of the Legion of Honour, while the king himself makes a tidy sum speculating on red ribbon, which has risen 200 percent in the market because of the number of ceremonial crosses he has been distributing.[31] The difference in the way Thackeray worked with emblems as he moved from his magazine writing to his novels raises a larger set of questions. Did the techniques of popular graphic caricature have a future within the expressive system of the novel despite Thackeray's propensity to discard them when it came to what he considered the serious business of novel writing? What implications would the political orientation of graphic satire have on the novel's subject and specifically on its relationship with public issues? In what exact ways would the counteremblematic, expressive strategies effect the novel's representation of persons and processes associated with power? I need to turn to *Bleak House* in order to engage more fully with these questions.

Ever since it was first published in 1851, *Bleak House* has provoked discussions on whether the novel as a form was equipped to engage with the great administrative structures of the state. The mid-Victorian quarterly press generally argued that the art of novel writing was inseparable from the everyday lives of the middle and upper classes and that writers who focused on the law or the bureaucracy were destroying the novel's status as a form of art. A more recent body of criticism, however, has demonstrated how resources internal to the novel form have enabled it to engage in unique ways with a society's great public institutions. D. A. Miller's seminal *The Novel and the Police,* for example, uncovers a properly historical negotiation whereby *Bleak House* metatextually pits its own internal procedures of uncovering the truth against, on the one hand, those of a moribund and self-serving Chancery that never redeems its promise of judgment and, on the other, those of an emergent Detective Police "whose shallow solution[s], merely gratifies our appetite for closure."[32] Miller's account, thus, combines a more sophisticated sense of the internal dynamics of the novel form than was available to the nineteenth-century reviewers, with a historical understanding that inserts Dickens's novel within nineteenth-century England's history of administrative reform. What Miller does not sufficiently historicize are the expressive resources that go into Dickens's attack on the Court of Chancery. In fact, Dickens's representation of Chancery proceedings is underpinned by techniques that developed in the radical graphic caricature of the late eighteenth and early nineteenth centuries, and the displaced afterlife of these counteremblematic techniques in the Dickensian novel equipped it with an expressive dimension that could not have been generated by either the novel's universal, structural features (such as its capacity to effect a closure) or by the realistic orchestration of details to constitute the ebb and flow of everyday life.

In Dickens's delineation of Chancery proceedings, emblems are never allowed to blend discreetly among the other details of the real but are, on the contrary, wrenched out of their naturalizing context, projected self-consciously as the consecrated iconography by which the Court of Chancery seeks to legitimize its arbitrary processes. Emerging out of one of England's sacrosanct traditional institutions, the legal process is shown, in *Bleak House,* to be "dignified,"[33] in Walter Bagehot's sense of the term. That is, the legal process is produced and received within "the institutional conditions" which authorizes its unfolding as "ritual discourse"[34]—with its ceremonial etiquette, its specialized vocabulary, and, above all, its traditionally sanctified symbolism. Conducted in "great state and gravity," displaying the mace and seals, the javelin men and the white wands, and presided over by the august Lord Chancellor who wears "a full bottomed wig" and a robe "trimmed with beautiful gold lace," Chancery proceedings are, to use Conversation Kenge's word, "imposing."[35]

Dickens's focus on ceremonial emblems as the dominant signifiers in his representational strategy points to a historicized sense of how an institution like the Court of Chancery deployed power. At the broadest level, Dickens's criticism is driven by the conviction—shared by radicals as different as Jeremy Bentham and Thomas Paine—that the institutional functioning of the state should be made rational and visible.[36] At this level the discursive attack against the conduct of the Chancery would be directed against the sanctifying metaphors it deployed in order to obfuscate visibility and continue its corrupt and self-serving practices. However, Dickens's satire on Chancery proceedings is also implicated in a tension that always underlay the radical demystificatory project: between the suspicion about the mystifying functions of icons, on the one hand and, on the other, the propensity, especially within the more popular strands of radical journalism, to work constantly with figures, analogies, and metaphors. Indeed, Dickens's own method is embedded not so much in the austere, rational skepticism of Paine that is so often directed against metaphors as in the irreverent play with seals, crests, and blazons that drove the counterimagistic assaults of Cruikshank, Hone, or Jerrold.

As someone whose work intersected at many points with the counteremblematic political caricature of both Cruickshank and Jerrold, Dickens always knew how to appropriate for a destabilizing counterimage the constituent details, the figurative and emblematic elements by which the symbols of power communicated. It was not until *Bleak House*, however, that he managed fully to novelize the subversive capacities of emblematic and juxtapositonal representation and to deploy these as a sustained strategy against the orchestration of consecrated symbolism that sanctified Chancery procedures. More specifically, in contrast to *Vanity Fair* or *Pendennis*, in which, as Thackeray said, a coat had to be a "coat, and a poker a poker and . . . nothing else according to my ethics,"[37] and in which an emblem would remain immutably a sign of power or of wealth, Dickens's basic representational strategy is to seize upon a ceremonial emblem or motif associated with Chancery practice, wrench it out of its context, and recombine it with ideas or motifs that suggest the primitive shapelessness or the gothic cruelty of the dark ages. Moreover, unlike pictorial satire, which can operate only with images and within a framed space, *Bleak House* unfurls the juxtapositional aesthetics of graphic satire across the vaster and more complex discursive domain that the novel form made available. For example, Miss

Flite's unstable mind emerges in *Bleak House* as one plane where the consecrated emblems of Chancery transform themselves spontaneously into medieval instruments of torture. Miss Flite speaks of the Mace and Seal at the Chancellor's table in hushed, reverential tones, but her experience of Chancery also compels her to think of these emblems as "Cold glittering devils!" that "draw people on, my dear . . . Draw peace out of them . . . Sense out of them" (457). The expressive system of the novel, however, also allows Dickens to move away from Flite's individual consciousness and to inscribe his counteremblematic improvisations on the objective world outside. Thus, the barbaric practices that Dickens associates with the Chancery find an emblematic victim in the "street of perishing blind houses with their eyes stoned out": the mark, as Jarndyce tells Esther, of "the Great Seal" (100).

The expressive energies of graphic satire that enjoy a vigorous, if displaced, existence in *Bleak House* sustain the novel's discursive destabilization of Chancery in other ways as well. Specifically, *Bleak House* achieves some of its strongest effects by drawing upon the greater freedom that had become available to the techniques of graphic satire as these moved from the visual to the linguistic domain. Unlike pictorial satire, linguistic representations, as we've already seen, did not need to pick on the emblem's visible details in order to work its metonymic transformations. Indeed, *Bleak House* often follows Jerrold's "The Order of the Poverty" in generating discursive improvisations around not the visible features of an icon but, more generally, the cluster of ideas that the icon consecrates. For example, *Bleak House* seizes upon and degrades the idea of antiquity that is conferred on the Chancery by its consecrating symbols. The opening paragraph of the novel pushes the Chancery's claims to antiquity into an antediluvian past and then associates it with the lethargic, purposeless activities of prehistoric creatures unfit to survive in modern times. Appearing barely a few months after the Great Exhibition and juxtaposed against that symbol of Britain's progress, the opening paragraph of *Bleak House* sensationally shows the Chancery neighborhood encrusted in as much mud "as if the waters had but newly retired from the face of the earth, and it would not be wonderful to meet a Megalosaurus, forty feet wide or so, waddling like an elephantine lizard up Holborn Hill" (15). Furthermore, in one of the earliest descriptions of Chancery proceedings, Dickens seizes upon the "horse-hair and goat-hair" used in the lawyers' wigs and, by only slightly shifting the connotations of these words, is able to transform the lawyers into half-human, half-animal figures who are so integral to the emblematic arts and who are shown, in *Bleak House,* to be "mistily engaged in one of the ten thousand stages of an endless cause, tripping one another up on slippery precedents, groping knee deep in technicalities, running their goat-hair and horse-hair warded heads against walls of words" (16).

The strongest example of the ways in which Dickens novelizes the expressive possibilities of graphic satire, however, is in the emblematic mirroring of the Lord Chancellor and the Court of Chancery in the sordid figure of Krook and his rag and bottle store. In his remarkable picture of Krook's shop, Dickens brings together the ceremonial symbols of the court—the lawyer's robes, the scales of justice—only to subject them to radical demystification:

> A little way within the shop-door, lay heaps of old cracked parchment scrolls, and discoloured and dog's-eared law papers. I could have fancied that all the rusty keys, of which there must have been hundreds huddled together as old iron, had once belonged to doors of rooms or strong chests in lawyers' offices. The litter of rags tumbled partly into and partly out of a one-legged wooden scale, hanging without any counter-poise from a beam, might have been the councellors' bands and gowns torn up. One had only to fancy, as Richard whispered to Ada and me while we all stood looking in, that the yonder bones in a corner, piled together and picked very clean, were the bones of clients, to make the picture complete. (59)

This passage could, at one level, be thought of as a straightforward transposition into language of some satiric, anti-Chancery print. Inserted within the expressive system of the novel, however, this satirical picture of the Lord Chancellor does not remain confined within the synchronic frame in which it is originally cast. Rather, Dickens's counteremblematic picture of the Lord Chancellor's domain develops as a metaphor. Thus, Dickens breaks through both the synchronic frame of the print as well as the limits of what contemporary critics would call "probability" when, in the climactic moment of his counterimagistic assault on the ceremonial processes of the law, Krook is discovered dead—burnt to cinders by Spontaneous Combustion. Krook's death by Spontaneous Combustion presumably prefigures, metaphorically, the self-induced explosion that awaits the Court of Chancery. From my point of view, however, the more interesting feature of Krook's strange death is the nauseating liquid that flows out of his body. As an image for unpurged accumulations of what Conversation Kenge calls "the very great system of a very great country" (786), the "thick yellow liquor which is offensive to the touch and sight and more to the smell" (417) suggests how one of the most widely used techniques of radical graphic satire—its capacity to make the most sacrosanct institutions and personages generate images that provide the basis of their own degradation—survives and continues to develop, through many displacements, in Dickens's later fiction.

This chapter has argued that the deeper effects of Dickens's radical inheritance are to be found not so much in the content of his criticism of Chancery practices as in his deployment of certain radical techniques to demystify the symbols by which arbitrary and oppressive Chancery procedures are sanctified. That is, it has been concerned with the ways in which radical techniques enter into and extend the internal expressive repertoire of the novel form. However, did Dickens's appropriation of the expressive resources of graphic satire[38]—a mode that the *Westminster Review* associated with disseminating "opinion" and promoting "discussion"[39]—enable his fiction to intervene in debates over public affairs?

One way in which to address this question is by revisiting the extended sequence around Krook's death and focusing not only on the brilliantly inventive manner in which Krook is made to die[40] but also on the use that Dickens makes of this death to directly address his readers. One could then argue that the "generic memory" of "radical expression" that is carried into the Dickensian novel not only influenced the latter's representational strategies but also "carnivalized" its structure. More specifically, "the stylistic aura" of the radical discourse enabled a novel like *Bleak House* to bring about, at any point of its evolution, what Julia Kristeva calls a "splitting of the mode of enunciation," in which the authorial voice "divides and faces in two directions"[41]—inwards, toward the world of the novel, but also, and more significantly, outwards, toward the real world inhabited by a socially aware audience who might be mobilized as a pressure group against the state's malfunctioning institutions. In these circumstances it is not surprising that immediately after Krook's death by Spontaneous Combustion, that is, immediately after the most obviously fictional event in *Bleak House,* Dickens can effortlessly discard his role as storyteller for that of public speaker addressing the queen herself on behalf of the people:

> The Lord Chancellor of that Court, true to his title in his last act, has died the death of all Lord Chancellors in all Courts, and of all authorities in all places under all names soever, where false pretences are made and where injustice is done. Call the death by any name your Highness will, or say it might have been prevented how you will, it is the same death eternally—inborn, inbred, engendered in the corrupted humours of the vicious body itself, and that only—Spontaneous Combustion, and none other of all the deaths that can be died. (418–19)

The presence of an extranovelistic mobilizing impulse encoded within the very structure of *Bleak House* raises several questions about the relationship that has been crucial to this chapter: that between the work of the radical publicists and of Dickens. Might Dickens's readiness to open, within his novel, a nonfictional discursive space from which he may address the general public be regarded as a politically displaced continuation of a process that William Hone, for example, began when he successfully transformed his 1817 trial for blasphemy into a forum for building public opinion against censorship? What is suggested by the discrepancy between, on the one hand, the mid-Victorian critical establishment's conviction that Dickens had abandoned the claims of the literary by transforming the novel from a "form of art" to a forum for political debates and, on the other, the enormous respect and effectiveness with which radical writers used literature and literary devices for their political writing? Is there a line of continuity between the kind of anxiety that the radical press aroused in the political establishment of the 1820s and the changes that mark the quarterly press's reception of Dickens after he published *Bleak House* and *Little Dorrit*? In what remains of this chapter, I will engage with these questions to bring to a conclusion the argument about whether Dickens drew on the language of radicalism to not only produce a new novelistic aesthetic but also to politicize the public sphere within which the novel operated.

Did the radical publicists anticipate Dickens in finding ways of mobilizing public opinion from within well-established public forms whose internal protocols did not necessarily sanction such mobilization? In her pioneering work on Dickens and radical culture, Sally Ledger demonstrates that Cobbett, Hone, and others frequently turned "the courtroom into a locus for cultural and political debate." However, this politicization that the radical journalists effected in legal procedures is, in Ledger's opinion, reflected in the *content* of Dickens's work and more specifically, in the frequency with which court scenes occur in Dickens's fiction:

> The persistence of the Fenning case in the popular cultural memory throughout and beyond the first half of the nineteenth century is strongly suggestive of the importance of the courtroom as a locus of cultural and political debate in the period. Dickens's novels and journalism are peppered with trial scenes: highlights include the hilarity of the Breach of Promise suit in *The Pickwick Papers,* Oliver Twist's poignant appearance before a magistrate, Jack Dawkin's comic bravado as his sentence is passed, the bullying judgement passed on Barnaby Rudge by a "gentleman" country magistrate, the extended Chancery suit in *Bleak House,* and

the high melodrama of the four trials of Charles Darnay in *The Tale of Two Cities*.⁴²

The connections that Ledger makes between the radical engagement with the law court and certain trial scenes in Dickens's novels are invaluable because they highlight the contribution of one more extraliterary discourse in the making of the Dickensian novel. What Ledger does not consider, however, is that a distinguishing structural feature of the Dickensian novel—its ability not only to split the mode of enunciation and address issues internal to its fictional world but also to discuss and take positions on events unfolding in the real world that its readers inhabit—may itself owe something to the radical journalists' propensity to turn trials into opportunities for public mobilization.

William Hone's 1817 trial exemplifies how radical publicists often managed to work from within the protocols of court procedure and, despite the resistance of the judge and the jury, to turn the court into a platform for propaganda. Hone's trial was an inherently political event in a way that the publication of a Dickens novel could never be. Unlike Dickens, who was never threatened by the state machinery, Hone found himself up against the harsh procensorship Chief Justice Lord Ellenborough and a jury that was predisposed to convict him. Hone also demonstrated, however, perhaps for the first time, how an established public form (in his case, a trial) could be made to turn outwards and draw in a far larger group of people than allowed for by the internal protocols of that form. In his self-defense against the charge of blasphemy, Hone drew on his knowledge of English literature and on his own skill with language to present a case that was so well researched and entertaining that it transformed the crowd, present throughout his three-day trial, into a pressure group against the much larger political issue of censorship. The impact that Hone made on the attending crowd can be gauged from the extremely strict measures that the judge and the jury took to control the crowd's behavior. Lord Ellenborough instructed the sheriffs to apprehend anyone in the crowd who showed appreciation of Hone's arguments by laughing at his jokes, and the Attorney General cited the laughter of the crowd as evidence of how radical publicists were "perverting" the unlettered masses by turning the law court into a platform for propaganda.⁴³

Some three and a half decades later, journals like the *Westminster* and *Quarterly Review*s would express very similar anxieties in relation to what Dickens was doing to the novel. These journals did, of course, recognize that the radical publicists and Dickens were addressing very different constituencies and that the political impact made by the former was incomparably stronger than what the Dickensian novel could achieve. However, the quarterly journals returned frequently to that precise feature in the Dickensian novel which most closely approximated Hone's ability to reach a popular audience even while remaining within the procedures of his trial. More specifically, the quarterly press invested a great deal in trying to understand the exact conditions that had enabled Dickens's emergence as a novelist who could provide fictional entertainment to isolated, individual readers and, at the same time, mold these readers into a semipolitical community brought together by their disaffection with the malfunctioning public institutions. Accordingly, reviewers focused not on subversive trial scenes that may have appeared in this or that Dickens novel, but on the aesthetic legitimacy of using the novel as a means of mobilizing public opinion.

As it happens, Hone's trial also brings into sharp focus the fraught relationship between the political and the literary—a relationship that continued to be discussed through the 1850s and '60s but was understood in very different ways by the radical writers and the literary establishment.

Hone, Cobbett, and many others considered literature and literary devices as strong allies of the radical project. Hone, for example, very effectively invoked examples from English literature while defending himself from the charge of blasphemy by arguing that some of England's most revered writers had preceded him in parodying the scriptures. Moreover, in a maneuver that seems to gesture paradoxically toward a basic discursive strategy of radical mobilization itself, Hone argued that parody was a popular medium of communication "which the common people had been accustomed to for centuries," and that its aim was not so much to mock the work parodied as to help the widespread dissemination of ideas. Put another way, Hone's defense—based, as Ben Wilson has suggested, on a "general discussion about the use of literature"[44]—not only suggests the alliance that several radical writers sought to forge with canonical English literature but also acknowledges the contribution made by literary devices in sustaining the popularity of the language of radicalism. This contribution is evident in the great popular appeal of Hone's own parodies, of the fantastic black dwarf in Wooler's journalism, and of Cobbett's self-consciously deployed rhetorical effects.

The allegories and parodies, the heightened rhetoric, and the metaphoric transformations that marked so much of radical writing elicited two intertwining responses in the elite press that remained active all the way up to the 1860s. On the one hand, this press dissociated radical writing from anything resembling literary value and, in this way, portrayed radical writing's exaggerations and distortions as indicative merely of its unreliability. The *Quarterly Review*, for example, had described Hone as a "poor illiterate creature," despite the knowledge of English literature he had demonstrated through the course of his trial. However, this mode of discrediting could not neutralize the deeper anxiety with which the *Quarterly Review* responded to the expressive power that enabled radical publicists to attract huge readerships. In the following extract from an article that he contributed to the *Quarterly Review*, Robert Southey clearly refuses to grant aesthetic value to radical writing but finds it impossible to get away from the expressive power that had enabled a Cobbett or a Hone to raise a whole new popular readership: "The weekly epistles of the apostles of sedition are read aloud in taprooms and pot houses to believing auditors, listening greedily when they are told that their rulers fatten upon the gains extracted from their blood and sinews; and they are cheated, oppressed and plundered."[45]

The mid-Victorian quarterly press never attacked Dickens in the kind of language that Southey uses to describe the plebeian milieu in which radical expression flourished. This press, moreover, was aware, as we've seen, of differences at the level of context, content, and modes of dissemination that separated Dickens from the radical writers. Nevertheless, the *Westminster* or *Saturday Review*'s response to Dickens's fiction continued to be characterized by an anxiety about the relationship that it articulated between the popular, the literary, and the political.

We can track the ways in which the mid-Victorian quarterly press configured the relationship between popular entertainment, literature, and politics by focusing on an important shift in its response to Dickens after he published *Bleak House*. As journals that addressed themselves self-consciously to the educated and the cultivated, the mid-Victorian reviews, unlike the radical writers, always preserved the distinction between the properly literary and the merely popular. Dickens's popularity, therefore, was never a reason for them to confer literary merit upon his work. After the initial shock that the lower realms of journalism could throw up a talent as prodigious as Boz, however, the reviewers seem to be benignly tolerant of a writer who could never, of course, attain the stature of a full-fledged serious novelist, but whose comic genius was universally entertaining and who was always careful not to give offense to any decent reader.[46] This universal appeal is what the term "popular" connoted when it was used in association with Dickens's early works. As one commentator wrote, "Indeed the great characteristic of Dickens's early popularity was this, that it was confined to no class, but extended to all classes, rich and poor, noble and plebeian. The Queen on the throne read him and so did Hodge at the plow."

Edwin Whipple, who offered this explanation of the young Dickens's popularity from the hindsight of 1877, went on to articulate an argument—deeply entrenched in the highbrow press—that Dickens's universal appeal began to fragment after the publication of *Bleak House* because his "educated readers" who had enjoyed his "humour and pathos" began to get irritated by his intrusions into "matters relating to social and economical science with which he was imperfectly acquainted."[47] In the post–*Bleak House* years, therefore, the word "popular," when used in association with Dickens in the quarterlies, began to acquire different connotations. In an influential piece, first published in the *National Review*, Bagehot argued that Dickens's great popularity was based on his hold over the indiscriminating masses that cared only for their "own multifarious, industrial, fig selling world."[48] Bagehot thought of Dickens's lowbrow readers not as a politically active group, but as passive consumers of literary entertainment. Moreover, Bagehot understood that, unlike Hone or Cobbett who wrote to rouse masses of people against a state that was both vulnerable and oppressive, Dickens wrote well within the bounds of what the far more self-confident state of the 1850s considered acceptable. Still, in an age when the novel was emerging as a major form of entertainment and when leisure itself was, in Peter Bailey's words, "a new, relatively uncharted area in the lifespace" of the urban masses,[49] the reading habits of large groups of people were bound to have some political significance. It was its changing sociology that made the novel, and especially the Dickensian popular novel, such a potentially harmful public influence for a man like James Fitzjames Stephen who might otherwise never have condescended to write about as lowbrow a novelist as "Boz."[50] Writing in 1855, Stephen argued that while the popularity of outdoor sports and even of the theatre and of spectacles had declined, "the habit of reading novels [had] become universal." This meant for Stephen that a "very considerable" number of "young people" took from novels "nearly all their notions of life." Stephen thought, therefore, that Dickens was behaving completely irresponsibly when he sent to his innumerable readers the message that "their Legislature is a stupid and inefficient debating club, their courts of law foul haunts of chicanery, pedantry and fraud, and their system of administration an odious compound of stupidity and corruption." Unlike Cobbett or Hone who found in canonical literature the resources as well as the justification for the kind of writing that Stephen criticizes, Stephen relegates Dickens's political satire to the realm of low entertainment. It is in the very process of his aesthetic denunciation, however, that Stephen betrays anxieties that are very similar to those articulated by Southey some three and a half decades ago.

Who, it may be asked, takes Mr. Dickens seriously? Is it not as foolish to estimate his melodramatic and sentimental stock-in-trade seriously as it would be to undertake the refutation of the jokes of the clown in a Christmas pantomime? No doubt this would be true enough if the world were composed entirely or principally of men of sense and cultivation. To such persons Mr. Dickens is nothing more than any other public performer—enjoying an extravagantly high reputation. . . . But the vast majority of mankind, unfortunately, think little, and cultivate themselves still less . . . and to these classes such writers as Dickens are something more than amusement.[51]

Stephen's tone may be dismissive, but his words implicitly acknowledge the many ways in which the work of the radical journalists had transformed the public realm of letters so assiduously cultivated by the journals for which Stephen wrote and by their eighteenth-century predecessors. On the one hand, Stephen finds it impossible to wish away the masses that the radical publicists had steadily drawn into public debates on the most significant social and political issues of nineteenth-century England. On the other hand, the expressive strategies of the radical journalists, which Southey associated with the lowest forms of entertainment but which Hone saw as his inheritance from such writers as Sterne or Swift, were beginning to enter and (from Stephen's point of view) contaminate the nineteenth-century's dominant literary form: the novel itself. Significantly, Stephen invokes that pivotal figure in the radical journalistic tradition, William Cobbett, as the person most responsible for diffusing the bourgeois public sphere and making possible the emergence of Dickens as the central writer in a vastly expanded world of letters. Stephen argued that as the writer who first demonstrated that it was possible to bypass sustained formal education, to write entirely "by the light of nature," and to convey opinions about public matters in the most emphatic language to a large, often subliterate audience, Cobbett began a process that Dickens would internalize for the novel.

> Though no two persons could resemble each other less in terms of character, the position of Mr. Dickens with respect to fiction is precisely analogous to that of Cobbett with respect of political discussion. The object of the arguments of the one was to drive his opinion into the dullest understanding—the object of the narrative of the other is to paint a picture that will catch the eye of the most ignorant and the least attentive observer. Mr. Dickens's writings are the apotheosis of what has been called newspaper English. He makes points everywhere . . .[52]

Hone had habitually drawn on English literature—on the status of parody within its canonical texts or on the speech habits of one of Laurence Sterne's characters[53]—to engage with the most contested political issues of his time. The resources of literature had, therefore, been a major and enabling factor in his political writing. For Stephen, on the other hand, the intersection between the topical and the literary is a contaminating process by which "newspaper English" threatened to radically compromise the aesthetic quality of the novel.

One of Stephen's responses to this threat was to develop, in the authoritative pages of the reviews, the audience-oriented subjectivity of the ideal bourgeois novel as the criterion of literary legitimacy.[54] Moreover, the major point in Stephen's criticism—that instead of realistically delineating the ebb and flow of everyday life Dickens habitually used the novel to "ventilate opinion" and to ply his "melodramatic and sentimental stock-in-trade"—was shared by some of the most influential critics of the nineteenth century. The significant thing, however, is that even Stephen (and the very powerful literary and political interests that he represented) could not arrest the process that has been outlined through this chapter: that despite many displacements—from its roots in a radical artisanal community to one strand among many within literary commodities consumed by a large, socially diverse audience; from the revolutionary political climate of the late eighteenth and early nineteenth centuries to the stability and prosperity of the mid-Victorian era—the "language of radicalism" not only survived in the Dickensian novel but also influenced its form, giving it a new public dimension and enabling Dickens to take on *as a novelist,* the role of what the *Westminster Review* half admiringly and half grudgingly described as that of "a recognised public instructor."[55]

CHAPTER 3

Re-Visioning the City

The Making of an Urban Aesthetic from Hogarth to the Stereoscope

MY FOCUS SO FAR has been on "radical expression" as an important presence in the print market of the early nineteenth century and on the ways in which it shaped Dickens's fiction. One way in which radical expressive techniques affected Dickens's fiction was in terms of moving it away from the more realistic forms of novel writing embodied in the work of Thackeray. This chapter will turn to the ways in which Dickens related to a second strand of popular expression that drew its energies not from the experience of political exclusion but from its location in that great, threatening, fascinating, and characteristically nineteenth-century formation: the big city.

England's giant metropolis—with its broad main thoroughfares, its palatial buildings, its slums, and its teeming, utterly heterogeneous population—continued throughout the eighteenth and nineteenth centuries to be the subject of prints, panoramas, entertainment-providing optical gadgets, novels, and other forms of literary entertainment. Yet these representations tended most often to domesticate the city; they reproduced the city through images that could be consumed in the safety of the home or the viewing gallery and mitigated, through a range of discursive strategies, the socially disconcerting implications of that very urban variety from which the city sketch or panorama drew its expressive energies. The classic statement of this domesticizing impulse is to be found in the opening pages of Pierce Egan's *Life in London*. Assuring the reader that he could enjoy the sights of

London without exposing himself to any of its dangers, Egan wrote: "The author . . . has chosen for his readers a *Camera Obscura* View of London, not only for its safety, but because it is so *snug,* and also possessing the invaluable advantages of SEEING and not been *seen*" (2; italics in the original).

Egan's metaphoric use of the camera obscura as his means of unfolding the city is significant. The camera obscura, Jonathan Crary has argued, is "inseparable from a certain metaphysic of interiority: it is a figure for both the observer who is nominally a free, sovereign individual and a privatized subject confined in a quasi-domestic space, cut off from a public exterior world."[1] In other words, Egan's metaphoric optical gadget—which is conceptualized as a portable machine in defiance of the stationary position from which real-life camera obscuras operated—promises not only to protect a comfortably positioned reader/viewer from the dangers of the streets but also to break up the seamless life of the city into discreet, manageable scenes for the study or pleasure of the "nominally . . . free, sovereign individual." The camera obscura, thus, registers the city as a passing show: it transforms the struggle of urban existence into subjects of entertainment. At this level, the camera obscura's articulation of the city is paradigmatic of a larger process: the nineteenth century's propensity to reproduce the city as a series of easily consumable linguistic and visual scenes, which would, moreover, be mobile and purchasable. Thus, for example, John Wright—author of the reasonably popular series called *Mornings at Bow Street* (1825)—found in police reports a source from which he could generate "pictures of what is passing in the streets," "the phraseology of the vulgar," and "secrets of low, and now and then high life" for the pleasure of consumers who might enjoy these with their "potted beef and buttered toast."[2]

We might, then, think of the mechanically produced urban image as a simulacra, sundered completely from the object that it represents, driven arbitrarily by market forces to a range of disparate locations: "floating *signs,*" as Shelly Rice says about the photographs that circulated in Haussmann's Paris, "without narrative support in the increasingly complex checker board of the modern image network" (italics in the original).[3] It would be a mistake, however, to dissociate the life of a photograph or of the city sketch from anything like a social imaginary and to relate it only to the passive act of consumption. More specifically, it is important to take into account that the process of uprooting, framing, and circulating that Crary and others have associated with the production and dissemination of the modern image was, in fact, double-edged in its effects. This process did, indeed, constitute the violent, harsh, but endlessly fascinating life of the streets into mechanically reproducible "scenes" that could be enjoyed in the safety of the home. But it was also implicated in the making of, adapting Michel de Certeau's term, a specifically urban "space." In *The Practice of Everyday Life,* de Certeau argues that "space is composed of intersections of mobile elements. It is, in a sense, actuated by the ensemble of movements deployed within it. Space occurs as the effect produced by the operations that orient it, situate it, temporalize it and make it function in a polyvalent unity of conflictual programs or contractual proximities."

What made the mechanically produced urban image a vital constitutive "vector" in the "polyvalent unity of conflictual programs" is that it unfolded as "the other" of those great organizing interiors of the Victorian moral universe:[4] the home, the workplace, the centers of administration. In this sense, expressive operations that sustained the "space" of the nineteenth-century urban imaginary are engaged, in their various ways, with probing, fortifying, breaching, and redrawing the boundary between the moralized interiors of the establishment and the chaotic, dangerous life of the streets.

A very powerful anticipation of the defining tensions of the nineteenth-century urban imaginary is to be found in William Hogarth's *Industry and Idleness* (1747). As is well known, Hogarth followed in *Industry and Idleness* a pattern that he had set with *A Harlot's Progress* (1732): he produced the pictures in the form of multiple prints that he sold to subscribers, and he continued to focus, at the level of content, on contemporary city life rather than on the mythological or historical subjects favored by high art.[5] Even more than *A Harlot's Progress,* however, *Industry and Idleness* helped to generate the demand for certain forms of urban representation that would attract consumers from all classes and influence the Dickensian novel itself.[6]

The popularity that *Industry and Idleness* enjoyed with both plebeian and middle-class audiences had a great deal to do with the extremely productive paradox inbuilt within its delineation of the contrasting careers of its protagonists. On the one hand, Hogarth takes advantage of Idle's immoral activities to give full and dramatic expression to the proliferating, always interesting life of the streets. (In the ninth plate of *Industry and Idleness,* indeed, he self-consciously anticipates the magnetic pull that these representations of street scenes were to have on viewers.) On the other hand, unlike the nineteenth-century city sketch, which saw itself merely as an entertainment-producing commodity, Hogarth's artistic investment in the life of the streets is mediated by a strong moral impulse that constitutes this life as immoral and dangerous. It is this tension in *Industry and Idleness* that throws into relief the defining dynamic of the urban imaginary as it was to develop in Dickens's novels as well: its propensity to reinforce the boundary walls of the orderly interiors that sustain the responsible and productive existence but, at the same time, to explore, express, and publicize the immoral but endlessly fascinating life that lay beyond these walls.

Any analysis of *Industry and Idleness* must start by recognizing the strong moral investment that it makes on a certain kind of social space. Goodchild's superiority over Idle is based on not only his industry and application but also his location within and absolute commitment to the long sequence of interiors across which his success story unfolds: to the workshop, the church, the home, the alderman's chamber. In the last plate, indeed, Goodchild carries the interiority of his office into the streets of London themselves (fig. 4). Barely distinguishable behind a rectangular glass window, Goodchild's presence amidst a London crowd is represented by the enclosure of his mayoral coach. This coach, indeed, seems to gesture toward a basic organizing principle by which Hogarth distinguishes the contrasting careers of Goodchild and Idle. Located in the middle ground, it marks the boundary between two clearly opposed modes of representation: the wavering, unpredictable movement of the crowd in the foreground and the rock steady lines that delineate the buildings in the background. A major assertion of the latter mode is the rectangular window of Goodchild's coach, which defines his location and which is replicated, moreover, in the rows of windows that run across the square building in the background.

The straight lines, rows, squares, and rectangles that connect the mayor's carriage to the more permanent places of inhabitation are crucial to *Industry and Idleness:* they constitute the basic visual units that go into Hogarth's representation of the spatial universe across which Goodchild's career moves. Thus, the all-important emblem of Goodchild's early career—the loom that he works in plate I (fig. 5)—may be viewed, despite its scale and three-dimensionality, as a structural variation on the window behind which he finally disappears in the last print of the series. Moreover, Goodchild's career, characterized though it is by incessant upward mobility, never moves out of the sort of enclosed space of which the workshop of the first plate is a paradigm. To be sure, the succession of spaces that sustain Goodchild's movement from the loom to the mayoral carriage are capable of registering a range of social differences as well as the internal variety within large-scale corporate activities. These spaces are, however, inexorably framed by the columns and rows that order the congregation which Goodchild attends as a young man or the horizontal lines (of the geometrically arranged tables) and the vertical lines (of the windows and the picture frames) in the banquet scene over which he presides in plate 8.

FIGURE 4. William Hogarth, "The Industrious 'Prentice Lord-Mayor of London," Plate 12 of Series *Industry and Idleness* (1747)

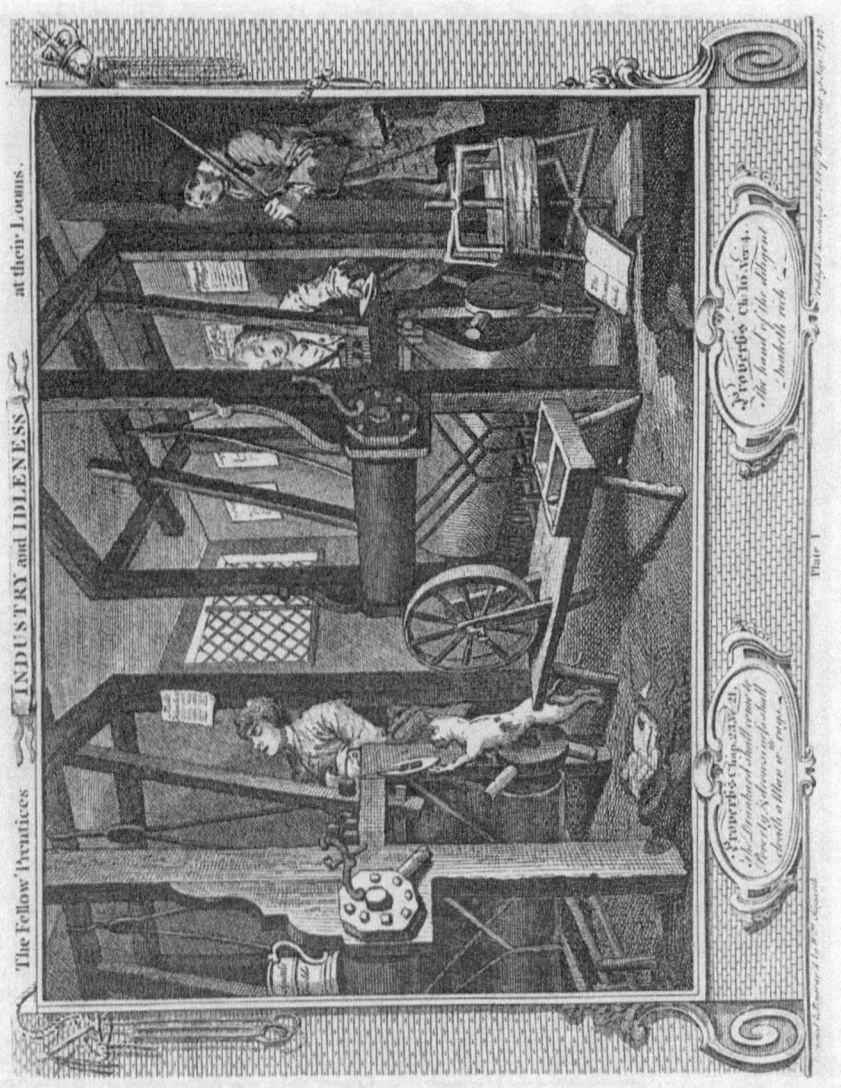

FIGURE 5. William Hogarth, "The Fellow 'Prentices at their Looms," Plate 1 of Series *Industry and Idleness* (1747)

The geometrically constructed spaces across which Goodchild's career unfolds reproduces the city as a network of organized, hierarchically ordered sites of production, administration, and responsible domesticity. This stabilization of social space makes possible the unfolding of the individual subject across time. However, instead of holding his place as a figure at the center of Hogarth's story, Goodchild's progress ironically seems to require his shrinkage. In several plates, he appears only as a distant figure of authority. Thus, Goodchild's career might represent an ideal version of success, yet it also results in his merger with the geometrical spaces that increasingly identify him and separate him from the world outside. Moreover, unlike the domestic novel, *Industry and Idleness* does not naturalize this separation. Hogarth's picture series structures city life around the principle of contrast, thereby making the delineation of Idle's reckless life in the streets and the vice dens of London an indispensable precondition for the articulation of Goodchild's improvement story. The beggary and disorderly grotesquery that are often prominent in the plates depicting Goodchild's rise—in plates 6 and 8, for example, grotesques occupy the foreground—even more obviously condition his plot line in the contrasting places of Idle's ruin. Idle's immorality obviously breaches the social boundary walls within which Goodchild's story unfolds, accessing the seemingly independent existence of another London, and in this way it sets into motion an expressive trajectory driven by the very social disparities that occupy the gap between the plates instead of unfolding smoothly within either contrasting series.

Hogarth's commitment to ordering and making visible does not, of course, disappear when he moves from the workshop or the alderman's chamber to the chaotic London streets. In fact, these streets help to link the very interiors that Goodchild inhabits and are consequently inseparable from the network of addresses, signboards, and official emblems mapping the city. But the creative excess, the sheer irresistibility of Hogarth's representations of the "other" London also suggests a complex representational system that is oriented toward not only surveying and containing but also multiplying urban contradictions. Coexisting, thus, with the parallel tasks of viewing and disciplining in *Industry and Idleness* is a trajectory of representation that draws its energies precisely from the most unclassifiable elements in London's street life: its shifting contrasts, its variety, and the irresponsible, reckless, brutal but endlessly proliferating activities of its crowds.

One way in which to uncover the expressive energies that lurk beneath Hogarth's demonized street scenes and that were to sustain a whole tradition of graphic representation right up until the mid-1830s is by focusing on that characteristically Hogarthian entity: the city crowd (fig. 6).[7] In *Industry and*

FIGURE 6. William Hogarth, "The Idle 'Prentice Executed at Tyburn," Plate 11 of Series *Industry and Idleness* (1747)

Idleness, the crowd is not only shown to congregate around the spectacle of a public hanging but is itself constituted as a spectacle. Uncontainable in the interiors that Goodchild inhabits, incapable of sustaining those rational and productive relationships that underlies the lives of the "industrious," the crowd in *Industry and Idleness* is vast, chaotic, and prone always to acts proscribed in the enlightened world. Thus, the predictability of Goodchild's regulated life gives way, in the Tyburn scene, to proliferating uncoordinated activities, random collisions between the most unconnected people, and to that sense of "quick, various movement, of surprise seen close" that Donald Gray sees as Hogarth's legacy to the relatively denuded city sketches of the nineteenth century.[8]

Moreover, unlike the typical nineteenth-century city sketch, the Tyburn plate is centered around a special occasion: it finds in Idle's public hanging the opportunity to bring together a very wide range of street folk within a single frame and to give free expression to activities that are hectic, heterogeneous, and completely free of the restraint that regulates behavior in Goodchild's world. Thus, the crowded foreground of Hogarth's picture is made up, among much else, of prostitutes who are getting drunk; a fellow who looks up a girl's skirt as he helps her climb into a cart; sellers of gin, oranges, biscuits, and broadsheets; a man who is about to throw a dog into the cart that carries Idle to the gallows; an enraged woman who claws the eyes of an astonished adversary; a soldier who is down on his haunches urinating; and two boys who laughingly watch him. The sheer surplus of figures that Hogarth spreads across the length and breadth of his picture, the vividness with which he details the people who inhabit the foreground, the sense of drama that he imparts to their expressions and activities, in short the artistic energy that he invests in his representation of the crowd, points to a paradox that runs through *Industry and Idleness* and that is particularly evident in the Tyburn plate.[9] On the one hand, Idle's public hanging is constituted as the culmination of a moral fable based on the segregation and moralization of urban space. On the other hand, like the public hanging, Hogarth's crowd is spectacular: it is sexual, violent, dramatic, grotesque, and, in this sense, capable of giving Hogarth's representations an expressive and commercial energy that threatens rather than reinforces the binaries around which his moral tale is built. A remarkable feature of the Tyburn plate is that it articulates, at the level of its content, the tension between its moral condemnation of a life led in the streets and its sense of the popular appeal and, by implication, of the commercial possibilities that adhere to any representation of such a life.[10]

Indeed, the story of Idle's life enters the print market even before he dies: the penultimate picture in *Industry and Idleness* focuses on his journey to the gallows but also on a woman who sells a broadsheet entitled "The Last Dying Speech and Confessions of Tho Idle." Hogarth's delineation of his wayward protagonist and of the details which surround him expresses powerfully the horror of the fate he has brought on to himself. The cart that carries Idle to the gallows also bears his coffin, and the dramatic gestures of the lean-faced, long-haired Methodist preacher who accompanies Idle suggests the enormity of the transformation that is about to overtake Idle. Above all, it is on Idle's tiny but finely etched face that Hogarth inscribes the force of his retribution. It is a shrunken, cowering face that is already stamped by death.

In an unexpected maneuver, however, Hogarth pushes the culminating image of his moral drama to the middle ground of the Tyburn plate. The figure who dominates this picture is located at the very center of the foreground and it is not Idle at all but a woman who hawks a broadsheet containing the last dying speech and confessions of Idle. What distinguishes her from the rest of the crowd, despite the ragged appearance that she shares with everyone else, is the purposefulness of her activities. For instance, the bleeding child who wallows in the mud to her right throws into relief the security that she is able to give to her own baby. Moreover, even as she manages her baby amidst the jostling crowd, she is able to channel her entire energy into the act of selling her broadsheet: her posture—the left hand covering the ear to shut out disturbance—suggests the concentration with which she works. Having turned her face away from the crowd in the direction of the real world with real people who are in the act of viewing Hogarth's picture series, the woman's open mouth holds in perpetuity her hawking shout.

But exactly what kind of document is the Tyburn woman selling? Generically, a broadsheet such as the one that the Tyburn woman sells descended from an official document that often accompanied the execution of a malefactor. As Peter Linebaugh explains, "The 'great Bishop of the Cells' (as the Ordinary was called) talked to the condemned malefactors in their last days. He summarized these conversations and published them in his *Account* along with his sermons. It was then sold in the streets before, during, and after the hanging for the edification of his readers." "The Last Dying Speech" derived from the *Account* but was "part of a broader library of the street, whose purveyors included reciters of dialogues, litanies, and squibs, taletellers and ballad mongers." Geared to street culture and to the expressive economy of ballads and legends, "The Last Dying Speech" contained an emotional excess that distinguished it from the *Account* and that supported "a mythic presentation of the malefactor."[11] *Industry and Idleness* vividly registers this process of unofficial mythification. Thus, Idle does not disappear from the life of the crowd even after he is executed. On the contrary, inscribed in a broadsheet called "A Full and True Account of the Ghost of Tho Idle," Idle's mythical afterlife circulates through the very procession that accompanies Goodchild's triumphal journey through London.

By representing the hawking woman's shout as a focused and powerful act of intervention, Hogarth, thus, seems to be recognizing the unstoppable energy that drives the print commodity and in this way helps morally ambiguous accounts of low life to circulate freely across the disparate social spaces of the city. Paradoxically, it is exactly the print commodity's capacity to "elude discipline without being outside the field in which it is exercised,"[12] which proves crucial for the making of the new urban aesthetic that would develop continuously from *Industry and Idleness* to *Bleak House* and beyond.

It is possible to uncover more precisely the relationship between the Tyburn woman's hawking shout and the making of the new urban aesthetic by comparing the process that Pierce Egan's *Life in London* advocates for its own circulation with the ways in which print commodities actually circulate in *Industry and Idleness*. Thus, unlike Egan's camera obscura-like book, which detaches not only the represented scene but also the viewer/reader from the city itself, and which generates its social knowledge within the placeless public sphere made up of isolated individual readers, the Tyburn broadsheet—and even more directly the one entitled "A Full and True Account of the Ghost of Tho Idle" which appears in the last plate of *Industry and Idleness*—belongs to the firmly located, physically concrete domain that David Henkin has designated as the "public sphere of urban letters."[13] Broadsheets are documents that circulate together with newspapers, calling cards, handbills, and posters amidst the shop signs, the buildings, and the alleys of the city, and they owe their very existence as print commodities to their integration with the human traffic of the streets. As unbound, uncovered, and always readable documents, they seek to draw the attention of every passerby, and ultimately to affect the series of exchanges that will result in their dispersal across the length and breadth of the city.

As part of "city reading,"[14] then, broadsheets based on Idle's life and death keep in constant circulation those images and discourses from the "other" London that pose such a danger to the organized and organizing centers of Hogarth's moral universe. In *Industry and Idleness* this threat is not just theoretical: its effects are evident not amongst some imagined community of consumers but directly, and very powerfully, within the internal world of the picture series itself. Thus, in the opening picture, a broadsheet very similar to the one that circulates in London's streets in the last plate is shown to have found its way into that geometrically fortified and highly organized site of production: the workshop. It hangs on the sleeping Idle's loom in the form of a down-market, broadsheet version of the story of Moll Flanders's promiscuous life. Certainly Hogarth moralizes Idle's reading habits: Idle's preference of the Moll Flanders story is at the cost of "The Prentice's Guide" (which lies torn and rotting on the floor) and it looks forward to a reckless life that will end with his hanging. However, the Moll Flanders broadsheet, together with the words "Spittle Fields" inscribed on the large ale measure that Hogarth strategically places in Idle's vicinity, also symptomize the mobility of urban texts and especially their capacity to carry fragments of the life of the "other" London to the geometrically enclosed sites of productive and responsible living. What is more, the urban text's propensity to bring together the differing social spaces of the city generates an important feature in Hogarth's own articulation of the metropolis.

This feature is evident above all in plate 3 (fig. 7) where the disruptive energies that Hogarth associates with the centers of urban debauchery and crime are, like the broadsheets that the Tyburn woman sells and Idle buys, shown to spill into and threaten the more organized sectors of the city. Every detail in the third plate—the sinking grave which serves as the gambling table; the vicious, hardened faces of Idle's gambling companions; the moldering skulls and bones that lie scattered chaotically in the immediate vicinity of the grave; the suggestions of unfair play and retaliatory violence—serves to imbue the gambling scene with the nightmare atmosphere that pervades the more permanent vice dens of London. However, if the prostitute's garret where Idle spends a night or the Blood Bowl where he is shown to divide the spoils of a robbery with a fellow criminal are enclosed interiors constituted, self-consciously, as the "other" of the spaces across which Goodchild's career moves, the vicious gambling scene in plate 3 unfolds tensely against a background that belongs clearly to the domain of rational, respectable existence. The wall of the brick church that constitutes the background in plate 3 is punctuated by the geometrically shaped doors and windows that remain throughout the picture series, the markers of control and rational organization. Indeed, it would not be unreasonable to think of the church wall as the external face of the sort of interiors that Goodchild inhabits. Yet the church wall is part of an urban scene characterized not by its settled homogeneity but by a series of dramatic contrasts: between a group of disreputable characters engaged in a tense, potentially violent activity and the last of the

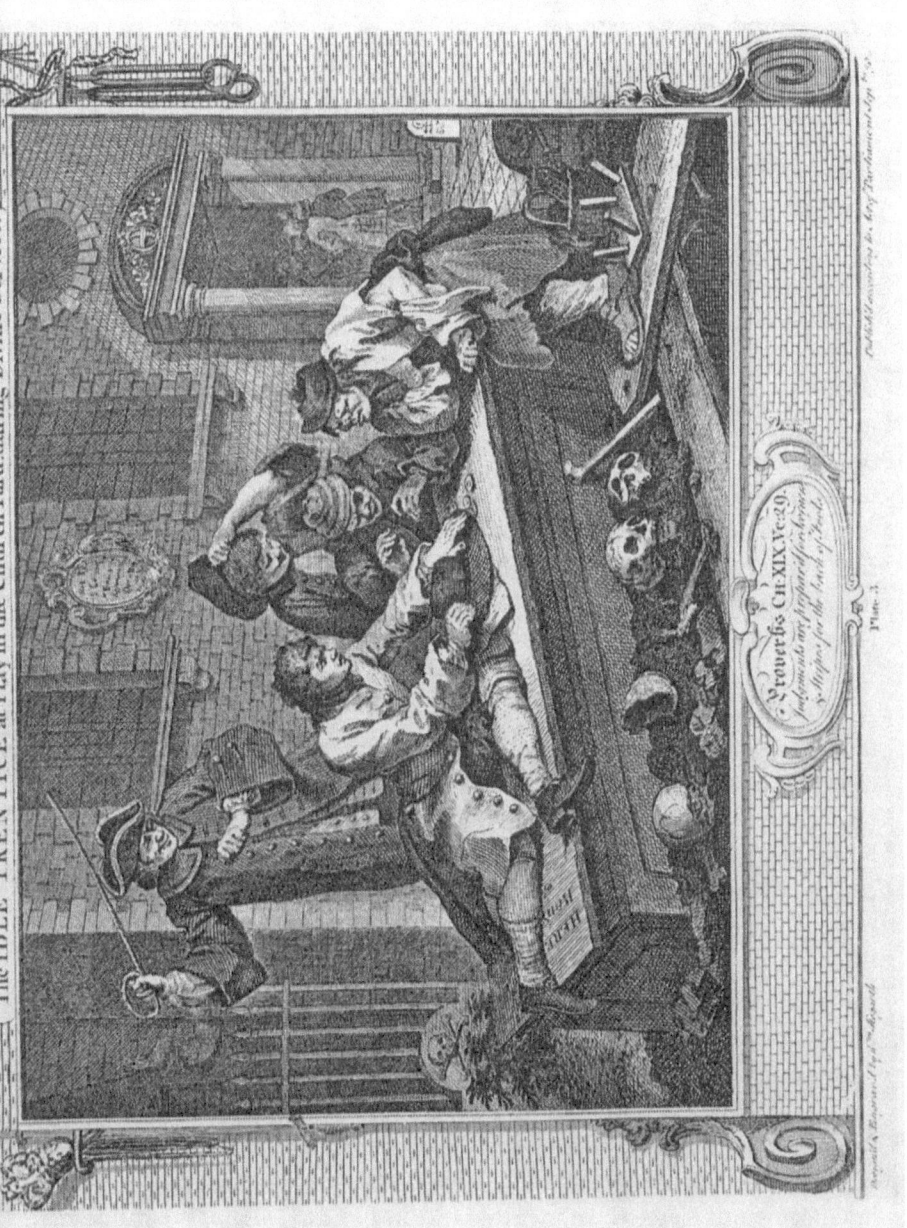

FIGURE 7. William Hogarth, "The Idle 'Prentice at Play in Church Yard, during Divine Service," Plate 3 of Series *Industry and Idleness* (1747)

congregation that files into the church in an orderly manner; between the official insignia of London that appears at the very center of the church wall and the dark, uncared-for, desecrated graveyard that stretches out under its very shadow.

It should be clear, therefore, that the importance of the Moll Flanders broadsheet cannot be limited to its (negative) role in Hogarth's moral fable. Rather, as a fragment of street culture driven by the circulatory energies of print capitalism to breach the fortified spaces of respectability, the Moll Flanders broadsheet embodies a second major impulse within *Industry and Idleness* that unfolds in tense opposition against Hogarth's attempts to map the city and to shut off its respectable and productive interiors from the contaminating effect of its streets. More specifically, this second impulse cuts through the binary structure established in *Industry and Idleness* by the classificatory, disciplinary trajectory within Hogarth's articulation of the city, and it is oriented not toward segregating the respectable quarters of London from the disreputable but toward bringing urban disparities together in relationships of tense simultaneity. Accordingly, the characteristic mode of this second trajectory is a "spatial phrasing" that is based on fragmentation and juxtaposition rather than on continuity and homogeneity.[15] This juxtapositional impulse was to coexist throughout the nineteenth century's representations of the city with the classificatory and segregating modes, to constitute what I am calling the urban aesthetic.

This chapter has dwelled at some length on *Industry and Idleness* because it exercised a very strong and enduring influence on nineteenth-century representations of the city. Not only did Hogarth's characters, plots, and locations continue to circulate throughout the first half of the nineteenth century in reprints and in dramatic and fictional adaptations but nineteenth-century practitioners routinely drew upon Hogarth's techniques in their representations of London's low life.[16] What is more is that the tension—between, on the one hand, the techniques with which Hogarth had sought to classify the city and fortify its respectable interiors and, on the other, the juxtapositional possibilities generated by Hogarth's "spatial phrasing"—never lost its relevance in the nineteenth century's imaginative articulations of the metropolis. I will now track the development of this tension through the first half of the nineteenth century, focusing on images of the city produced by three popular forms of the nineteenth century: the city sketch, especially as it worked in tandem with Pierce Egan's written text in *Life in London,* the panorama, and the stereoscope.

The London of the 1820s that Egan depicts was a less menacing, more precisely mapped-out city than the metropolis of *Industry and Idleness.*

Writing about Paris in 1836 Balzac points to the nature and some implications of such mapping:

> Poor women of France! You would probably like to remain unknown in order in order to carry on your little romances. But how can you manage to do this in a civilization which registers the departures and arrival of coaches in public places, counts letters and stamps them when they are posted and again when they are delivered, which provides houses with numbers and will soon have the whole country down to the smallest plot of land in its registers.[17]

The classificatory work, whose administrative manifestations Balzac describes, had begun in England during the eighteenth century itself. As John Marriott suggests:

> when the ethos for improvement gathered momentum in the course of the eighteenth century, it was framed in terms of the physical rather than the human environment. Such improvement was, therefore, predicated on a detailed knowledge of metropolitan topography; cartographers, surveyors, travel writers and poets applied themselves to the task of mapping the streets of the city so opening them up for the bourgeois traveler.[18]

The classificatory impulse, already evident in Hogarth's work, becomes considerably stronger in *Life in London*. The well-known frontispiece of *Life in London* (fig. 8) visually articulates the fantasy of a hierarchically organized London that nevertheless made the city's social extremes available for observation. In the Cruikshank picture, London's social life descends vertically from the court to the garret. But the Cruikshank brothers (George and Robert) also use the clearly demarcated segments and niches of the Corinthian pillar (which serves as the allegorical ground for the picture) to separate the social groups and offer them as exhibits for the benefit of the viewer. The Cruikshanks, thus, offer readers a view of London's heterogeneous social life and extend Hogarth's system of geometric divisions between segments of the social spectrum.

Egan's written text, following the Cruikshank frontispiece, deals only with the two extremes of the social spectrum, but like many other forms of representing the city discussed in this book, *Life in London* seeks not only to contain but also to *work with* the intersections and mutations incessantly produced by the mobility and radical social diversity of urban life. This double trajectory within the urban aesthetic is encoded in the image of

FIGURE 8. I. R. and G. Cruikshank, frontispiece to Pierce Egan, *Life in London* (1821)

the encyclopedia that Egan uses to describe London. As a discursive mode, the encyclopedia suggests, at one level, the idea of cataloging—of recording every detail that may contribute to the reader's knowledge of London. At the same time, however, the diverse entries that randomly follow each other in the encyclopedia also approximate the endless sequence of unrelated but contiguous scenes in *Life in London,* activities that turned Egan's London into a site where, as John Marriott puts it, "the extremes and paradoxes of life happily coexist."[19] In a very real sense, indeed, the whole of Egan's discourse is generated by the conviction that the extremities in the "complete CYCLOPAEDIA" (23), that is, London, can be experienced: the paradigmatic character of *Life in London* is Bob Logic who, as a "complete walking map of the metropolis—a perfect pocket dictionary of all the flash cant, slang patter, either of St. James's or St. Giles's,"[20] opens up passages between dramatically different areas of London and in this way sustains an important dynamic of the book. Focusing on this commitment to the unfolding of urban variety and, more specifically, on the behavior of Egan's protagonists as they move *between* those utterly disparate social worlds frozen in the Corinthian pillar makes it possible to track the continuing unfolding of the juxtapositional trajectory within the urban aesthetic.

In *Life in London* Egan finds, perhaps *invents,* ways by which he might register the city's diversity on the figures of his protagonists. One way in which he does this is by fabricating for his book an arrangement of time and space that differs significantly from the ways in which these elements are organized in the realistic-domestic novel. Time, in the domestic novel, works to generate, among other things, the effect of everyday life—its rhythms and its more or less set routines. Moreover, these regular temporal sequences ensure that the socially homogeneous individuals and groups who inhabit the domestic novel meet at regular intervals in such spaces as the parlor, the park, or the church. In this sense, time becomes the taken-for-granted, almost invisible element in which interpersonal relationships and, indeed, individuality itself develop. *Life in London* totally disrupts the normal, everyday pace of time: "Jerry, who used to rise with the lark when at *Hawthorne Hall* . . . had, since his arrival in London, reversed the scene altogether. His acquaintances, Tom and Logic, had bid adieu to anything like regularity of living, long before . . . and had only gone to *repose* or left their beds as circumstances required" (234; italics in the original).

The regular temporal sequence that sustained the unfolding of subjective life in the domestic novel gives way here to an arrangement of time oriented toward exposing Egan's protagonists to the random variety of the city: to its night life and more generally to its innumerable unforeseen and unforeseeable encounters. In fact, Egan's basically *spatial* imagination, the individual figure, for all its lack of inner depth, often emerges as a site where the diversity—often the internal contradictoriness of the metropolis—can be vividly registered. Tom and Jerry may be "superficial" as characters, their unreflective enjoyment of urban contrasts being utterly incapable of sustaining anything like a developing inner life. But Egan's characters might also be considered instruments of that "complex kind of training" to which the experience of urban modernity subjected "the human sensorium."[21] Thus, Tom and Jerry do not simply relay to the readers of Egan's book the scenes that they encounter during their sprees and rambles through London. Their behavior also focuses on their persons the city's propensity to destroy the internal integrity of things and to habituate the mind, instead, to the experience of random diversity and juxtaposition, fragmentation, and superimposition. Indeed, Tom and Jerry can sustain their situation as connoisseurs of urban variety only by learning how to rapidly erase from or superimpose upon their personalities such markers of social class or station that may or may not be relevant to a particular social encounter. As Egan's protagonists prepare to enter the "*classic ground*" "of fashion, style, elegance, and manners" in Allmacks very soon after having spent an evening among the "Lascars, Blacks, jack tars, coal heavers, dustmen, women of colour, old and young of All Max," Tom invokes the "waters of LETHE" to cleanse Jerry's "pericranium" of any evidence that might betray their recent association with "the flash part of mankind" (293, 286, 293; italics in the original). On the other hand, when Tom moves around in the Back Slums of London, it is no longer absolutely imperative for him to sustain an unambiguous social identity. He disguises himself as a beggar, yet, Egan writes, "he did not lose the traces of a *gentleman*" (346; italics in the original). Tom's situation as a conduit between the contradictory social spaces that make up the city and his consequent propensity to bear on his person the signs of urban contradictions symptomize a strand within the urban aesthetic that will turn out to be important for this book. To be sure, Tom's situation as both beggar and gentleman carries no significance beyond his (and Pierce Egan's) enjoyment of the social diversity of the city. Corinthian Tom's many interactions with beggars and whores are not mediated by that self-conscious ideology that inexorably leads Thomas Idle to his hanging ground. Furthermore, Tom and Jerry's propensity to bring together in relationships of simultaneity the extremities of the social world do not generate the sort of anxiety that comes through so powerfully in the discourses (both fictional and nonfictional) of the 1850s. Nevertheless, Egan's early attempts to articulate the unstable diversity of the city and, more specifically, its propensity to fragment but also to generate unexpected convergences does suggest a trajectory of representation that would ultimately produce novels like *Bleak House* and *Our Mutual Friend*. For example, Egan's propensity to present Corinthian Tom as a collage of socially contradictory signs rather than as an introspective subject would energize, in Dickens's novels, an urban mode of characterization whose effects were very different from those that realism sought to achieve. Moreover, unlike Hogarth who exploited but did not acknowledge the expressive possibilities offered by a fractured cityscape, Egan explicitly finds in the city the source of an expressive dynamic that runs counter to domestic realism's focus on the everyday life of the middle classes as the only proper subject for the novel. Corinthian Tom speaks for Egan when he insists that a "view of real life" is to be obtained not in those typical sites of novelistic representation—"the CLOSET" or " in the circles of fashion [where] you scarcely meet with any contrast, whatever"—but at the entrance of the Westminster-Pit where dogs are fought and where "*flue flakers,* dustmen, lamp-lighters, stage coachmen, bakers, farmers, barristers, swells, butchers . . . weavers, snobs, market-men, watermen, honourables, sprigs of nobility, M.P.s" jostle for admission (223, 222; italics in the original).

The popular discursive engagement with the city, of which Pierce Egan's *Life in London* is an early example, continued well into the 1850s, and one form in which the effects of this continuing engagement are clearly visible is the panorama. More specifically, the panorama deployed its enhanced technological resources to sustain in new ways the central paradoxical dynamic of Egan's work: the impulse, on the one hand, to topographize the city, to fix and to make visible its details and, on the other, to uproot these details from the discourse of objective geography to set them into circulation. One way in which to unfold the tension between the centripetal and the dispersive forces within the panorama is by focusing on certain significant differences in the conditions in which early nineteenth-century England's most famous panoramic work—Thomas Horner's gigantic representation of London—was produced and disseminated.

When in 1823 Thomas Horner first established his "observatory" on the very top platform of the scaffolding erected for the purpose of renovating St. Paul's Cathedral, he conceptualized his panorama of London in relatively modest terms. As he went on, however, he was more and more impressed by the view he commanded and in the end he produced a panorama of truly gigantic proportions. When it was finally displayed in a massive, specially designed building called the Colosseum, it "enclosed a circle 130 feet in diameter, was 60 feet high, and covered a surface of more than 24,000 feet."[22] Horner's goal was to achieve an "absolute perfection of detail" in his panorama such that even the tiniest feature of the metropolis could be easily recognizable in it. It is clear that he succeeded to a considerable extent. One contemporary described the finished picture as "*a cyclopedia of information*" (italics in the original) that offered a far more detailed inventory "of the largest and most influential city in the world" than "[h]istories, descriptions, maps and prints."[23]

Evidently, therefore, one element in Horner's panorama that impressed his first viewers was its *comprehensiveness*—its successful presentation of the most immoderate of social formations as a topographically accurate whole. But Horner was able to achieve this only because he had managed to find a godlike vantage point above the dome of St. Paul's. It is exactly this undisturbed and fixed situation from which Horner produced his panorama that may be contrasted against the conditions in which his audience viewed it.

The view of London that Horner's panorama offered spectators was, in every sense, spectacular. Horner's gigantic picture spread cylindrically across 24,000 square feet of painted surface under the 15,000 square feet dome of the Colosseum, which was painted as the sky. Moreover, by affecting what Gillen D'Arcy Wood has called "a very modern marriage between entrepreneurship and visual technology,"[24] Horner's exhibition offered the visitor a range of viewing positions. The exhibitors devised an ultramodern system made up of pulleys, trolleys, and, most sensationally, the first hydraulic elevators ever used in London[25] to lift the viewer off the ground and to transport her or him to several points in the gigantic, empty hemisphere that the Colosseum enclosed. These spectacular technological arrangements gave to the viewer considerable ambulatory freedom and, by implication, access to certain visual effects that could not have been available to Horner himself when he was painting his panorama from his fixed position on top of the dome of St. Paul's. More specifically, the shifts that the exhibiting machinery affected in the viewer's position enabled her or him to grasp the city as fragments, to think of the city as a collage of dispersed details that did not necessarily have to conform to geographical continuity. In an important sense, Horner himself encouraged his viewers to abstract and compare the disparate details of his panorama. For one thing, Horner's gigantic painting completely subsumed tonal values to comprehensiveness and clarity in detailing: it sought to ensure that no effect of light or shade got in the way of a viewer's appropriation of this or that feature of the city. Indeed, Stephan Oettermann has attributed the "hyper clarity" of Horner's detailing to a real estate agent's view of London aimed at putting into circulation "the dimensions and price of the listings."

It is important not to take Oettermann's comparison between Horner's panorama and "a mail-order catalogue" too literally.[26] What makes Oettermann's insight valuable, however, is that it points to certain impulses within the panorama that tended to fly against its maplike ability to fix the exact locations of places. More specifically, it points to the ability of the panorama, as a form, to register what, following Jonathan Crary, may be called modern capitalism's propensity to "uproot . . . and make mobile that which is grounded, clear . . . away and obliterate that which impedes circulation, and make . . . exchangeable what is singular."[27] In a couple of prints that he published in 1851 on the subject of the Great Exhibition, Cruikshank demonstrated just how far panoramic representation could go in this direction. Cruikshank found in his very subject a mode of organization that privileged the dispersive impulses that Crary associated with modern capitalism over the traditional panorama's commitment of replicating a realistic topography from a fixed point of view. *All the World Going to See the Great Exhibition of 1851* represents the world itself as a dream space, depicting a densely detailed crowd of ships, trains, pyramids, and camels that move along the rims of the earth toward the Crystal Palace, which is located at the center of the upper hemisphere. *The Dispersion of the Works of All Nations from the Great Exhibition of 1851* is even more vivid in its dramatization of the unrelated simultaneity of diverse, far-flung images and commodities brought together by the imperatives of trade. The print holds together tiger skins, oriental umbrellas, exotic headdresses, cannons, cellos, clocks, railway engines, and dresses that float without people in what seems uncannily like a postmodern collage.

We could, thus, argue that although the panoramic mode was oriented primarily toward mapping the city's streets and buildings, it also demonstrated the possibility of holding together, within a single frame, elements that were widely dispersed in space. Cruikshank was to draw upon and extend even further the panorama's expressive possibility in the most elaborate picture of his later years. Cruikshank's *The Worship of Bacchus* (1860–62) is a massive oil painting, over thirteen feet wide and seven feet long, and it is inhabited by over a thousand figures. What unifies the picture is that all the figures exemplify, in some way or another, the evil effects of drinking. On the other hand, the figures are also divided into various self-contained, often disconnected tableaus that range from elegant, elite interiors to brutal and drunken scenes enacted in the streets of London. Cruikshank was drawing on the panorama's capacity to bring together disparate locations while attempting to map the evils of drinking across the whole spectrum of English society, but he was also extending the panorama's expressive possibilities by saturating his locations with a social content that panoramas did not always have. What is more, in an extraordinary lecture he gave during an exhibition of his painting, Cruikshank demonstrated that it was possible to discursively activate the figures and groups in his picture in a manner that a picture could not, on its own, have done. Cruikshank hoped that his picture would be "read" rather than merely viewed and that viewings would often be accompanied by lectures, so that "the mind may be operated upon through the *ears* as well as the *eye* at the same time." In his own lecture Cruikshank explained what was literally happening in the "diagrams" scattered across his canvass, but he also used the resources of language to improvise anecdotes—for example, around "acts of [drunken] violence that he had witnessed in the city"[28]—to make unexpected connections between this or that group.

Cruikshank's pieces are important because they suggest the possibility of a panoramic *imagination* where London's streets, buildings, and localities would appear not as markers in the discourse of objective geography but rather as floating urban signifiers, saturated with this or that semantic content and capable of entering into relationships of "opposition, alteration and juxtaposition" with other urban signifiers to create what Roland Barthes has called "the basic rhythm of signification."[29] In this sense, the panoramic mode would, indeed, have a special kind of significance for any articulation of the London of the 1850s when metropolitan improvements, rising standards of living, and the pervasive rhetoric of progress tended to overshadow the problem of poverty and when doctors, sanitary inspectors, journalists who wrote about "the residuum" or the "sunken sixth" often compared themselves to "explorers investigating foreign, 'savage,' and uncharted territory."[30] On the other hand, as a mode always capable of bringing together the socially disparate and spatially dispersed parts of the city in relations of "opposition, alteration and juxtaposition," the panoramic imagination had the potential of breaching the structural demarcations by which respectable London sought to separate itself from its unregenerate "other." In "The Last Words of the Old Year," an essay that appeared in *Household Words* in the same year as Cruikshank's prints, the Great Exhibition remains one of capitalism's dream spaces: "a great assemblage of the peaceful glories of the world." But the panoramic imagination can now emulate, at the discursive level, the circulatory processes of modernity that had brought together goods from all over the world in the Crystal Palace, wrench the "Great Exhibition" itself from an environment overlain with connotations of progress, and pit it against virtual spaces of other kinds: "the dark exhibition of the bad results of our doings."[31]

Re-Visioning the City

It is now possible to propose certain specific ways in which the panorama contributed to the making of an urban aesthetic. At the simplest level the panoramic mode was capable of registering, more vividly than ever before, the random diversity of the city. Henry Mayhew focused on precisely this function of the panoramic mode when he described the experience of viewing London from high up in the sky as a passenger in the Royal Nassau Balloon: "Indeed, it was a most wonderful sight to behold that vast bricken mass of churches and hospitals, banks and prisons, palaces and workhouses, docks and refuges for the destitute, parks and squares, and courts and alleys, which make up London."[32]

About fifteen years before Mayhew wrote this, Dickens was, perhaps, already sensing possibilities the panoramic mode would open up for novelists. In an 1847 letter to Edward Tagard, he invoked the moving panorama as the form most capable of registering a radically fractured cityscape. Dickens described Paris as a succession of "gaudy or ghastly" sights, and he added that as he walked through the streets of Paris, "Hospitals, Prisons, Dead-houses, Operas, Theatres, Concert Rooms, Burial-grounds, Palaces, and Wine shops" passed before him "as in a rapid Panorama."[33] In *Bleak House*, which he began some three years after his visit to Paris, Dickens would demonstrate how a basic feature of the panorama—the long, unbroken sequences that moved across a bewilderingly diverse cityscape—could be absorbed within the expressive economy of language and in the process transform spatial parameters within which novels usually worked.

But the panorama contributed to the emerging urban aesthetic at another closely related level as well, a contribution that flowed from the ambiguous status of the details that went into the making of the panorama. Thus, as parts of an accurate topographical representation, the buildings, monuments, and streets that made up the panorama could only have fixed locations. However, these details were also capable of freeing themselves from the topographical imperatives of the panorama, of circulating as independent urban signifiers, and of precipitating conjunctions and intersections unimaginable within the discourse of scientific geography. It was the panorama's capacity to produce potentially mobile details even as it focused on the city as a whole and, thereby, to suggest unexpected connections between widely dispersed and socially disparate locations of the city that Dickens seized upon when, in *Bleak House* for example, he cut a discursive path across London that would lead from the Dedlock townhouse to the paupers' graveyard.

More than any of the forms discussed so far, it was the technologically advanced operations of the stereoscope that demonstrated the range and sophistication of effects that could be brought into play in nineteenth-century simulations of the big city. As something fabricated out of objects that were simply added to "others in a succession that only underscores their disconnection,"[34] the stereoscope articulated, in an extreme form, an image of the city built out of randomly circulating details. Unlike the city sketch or the conventional panorama, it dispensed even with contiguity in real space as the basis of its organization. However, if the stereoscopic representation completely disregards the real location of an urban detail or the relationship that it bears to the objects that actually surround it, it also promotes relationships of other kinds. As Rosalind Krauss put it, "The file cabinet is a different object from the wall or the easel. It holds out the possibility of storing and cross-referencing bits of information and of collating them through the particular grid of a system of knowledge."[35]

The system of "cross-referencing" to which Krauss refers could, of course, produce manufactured knowledge or even pure illusion. Indeed, as "the technical reconstitution of an already reproduced world,"[36] the stereoscopic scene was, in many senses, the ultimate example of the nineteenth century's increasing propensity to *simulate* the domain of the visible. Thus, "Photography"—an essay that appeared in *Household Words*—describes the operations of the stereoscope in a way that highlights precisely the illusion-producing trajectory that so often underlay the operations of Victorian optical gadgetry. The stereoscope, in this essay, produces an amazing spectacle: a groom "biting the puppy's tail off, with an expression of enjoyment." Equally, however, "Photography" reiterates Rosalind Krauss's sense of the representational possibilities generated by the way in which the stereoscope organizes its signifiers. The stereoscope, like the camera, trained the mind to respond to a new kind of discursive experience: "the art of judicious groupings."[37]

"[T]he art of judicious groupings" will have major implications for the Dickensian urban aesthetic. What I want to emphasize now is that the stereoscope made it possible to extend these groupings across not only two- but also three-dimensional space. Here again the stereoscope's representation of receding space was very different from the realism that the use of perspective achieved for painting. As Jonathan Crary puts it:

> The stereoscopic relief or depth has no unifying logic or order. If perspective implied a homogeneous and potentially metric space, the stereoscope discloses a fundamentally disunified and aggregate field of disjunct elements.... When we look head on at a photograph or a painting our eyes remain at a single angle of convergence, thus endowing the image surface

with optical unity. The reading or scanning of stereo image, however, is an accumulation of differences in the degree of optical convergence, thereby producing a perceptual effect of a patch work of different intensities of relief within a single image.

It would seem, thus, that by dispensing with the imperative of optical unity, the stereoscope made it possible to fabricate the depth of a scene and bring together two visual planes inaccessible by the stationary eye. Moreover, the "hallucinatory clarity" with which the stereoscope imbued certain objects,[38] while leaving others in the shade, suggested the possibility of establishing visual relations based on differing intensities of focus. Therefore, if the machine-based transformation of vision destroyed any direct link between the eye and what it was seeing, it also reconfigured the domain of the visible, ensuring its unfolding on a vast scale and in relation to an increasingly complex set of coordinates.

It may be argued that the technologically induced transformation of vision could have little consequence for the novel, since the novelist's omniscient eye was, in any case, capable of limitless mobility and vision. But this is an ahistorical argument. As Sharon Marcus has shown so effectively in the context of nineteenth-century France, authorial omniscience could work only within certain historically determined parameters. More specifically, what Marcus does is to track the changing functions of Asmodeus, a mythical figure whose supernatural powers traditionally helped to sustain authorial omniscience in a certain form of French literature. Thus, in its earliest version—as the devilish hero of Lesage's *Le Diable boiteux* (1707)— Asmodeus simply removes roofs and peers inside houses. When Jules Janin revived him in an 1831 preface for a fifteen-volume collection on Parisian scenes, Asmodeus is capable of generating a bird's-eye view that will organize "buildings as a series of scenes" and "the apartment house as a planar picture to be observed, as a live, three dimensional scene." It is only in the 1840s that Asmodeus's eye begins to approximate the elasticity as well as the alienated nature of the truly modern vision. Asmodeus is now able to align his viewpoint to a building's vertical front even as he approaches it from the sky and to transform a building's walls into transparencies so that everything that happens there appears before the viewer as "so many moving pictures framed under glass."[39]

The changing powers of Asmodeus symptomize the modernization of vision or, more specifically, the modernization of the ways in which the city could be visualized. By the 1840s the omniscient authorial eye had far outreached its early, relatively simple functions. The technology that underlay stereoscopes and the viewing conditions for Horner's gigantic panorama suggested the possibility of unfolding the city not only as a linear sequence, but also from different heights and angles. Moreover, the "hallucinatory clarity" of focus which the stereoscope achieved enabled the omniscient authorial eye to imagine and fabricate unexpected juxtapositions or sequences based on vividly articulated details dispersed over not two but three dimensions of urban space. These new ways of seeing would turn out to be vital for the making of novels like *Bleak House* or *Our Mutual Friend*, and they would determine the internal dynamics of not only the discursive unfolding of London but also such properly novelistic features as plot construction and characterization.

The last mode that this book associates with the production of the urban aesthetic is perhaps the oddest. Walking, on the face of it, has little in common with the workings of machines or the effects of writing and, as a mode of observing the city, it did not, of course, originate in the nineteenth century. But in contemporary accounts, virtually everything that this chapter has discussed—the writing, sketches and the optical gadgets—become associated with the activity of walking. The title page of Pierce Egan's *Life in London* equates Tom's and Jerry's "Rambles and Sprees" with the camera obscura's ability to discover and record the scenes of the metropolis, and, in a passage quoted earlier, Dickens had compared a walk through Paris to the experience of viewing a panorama. These comparisons suggest that the activity of walking enabled the nineteenth-century urban pedestrian to sustain the by-now-familiar experience that underlay the urban aesthetic: to remain both aloof from and immersed in the chaotic, socially diverse life of the city.

As it happens, it is precisely walking and its capacity to sustain the doubleness associated with the urban aesthetic that drives Dickens's first attempt to write the city. Several critics have demonstrated how *Sketches by Boz* adapts and transforms the mediating strategies developed by Egan to socially separate himself and presumed readers from the characters and scenes that he describes. Dickens may not invoke the metaphoric camera obscura to protect his readers from the brutality of street scenes they will be made to witness, but, as Deborah Epstein Nord shows, he finds in humor a very effective distancing device.[40] Again, the sympathetic mode in which Dickens sometimes describes a character or scene from low life is invariably mediated by what Audrey Jaffe has called "a self consciousness about [the] social position" that binds Boz to his middle-class readers.[41]

It seems to me, however, that in Jaffe's fine account of narrative positioning in *Sketches by Boz*, the problem of the social works exclusively at a synchronic level. Jaffe unfolds convincingly the social nuances that are invariably encoded within the narrator's transactions with his characters and his readers. She does not, however, acknowledge that Dickens's attempt discursively to separate himself and his readers from his low-life characters is always in danger of becoming undermined by the central activity of the book: walking.

The starting point of *Sketches*, the indispensable precondition for its existence, is, of course, the ambulatory freedom that, as the narrator claims, distinguishes him from those who "brush quickly by," "steadily plodding on to business" (59). This distinction does, indeed, reiterate the author's sense of superiority over the subjects that he describes—it constitutes Boz as, in Jaffe's words, "the untrammelled individual" who finds "interest in what the man on his way to business cannot take the time to see."[42] But Dickens's opening declaration might also be understood diachronically as "a process of *appropriation* of the topographical system" (italics added), to adapt Michel de Certeau's terms.[43] That is, the "speculative" pedestrian's walk through London is not something that involves a superior, *flâneur*-like enjoyment of the endless variety of urban life but is an act that will join together socially and geographically disparate parts of the city to produce a "story."

One way to track the process of fragmenting and joining that transforms walking in *Sketches by Boz* into a "spatial *practice*" is by turning to a piece like "The Hospital Patient."[44] The starting point of "The Hospital Patient" is, of course, a typically productive encounter between the urban perambulator, not tied down to any routinely taken path, and a dark, unfrequented bit of urban space. But for Boz the hospital interior he glimpses from the outside is not merely a possible subject for a sketch. Rather, it is something he stores in his memory, transforming into a potentially mobile signifier that can, like the low life described in the circulating broadsheets in *Industry and Idleness* or the detachable locations of Horner's panorama, be made to relate, discursively at least, to other forms of life that proliferate in the city. In fact, it is precisely the activity of walking that provides Boz with the opportunity to connect the hospital room to another section of the city. The story of the woman battered by her lover that Boz picks up while "strolling through Covent Garden" ends inexorably in the very hospital whose "gloomy and mournful scenes" are, for Boz, already a subject of intense interest (241, 240).

In "The Hospital Patient," then, the hospital interior and the police station at Covent Garden no longer remain undifferentiated locations within the city. Rather, they become part of a discursive economy, spaces that will sustain the unfolding of what might properly be called a story. This story, moreover, uncovers a social domain that is organized not as hierarchically separable positions where the author and his readers are situated above the subject but rather as a continuum made up of radically disparate spaces. It stitches together within the virtual space of the middle-class reader's mind a dark social landscape made up of a desolate London pavement "hours after midnight," "the gloomy and mournful scenes" within the hospital, and a police station near Covent Garden filled with criminals (240). Boz's perambulations thus help, in de Certeau's words, to "traverse and organize places; . . . select and link them together; . . . make sentences . . . out of them" and, in this sense, to replicate that "spatial phrasing" with which the panorama or the stereoscope had helped to produce the urban aesthetic.

The aesthetic investment that Dickens made in "city stories"[45] is brought into sharper focus when considered alongside the consistent skepticism with which Thackeray responded to the figure of the urban pedestrian. In a brief commentary on Egan's book, for example, Thackeray picked not on the pedestrian's ability to register urban contrasts but on the "varieties of lounge in which the young men indulge—now a stroll, then a look in, then a ramble, and then presently a strut."[46] This skepticism unfolded more elaborately in a subsequent series of articles that he contributed to *Punch*. Here the "speculative pedestrian" is reincarnated as Mr. Spec—a journalist who undertakes a tour of London, not because he believes that any kind of literature can come out of the streets but because his editor orders him to travel "in London and bring me an account of your tour" in an attempt to cash in, yet again, on a best-selling formula.[47] Like Tom and Jerry, Mr. Spec does try to move between the highest and lowest levels of social life in London—"out of mere love of variety and contrast" (194)—but all that he can recover from this experience is the "leer" and the "wink" of a street sweeper and a vision of veterans so resplendent in "scarlet and gold lace" that it seemed strange "they did not mount their chargers to go to dinner" (181, 196). Similarly, Spec uses exaggeration to reduce to absurdity the speculative pedestrian's ability to read the city and uncover its hidden stories. Every man or woman in the streets of London, Spec claims, is "invested with an awful character" and is, therefore, nothing less than a "riddle to be read henceforth" (181). Indeed, the "very dummies in the hairdresser's" invite Spec to interpret "their new and dreadful significance." In these circumstances Spec can only confess to a mock helplessness in dealing with a "subject so tremendous" (182, 181).

Thackeray's skepticism about the city's potential to generate meanings beyond what adheres to its surface details and, more specifically, about "stories" fabricated out of the social diversity of the city points again to the very different ways in which he and Dickens related to the popular expressive resources to which both had equal access. These differences would have surprisingly precise effects on their novel writing and, in this sense, demonstrate the extent to which the novelistic aesthetic that Dickens developed with the help of popular expressive resources deviated from a more properly literary form of novel writing associated with Thackeray's fiction.

CHAPTER 4

Novelizing the City

Bleak House, Vanity Fair, and the Hybridizing Challenge

∞

HOGARTH'S DREAM of a comprehensively mapped city that would allow access to its darkest and most criminalized corner continued to remain potent in *Bleak House*—a novel that appeared more than a hundred years after the publication of *Industry and Idleness*. Thus *Bleak House* makes a powerful ideological investment in Inspector Bucket as an agent of surveillance capable always of penetrating into London's most obscure corners, of bringing these within the domain of visibility and, thereby, of sustaining always a panorama-like picture of the city in his mind. Thus, Bucket's activities may be thought of as carrying forward that fantasy of control whose unfolding across a range of visual forms has been documented in the last chapter.

Dickens's sympathetic portrayal of Bucket, and, by implication, his allegiance to modern and efficient forms of surveillance capable of penetrating the nooks and crannies of the metropolis, of registering all its transactions, and of tracking the movements of those who inhabit it, has been extensively discussed by critics like D. A. Miller and Deborah Epstein Nord.[1] What has not been discussed as often is the extent to which *Bleak House* is constituted by the second impulse that drove the representational modes discussed in chapter 3 and that was concerned not so much with surveillance as with the city's disconcerting contradictions. *Bleak House* works at many levels with the juxtapositional possibilities made available by Hogarth's prints, the city sketches, as well as the panorama and the stereoscope. For example, the broadsheets of Hogarth's picture series may mutate in Dickens's novel to newspapers or reprints of fashionable portraits, but, as print commodities whose circulation is impossible to regulate, they continue to precipitate unthinkable connections between dramatically disparate parts of the city. Indeed, the urban aesthetic—that "child of the giant city" capable of registering "the intersections of its myriad relationships,"[2] as Baudelaire might have described it—helped to constitute some of the basic features of *Bleak House* as a novel: its arrangement of time and space as well as its modes of characterization and of plotting.

We can begin to unfold the effects of urban aesthetic on *Bleak House* by comparing the differing ways in which Dickens and Thackeray treat a relatively minor urban figure: the ubiquitous street urchin. In *Vanity Fair* street urchins merely fill the background in scenes that happen to be set in the streets: they cannot, in any sense, be said to have a place in the plot connections that the novel makes. For instance, the "damp urchins" (260) who hang about the chapel door during George Osborne's wedding help make up the gloomy atmosphere in which Thackeray envelops the apparently happy event, but they disappear forever from the novel immediately after they have served this purely local function.

Like *Vanity Fair, Bleak House,* too, contains a description of the church and its surrounding scenes, but here the street urchin Jo, far from fading discreetly into the background, becomes the focal point of an emblematic street scene that aims, above all, at holding together the contradictions of a stratified landscape in a tense, disconcerting juxtaposition:

> And there he sits, munching and gnawing, and looking up at the great Cross on the summit of St. Paul's Cathedral, glittering above a red and violet-tinted cloud of smoke. From the boy's face one might suppose the sacred emblem to be, in his eyes, the crowning confusion of the great, confused city; so golden, so high up, so far out of his reach. There he sits . . . the crowd floating by him in two streams—everything moving on to some purpose and to one end. (255)

This passage sustains its destabilizing project by not only drawing upon but also setting itself off against various visual modes of representing the city. One might, for example, read in Dickens's tensely juxtapositional "sketch" a polemic against the numerous "topographies" or "views" of St. Paul's, which artists like Boys or Nash produced in the first half of the nineteenth century and which, with their emphasis on "order and firm composition"[3] and their propensity to blank out the confusion, crowdedness, and the squalor of the adjoining streets, would be very much in consonance with the general climate of the 1850s. This decade, as several historians have shown, was characterized by rising standards of living and massive street clearance drives that tended to push the poor to the realm of the "residuum" or "the sunken Sixth," morally and even biologically demarcated from those capable of participating in the processes of progress.[4] Such a polemic would obviously draw a great deal on William Hogarth's ability to register the radical social disparities of the cityscape. In fact, in a review of Cruikshank's *The Drunkard's Children* (1848), Dickens explicitly comments on Hogarth's ability in *Gin Lane* (1751) (fig. 9) to juxtapose the densely detailed landscape of urban poverty where the drunken mother is situated against "the prominent and handsome church" that coldly surveys the squalor "under the shadow of its tower."[5]

As is well known, Dickens's overt purpose in the review was to set off Cruikshank's didactic approach to drunkenness against the social complexity that Hogarth brought to bear on the subject. But Dickens's comment seems also to gesture toward his own juxtapositional method of charting the city and toward the debt this method owed to Hogarth's work. More specifically, the scene which brings together, in a recognizably Hogarthian configuration, the dome of St. Paul's and the figure of a boy who is poor, homeless, and utterly primitive already contains within the synchronic mode of its articulation the germ of a plot that would wrench the action of *Bleak House* from the social spaces within which a novel like *Vanity Fair* moves. Furthermore, the scene forces Dickens's predominantly middle-class readers to take cognizance of "the residuum" and of the contiguity and connectedness of this unspeakable realm to that which they inhabited.

The basic framework for such a mode of novelistic organization had already existed in the panorama—a form that, as we've seen, was capable of tracking sequentially the random diversity of the city, but also of bringing together disparate urban details in significant juxtapositions.[6] Thus, in a letter already quoted, Dickens had drawn attention to the panorama's capacity to register in a single, unbroken sequence the bewildering diversity of the cityscape. In a separate piece, moreover, Dickens also discussed a second discursive possibility suggested by the experience of *viewing* a panorama. He concluded a remarkable review of *Banvard's Geographical Panorama of the Mississippi and Missouri Rivers* with a paragraph that has significant implications for understanding the urban aesthetic that he was developing: "It would be well to have a panorama three miles long of England. There

FIGURE 9. William Hogarth, *Gin Lane* (1751)

might be places in it worth looking at, a little closer than we see them now, and worth thinking of a little more profoundly. It would be hopeful, too, to see some things in England as part and parcel of a *moving* panorama."[7] In this passage Dickens gestures toward the expressive possibilities that the panorama and (implicitly) even the stereoscope held for the novel. What Dickens proposes is the possibility of novelizing the moving panorama's capacity to generate relationships between geographically dispersed and socially disparate objects, scenes, or people. However, the panoramic mode Dickens has in mind also approximates the stereoscope's propensity to disregard optical integrity of scenes by focusing sharply on certain details while leaving others in the shade. Thus, Dickens imagines a way of writing the city that is capable (like the panorama) of ranging across the length and breadth of an internally fractured metropolis and also of bypassing the laws of objective geography and of bringing into stereoscopic focus those dispersed locations that were "worth thinking of a little more profoundly."

One way to uncover Dickens's "panoramic" way of seeing more clearly is by turning back to *Vanity Fair*—a novel whose spatial orientation is best embodied in the sharply focused scenes that Becky catches so often in her telescope or her opera glass. More specifically, the telescope with which Becky picks out the figure of Briggs in a fashionable spa and, even more, the opera glass which characters in *Vanity Fair* often use to spy on each other offer views that are sharply detailed but enclosed, unrelated to anything in the larger world outside the social milieu in which they are embedded. Indeed, Thackeray preserves both his vividly realistic detailing as well as the homogeneousness of his social groupings even when he moves characters like George Osborne and William Dobbin across the vastly stratified landscapes of different nations and even continents.

In contrast, consider the sixteenth chapter of *Bleak House* which begins in Chesney Wold, that exclusive seat of the Dedlocks that will not allow the slightest breath of vulgarity to contaminate its hallowed portals. Dickens's narrative (impelled, clearly, by an organizational possibility first articulated in the panorama) then sweeps across Lincolnshire, pauses briefly at the Dedlock residence at London, and then takes the reader to the heart of outcast London, that pestilential terrain unmarked on the map of progress, where ruined shelters "have bred a crowd of foul existence that crawls in and out of gaps in walls and boards" (206). The intensity of the language suggests that a passage such as this is not meant as an entertaining example of metropolitan variety or even as the sort of social exposure with which Mayhew had amazed his readers.[8] Rather, the unbroken passage of Dickens's narrative from Chesney Wold through Tom-all-Alone's may be grasped as the unfolding of a trajectory within the urban aesthetic that aims at disrupting, on the one hand, the comfortable assimilation of social contradictions within the set formats of urban entertainment and, on the other, the social isolation of what one contemporary called the novel's "legitimate province":[9] the network of socially contiguous spaces inhabited by the middle and the upper classes.

Moreover, the panoramic sequence that unfurls through this chapter of *Bleak House* also draws on the resources of the stereoscope to focus on dramatically disparate scenes and characters spread across three-dimensional space. For example, during this sequence, the narrator moves from the unlettered Jo to the book-lined, first-floor apartment of that master of legal procedure, Mr. Tulkinghorn, and from there directs our, but not his, eyes to the figure of Lady Dedlock disguised as a servant as she walks across the street below. Thus, Dickens's unanchored narrative deploys the stereoscope's ability to manipulate perspective and depth and a spatial freedom available only to language, to move not only back and forth but also up and down, to intrude into upper-floor interiors or, on the contrary, to sharply focus on a chosen subject in the street below.

As part of a developing urban aesthetic, however, the details that make up the Dickensian cityscape—a street urchin emerging out of the heart of outcast London, a lady disguised as a servant looking for the paupers' graveyard, a lawyer's chamber overlooking the street where the lady walks—are not random impressions of detached observers, entertaining themselves on a spree through London. On the contrary, they both approximate the arbitrary assemblages of the city and become, at the same time, the nodal points that will generate the lines of action whose intersections will constitute the montage progression of the Dedlock plot.

Unlike Thackeray, in whose precisely mapped interiors people are brought together only by social or kinship ties, Dickens draws on a range of popular forms—from the city sketches to the stereoscope—to constitute the city in what Raymond Williams calls its "double condition":[10] on the one hand, as a bewildering collage of contrasting scenes and people and, on the other, as something that promotes inescapable connections between its dispersed inhabitants. Yet since the linkages that Dickens makes in the vast, unwieldy, and radically stratified world of *Bleak House* tend to destroy rather than maintain the "wholeness" or "organicity" of the world as it is constructed in the realistic novel, the more educated traditions of novel criticism, especially as they were articulated in the Victorian quarterly press, quite often responded merely to the fragmentedness of Dickens's novels. One significant image that the quarterly press used to describe the dispersed quality of Dickens's novels was that of the newspaper. As Walter Bagehot put it:

> Mr. Dickens's genius is specially suited for the delineation of city life. London is like a newspaper. Everything is there, and everything is disconnected. There is every kind of person in some houses; but there is no more connection between the houses than between the neighbors in lists of "birth, marriages and deaths." As we change from the broad leader to the squalid police report, we pass a corner, we are in a changed world. This is advantageous to Mr. Dickens's genius. His memory is full of instances of old buildings and curious people and he does not care to piece them together. On the contrary, each scene, to his mind, is a separate scene—each street a separate street.[11]

At one level, Bagehot's threefold comparison between London, the newspaper, and the Dickensian text seems entirely apt. As what Richard Terdiman calls "the first culturally anti-organicist mode of modern discursive construction," newspapers "trained their readers in the appreciation of detached, independent, reified, decontextualised articles."[12] Indeed, like the city sketches, which may be said to represent graphically what the newspapers embodied formally, the newspaper articulated the sense of randomness of the urban experience that Dickens was to incorporate within his novelistic aesthetic.

Yet if the newspaper bears its contradictions on its face "in a clashing, conflicted disposition of its discursive surface,"[13] it is also the ultimate example of the standardized, mechanically produced cultural product. It bears not even the memory of an "aura." It cannot, in any sense, be said to belong to an individual or to a fixed place. On the contrary, its existence is predicated on its *circulation,* its accessibility to anyone who can read or acquire a copy. Unlike a novel, the newspaper does not even have to be read through but offers the reader the option of choosing, from within a standardized layout, what she or he requires. For these reasons, the newspaper not only approximates the random, unconnected sights of the city but also emerges as one of its great systems of communication—the means by which information about sordid slums reach the mansions of the rich and the powerful and by which business relations are struck between the most unconnected of individuals.

It would seem, therefore, that Bagehot is sensitive to only one side of the metaphor that he uses to describe Dickens's fiction. With its array of seemingly unconnected characters and places, *Bleak House* does bring to mind the random juxtapositions of newspaper columns. But the critical snobbery that makes Bagehot pick the metaphor of the newspaper—merely so that its fragmentedness can be set off against the "wholeness" of the higher forms of writing—blinds him to the role that newspapers actually play in a novel like *Bleak House*. In fact, newspapers are ubiquitous in the world of *Bleak House*, read as much by Lady Dedlock as by that wizened product of inner London, Chickweed. It is a newspaper report of the death and burial of Hawdon that enables Lady Dedlock to locate Jo and, thereafter, the terrible place where her former lover lies buried and in this way to open up, for the first time, the unimaginable connection between Chesney Wold and the paupers' graveyard. Again, an enquiry that Smallweed had made in the papers regarding the whereabouts of Hawdon elicits a response not only from George but also from Tulkinghorn and provides the latter with the final piece of evidence to establish Lady Dedlock's relationship with the recently dead, opium-eating pauper.

In *Bleak House*, newspapers are not the only means that help to establish contacts between people unconnected by social or familial ties. It may be possible for the individual inhabitant to disappear within the vastness of the metropolis and lead a nameless existence as Nemo literally does, but the masses of registration—the records of the Chancery, Post Office directories, even entries in the registers of the moneylender or the law stationer—both yield unexpected clues about the whereabouts of unknown persons and facilitate contacts between strangers. Jarndyce, for example, is inundated with begging letters from individuals and charitable organizations who have procured his address from the Post Office directory. More significantly, the Lady Dedlock plot, whose movement depends on information carried in newspapers, is set into motion when Tulkinghorn locates, from an entry in Snagsby's register, the whereabouts of a mysterious man whose handwriting had startled the normally imperturbable Lady Dedlock.

In the world of *Bleak House*, therefore, the newspaper as well as the proliferating system of registrations emerges as the underlying, almost unnoticed vehicles that both record and promote meetings between people who are unrelated by social or familial ties but who are brought together by the innumerable impersonal transactions that the city spawns every day. Therefore, Bagehot's (derisive) newspaper metaphor might be defined as expressive not only of the dispersed quality of the city but also of its capacity to forge unexpected connections and, indeed, of a trajectory within the urban aesthetic that will register and bring within the scope of its plot connections the turbulent unregulated life that lies beyond the familial and social relationships within which the middle-class novel usually works.

One way to respond to the newspaper as a complex rather than a simple metaphor for the city and for the whole urban aesthetic that it spawned is by examining the role that newspapers play in the sort of novel that might have served as Bagehot's yardstick when he spoke of the fragmentedness of Dickens's fiction. As it turns out, a work like *Vanity Fair* is just as full of newspapers as *Bleak House,* but one way in which the former novel is able to preserve its internally integrated social world is by dissociating its newspapers from the social unevenness of the city. Thus, the *Morning Post,* which is a representative newspaper in *Vanity Fair,* circulates more or less within the social domain of the elite carrying, for instance, the news about Becky's invitation to Gaunt House to a jealous Mrs. Crawley and reinforcing the novel's projection of a closely knit social milieu in which everyone knows each other. A rare example of a newspaper in *Vanity Fair* that does seem to perform the sort of dispersive function that Bagehot associated with it is the *Times* and, more specifically, its last page, which carries announcements of public auctions. Moreover, as something that redistributes "the library, furniture, plate, and choice cellar of wines" (150) of a single household across various unconnected locations, the auction itself may be seen as one of the very few centrifugal tropes in *Vanity Fair.* Yet, like the newspaper, the auction in *Vanity Fair* never functions as a means of forging connections between people separated by the wide social disparities of the city. Thus, the auction at the Sedley household does not relocate Amelia's piano to some remote, unexpected corner of the metropolis and in this way bring this new domain into the ambit of the novel's plot connections. Instead, Amelia's piano is bought by the utterly familiar Dobbin and then relayed back to her humbler home at Brompton.

The different ways in which Thackeray and Dickens treat the newspaper (and related tropes such as systems of registration or the auction) symptomize differing responses to a larger problem at the center of the urban aesthetic: the tension that always existed within the experience of urbanization between the known world of the home and the chaotic, unpredictable streets. More specifically, the auction as it is used in *Vanity Fair* may be said to incorporate within the internal economy of the novel the function that Walter Benjamin's arcades performed at the level of architecture: both extend the threshold of the interior into the streets to such an extent that the streets themselves become interiorized.[14]

Interiors in *Bleak House,* on the other hand, do not seek to colonize the outside, and although the novel does follow *Industry and Idleness* in constituting certain domestic spaces such as Bleak House itself as the idealized "other" of a chaotic outer world, it also exposes other interiors to the disorderly traffic of the streets. Cook's Court, for example, consists of a row of houses with shop fronts that extend into the open streets. However, in contrast to the arcades, where the attempt is to interiorize exteriors, the relationship between the open Cook's Court and its adjoining houses is interactive and conflictual. Mrs. Snagsby's shrill voice spills into Cook's Court all the time, but what she has to say is very much part of her domestic affairs. At the same time Snagsby's law stationery shop, which extends his home into the street, attracts a bewildering array of customers and, in this way, exposes the inner living quarters to the socially unpredictable encounters of the world outside. For Mrs. Snagsby, Jo's sudden emergence from the street into the midst of a tea party that she is hosting for the Reverend Chadband and his wife signifies more than a stray intrusion. When she hears Jo's account of his strange encounter with a lady who apparently wanders about in the streets looking for the paupers' graveyard, and when she observes her husband's sympathetic attitude to Jo, she begins to entertain dark suspicions about Jo's paternity.

Mrs. Snagsby's suspicion is, of course, entirely unfounded, but it does anticipate, in its absurd way, the other unthinkable liaison in the novel and, even more importantly, the breaching of the domestic threshold that this will involve. That breach is, of course, inseparable from Lady Dedlock's sexuality, and I will try to show soon how Dickens works with techniques that developed in city sketches to find in Lady Dedlock's sexual transgression the means of holding together in her figure the marks of those dramatic social disparities that make up a city. But before moving to Lady Dedlock, it is necessary to discuss a related set of problems pertaining to Thackeray's representation of Becky's body and her sexuality.

In comparison to Dickens, Thackeray's handling of the problem of sexuality is paradoxically both more and less expressive. Becky's situation—the air of uncertainty that surrounds her social (and, in the early parts of the novel, even marital) status, the nature of her intelligence, and her ambitions—makes possible a far freer articulation of a woman's sexuality than Victorian novels usually allow for, but it also confines Becky's unanchored sexuality within the network of interiors that make up the novel's characteristic social spaces. Despite the relatively homogenous social parameters within which Thackeray unfolds Becky's career, however, the representation of Becky's sexuality turns out to be radically split: characterized, on the one hand, by the unrestrained and fascinated articulation of its enabling aspects as Becky, freed from the constraints of conventional domesticity, goes about finding her way with great skill through the system of signs by which social superiority is asserted and power wielded in the world of *Vanity Fair* and, on the other, by the determination to expose this sexuality to the retributive backlash of a patriarchal domestic morality. Moreover, as with the protagonist of *Bleak House,* the effects of Thackeray's split representation of Becky's sexuality are marked above all on her body. Thus, unlike Amelia's domesticated body, which bears no signs of her sex except those that can be contained within the organicity of domestic reproduction, Becky's body is stared at, publicly discussed, reified into a sex object. Squills, for example, describes her entirely in terms of her anatomy: "Green eyes, fair skin, pretty figure, famous frontal development" (177). What makes Thackeray's delineation of Becky's body truly paradigmatic of the social dynamics that underlie the novel, however, is that the moralized trajectory of representation coexists with a fascinated exploration of the socially empowering aspects of Becky's sexuality. At this level Becky's body, far from being a passive object of male fantasies, is shown to be something that is deployed, with brilliant effect, by a gendered intelligence so developed that its maneuvers in the social arena are often compared to those of Napoleon in war. The important scene in which Becky entertains Lord Steyne provides a good example of the effectiveness with which Becky is able to deploy her body in her attempts to gain a position in high society:

> The great Lord Steyne was standing by the fire sipping coffee. . . . There was a score of sconces, of gilt and bronze and porcelain. They lighted up Rebecca's figure to admiration, as she sate on a sofa covered with a pattern of gaudy flowers. She was in a pink dress and looked as fresh as a rose; her dazzling white arms and shoulders were half covered with a thin hazy scarf through which they sparkled; her hair hung in curls around her neck; one of her little feet peeped out from the fresh crisp folds of silk—the prettiest little foot in the prettiest little sandal in the finest silk stocking in the world. (177)

In contrast to Lady Dedlock, who (as I will show) is freed by her relationship with Hawdon from the specificity of her environment and even of a distinctive individuality, Becky's body is constituted by an internally consistent system of signs that not only projects a sharply individualized sexuality but also registers the whole process by which the signs of class are acquired and redeployed. It is precisely because Becky's body is implicated inextricably in the system of signs that may be said both to energize and to demarcate the limits of social behavior in *Vanity Fair* that it becomes impossible for Thackeray to use the social ambiguity that distinguishes Becky's position from that of every other character in *Vanity Fair* to stretch her figure beyond the social spaces described in the novel—to loosen it in such a way that it becomes capable of registering simultaneously the signs of the contradictory social worlds of her childhood and her adulthood. In fact, in contrast to the methods of Dickens (and of urban forms such as the city sketches), which often draw their energies from the play of diverse or contradictory social surfaces, Thackeray's characters develop not horizontally but vertically in space. This striving for depth rather than breadth points to a second critical element in Thackeray's characterization: the extremely productive way in which it uses time.

Time, in *Vanity Fair,* is the element that most clearly embodies Thackeray's movement away from magazine writing toward realistic characterization:[15] it may be thought of as an invisible hinterland that gives depth to character, as the all-important element whose apparent invisibility disguises its indispensability in any articulation of a changing inner life. This inner significance of time becomes visible in *Vanity Fair,* above all, during the moments of crisis, for instance, when after deciding finally to disinherit his son, old Osborne retires to his study that is now thick with the details of his past, and, in a representative moment, turns to his escritoire:

> In the large shining mahogany escritoire Mr. Osborne had a drawer especially devoted to his son's affairs and papers. Here he kept all the documents relating to him ever since he had been a boy; here were his prize copy books and drawing books, all bearing George's hand, and that of the master, here were his first letters in large round-hand sending his love to papa and mama, and conveying his petition for a cake . . . They were all marked and docketed, and tied with red tape . . . his letters from the West Indies—his agent's letters, and the newspapers containing his commissions: here was a whip he had when a boy, and in a paper a locket containing his hair, which his mother used to wear. (216)

Clearly the critical element in Osborne's crisis is time, not only because time here loses its discreet everyday quality, becomes self-conscious as it were, makes visible its own passage, but also because by doing this, it humanizes old Osborne, exposes his rigid, selfish personality to the inescapable pain of memory, and thus gives to it an unexpected emotional depth.

In the main plot of *Bleak House,* on the other hand, time does not move in its everyday, "realistic" pace: it does not emerge as the element in which individuals and personal relationships gradually develop; as the major if almost unnoticed feature in the making of the plot. Instead, the arrangement of time in the main plot of *Bleak House* is characterized not by its continuity but by its breaks: it is organized as a series of "crises," in Bakhtin's sense of the term—points where a "radical change, an unexpected turn of fate takes place, where decisions are made, where the forbidden line is over stepped."[16] An example of this kind of use of time is the moment that sets into motion the Lady Dedlock plot. As Lady Dedlock reclines in her usual languid manner near a fire in the drawing room of Chesney Wold, her face is suddenly animated by her recognition of the handwriting in a legal paper that Tulkinghorn carries. She strives to suppress her agitation but, despite her tremendous will power, fails and is taken ill. The handwriting that Lady Dedlock recognizes is that of her former lover who is now an opium-eating pauper. The surfacing of Lady Dedlock's past thus introduces a sharp break in the languid pace of her everyday life, brings her to a turning point, and threatens to expose her to a radically new *space*. Put another way, the mass of time that constitutes Lady Dedlock's past is important not because it sustains her subjective evolution, but because it enables Dickens to stretch her image across the "great gulfs" (208) of the metropolis. Thus, the "crisis" in the Lady Dedlock plot is a pivotal point in a compositional method that is energized by the shocks of the street rather than the psychological and social complexities developing through the interactions of a group of socially homogeneous people and that has as its end the distinct individualization of characters.

Until quite recently, few critics even recognized that the urban mode of characterization that produced Lady Dedlock could have its distinctive expressive logic.[17] Instead, the privileged status given to the psychologically authentic character—which spontaneously unfolded its "humanity," "its natural sense and natural feelings"—enabled critics to reduce Dickens's "figures" to a "community of eccentrics."[18] Alex Woloch's recent work has, however, complicated the liberal humanist propensity to predicate the literary success of novels on their ability to indefinitely sustain characters in and for themselves—"character in its inward and outward workings, in its involuntary self-betrayals and subtle self-sophistications," as George Henry Lewes puts it.[19]

Alex Woloch's seminal *The One vs. the Many* shows that the potential limitlessness of a character's unfolding self is, in novels, limited by its insertion within "the definitively circumscribed form of a narrative."[20] This means that the unfolding of even the most psychologically complex character must come up against, and be continuously moderated by, the demands made by the plot as well as by other characters. The great value of Woloch's work, for this book, lies in its recognition that in the "chaotic urban field" of Dickens's novels, "other characters" can expand into a crowd. Thus,

Woloch argues that individuality in a novel like *Bleak House* is threatened always by the "sheer fact of urban multiplicity." The "tens of thousands of people" who "lose their footholds" and stumble on the tracks of "other foot passengers," to follow Woloch in quoting from the famous first paragraph of *Bleak House,* have little chance of emerging as sharply delineated, freely developing individuals. This erosion of individuality corresponds, in Woloch's account, to the way Dickens organizes light in his novels and, by implication, to what he allows his readers to see. For example, in the London of *Bleak House* where the fog never lifts, things "are continuously presented as half visible," and what "incompletely *seeing*" produces is, in Woloch's brilliant phrase, "obscure or eccentric *sights.*"[21] Unlike Henry James, thus, Woloch uses the term "eccentric" to describe not the lack of inner lives in Dickens's figures but rather the (peculiarly modern) experience of fragmentation that is attendant on their urban existence.

Woloch is right in relating Dickens's characterization to the city and, more specifically, in focusing on the city's fragmenting visual field "from which human beings themselves emerge only partially."[22] What he does not consider is the city's propensity to promote unexpected intersections, and the effects that this might have on an urban mode of characterization. For George Cruikshank, on the other hand, the urban mode's freedom from the internal consistency demanded by realistic characterization made it capable not only of registering the fragmenting effects of the city but also of bringing together, within the figure, the city's dramatic discontinuities. In a passage full of the most interesting resonances, Cruikshank digs out from inner London an image that, in its grotesque incongruities, would approximate the realistic critic's ultimate nightmare—"a pug nosed Apollo or a Jupiter in Great Coat."[23]

> There was, in the neighborhood in which I resided, a low public house . . . It was frequented by coal-heavers only; and it stood in Wilderness Lane . . . To this house of inelegant resort . . . which I regularly passed . . . my attention was especially attracted by the sounds of a fiddle, together with other indications of festivity; when glancing towards the tap room, I could clearly discern a small bust of Shakespeare placed over the chimney piece, with a short pipe stuck in its mouth. This was not clothing the palpable and the familiar with golden exhalations from the dawn, but it was reducing the immortal beauty of Apollo himself to a level with the commonplace and the vulgar. Yet there was something not to be quarreled with in the association of ideas to which the object led. It struck me to be the perfection of the human picturesque; it was a palpable meeting of the Sublime and the

Ridiculous; the world of Intellect and Poetry seemed thrown open to the meanest capacity; extremes had met; the highest and lowest had united in harmonious fellowship . . . it was impossible not to recognize the fitness of the pipe. It was only the pipe that would have become the mouth of the poet, in that extraordinary scene, and without it, he himself would have wanted majesty and the right to be present.[24]

In this description of a low-life scene from the giant metropolis, the coal heavers show little respect for the integrity of Shakespeare's image: they add to it new and incongruous features, vulgarize it, and transform it into an object whose significance lies not in its replication of a real-life figure but in its ability to hold together the dramatic incongruities of the city. Put another way, anything in the bust of Shakespeare that might convey a sense of flesh and blood individuality—a facial expression, a look in the eye that might communicate some facet of inner life, or even a distinctive physical profile—is either consciously blanked out or distorted. But what Shakespeare's image loses in terms of psychological depth, it gains semantically by the unrestrained play of surfaces that its freedom from any commitment to lifelike replication makes possible.

As with Cruikshank, the diverse, contradictory impulses of the city—its "magic-lantern"-like quality—were vitally important to Dickens's art of characterization, something without which, as he wrote from the relative quiet of Laussane, his "figures were disposed to stagnate."[25] Indeed, an unknown correspondent of Hotton went so far as to claim:

The grand object of Mr. Dickens, as a novelist, has been not so much to depict human life as human life in London, and this he has done after a manner he learned from "The Life in London" of Mr. Pierce Egan. If you remember that once famous book, you will call to mind that he takes his heroes—the everlasting Tom and Jerry—now to a fencing saloon, now to a dancing house, now to a chophouse, now to spunging-house. The idea is not to evolve the characters of Tom and Jerry but to introduce them in new scene after scene. And so you find with Dickens. He invents new characters, but he never invents them without at the same time inventing new situations and surroundings of London life.[26]

Hotton's correspondent is right in noting that in the urban aesthetic that the Dickensian novel helped to develop, space is often privileged over time, and that the object seems to be to take the reader through "scene after scene" rather than offering her or him an internal view of a character's evolution.

What he does not comment on, however, are the expressive strategies—noted in the previous chapter—by which Egan managed to superimpose on his figures the contradictory marks of the socially diverse spaces across which they move. These strategies are developed and deployed in several socially significant ways in Dickens's characterization of Lady Dedlock.

Like the bust of Shakespeare, Lady Dedlock's figure is not enclosed within what Bakhtin would call an "individual, closed sphere." She develops not so much vertically within herself as horizontally in space. She is physically freed, in a far more radical sense, than Becky from the framework of "relationships of family . . . of social status and social class," which are, as Bakhtin argues, the "stable, all determining basis of plot connections" in the middle-class domestic novel,[27] precisely so that her body can hold together, in a relationship of tense simultaneity, the contradictory marks of the social extremities through which it is stretched. Thus, if Becky's unanchored sexuality becomes the paradoxical means of focusing on her body the signs by which social status is acquired and asserted, the effect of Lady Dedlock's liaison with Hawdon is to shatter the integrity of her social existence. Significantly, a key element in Dickens's delineation of Lady Dedlock is the transforming device of the disguise. It is this device that enables Dickens, for example, to superimpose on her figure two sets of contrasting signifiers, such as a diamond ring under the sleeve of a servant's dress. In this way Lady Dedlock's frequent disguises split her body in a way that would never be possible in the more realistic modes of characterization: they prod the reader into seeing Lady Dedlock as *both* servant and lady, *both* lady and brick maker's wife, and they lead inexorably to the climactic emblem in the Lady Dedlock plot, in which Lady Dedlock's corpse, dressed in Jenny's clothes and with one arm around a bar in the gate of the paupers' graveyard, suggests powerfully how expressive modes generated in the popular forms of the city are used to break down the integrity not only of the individual subject but also of any conception of "civilization" that seeks to sustain itself by shutting itself off from the harsh realities that lie beyond it.

This chapter has been concerned so far with the relationship between certain ways of representing London that developed in popular forms such as the city sketches and a mode of characterization that seeks not to project but to shatter the physical, social, and psychological integrity of its subject. But the fracturing of Lady Dedlock's social identity also opens up for analysis a larger set of questions. These relate to the ways in which *Bleak House* engages with various extrafictional discourses, such as the highbrow literary criticism that appeared in the Victorian quarterlies or the reports of sanitary reformers such as John Simon and especially with their response to the many discursive, but also material, crossings across social spheres that became inevitable once dramatically divergent social groups began to inhabit and write about the metropolis. I will show that all these discourses regularly deployed the metaphor of disease or infection while negotiating the sort of crossings described above but will also focus on the changing connotations of the disease metaphor as it moved from the Victorian quarterlies to a novel like *Bleak House*. This will bring to the surface, once again, the tension that has been the starting point of this book: on the one hand, the threat that the discursive churning induced by the uncontrollable circulation of mass-produced print commodities posed to the more educated theories of novel writing and, on the other hand, the emergence out of this churning of paradigms that aimed at breaching precisely those social and cultural boundaries with which the higher traditions of novel writing sought to preserve their internal integrity.

As it happens, *Bleak House* contains a scene that seems to self-consciously connect the fracturing of Lady Dedlock's image within the novel to the larger process of fragmentation and reactivation that was a basic feature of the popular print market of the early nineteenth century. This scene occurs in chapter 7, when Guppy, clerk at Kenge and Carboy, finds his way into the splendid drawing room at Chesney Wold and is immediately struck by Lady Dedlock's portrait:

> "Blest!" says Guppy, staring in a kind of dismay at his friend, "if I can ever have seen her. Yet I know her! Has the picture been engraved, miss?"
> "The picture has never been engraved. Sir Leicester has always refused permission." (92)

It is the uncanny likeness that Lady Dedlock's portrait bears to Esther that catches Guppy's attention, but Guppy is, in fact, right in his conjecture about Lady Dedlock's portrait having been engraved.[28] Sir Leicester may strive to preserve the unrepeatable uniqueness, the "aura" of the Lady Dedlock portrait that adorns the drawing room at Chesney Wold, but the techniques of reproducing artworks such as Lady Dedlock's portrait and the existence of large markets for such reproduced prints, in fact, prove to be too strong for Sir Leicester's prohibition. They wrench Lady Dedlock's image from its unique existence at Chesney Wold, reproduce it in innumerable copies, modify it at various levels according to the tastes of consumers, and relocate it in the most unexpected of places. Thus, Tony Jobling's "Galaxy of British Beauty, representing ladies of title and fashion in every variety of smirk that art, combined with capital, is capable of producing" (267), includes a somewhat down-market version of Lady Dedlock's portrait. Clearly the free circulation of Lady Dedlock's image results in what Benjamin describes as a "tremendous shattering of tradition":[29] it breaks down an important barrier that separates Chesney Wold from Tony Jobling's modest room and, in this way, encourages the intermingling of expressive resources and ways of seeing bred in widely separated social spheres. Such a process would, obviously, be very dangerous for any culturally exclusive theory of art. Thus, Sir Leicester's anxiety about his lady's portrait is paradigmatic of a larger process in the world outside. It gestures, on the one hand, toward conditions that facilitated not only the multiplication of works of high art but also the circulation of more ordinary images, motifs, and ideas through an array of socially disparate genres and media and, on the other hand, toward the consolidation, in the pages of the Victorian quarterlies, of a discourse whose fear and loathing of such cultural intermingling is expressed above all in the metaphor of contamination or infection.

One example of the sustained use of the infection metaphor to express elite cultural anxieties can be found in reviews of the "sensation" novels carried by journals like *Temple Bar* and the *Edinburgh Review* through the 1860s. The reviewers were offended not only by the sensational and immoral subjects of "sensation" novels, but also by the acceptance these novels had gained among the middle-class reading public. As a reviewer in the *Temple Bar* wrote despairingly, after tearing apart what she or he saw as a particularly repugnant example of a sensation plot: "But . . . we have not been speaking of a serial story of 'Reynolds's Miscellany' or the 'London Journal,' but of a novel 'large numbers' of which, it was advertised upon its appearance, would be 'taken by circulating libraries, where well appointed carriages do most congregate.'"[30] The quarterly press responded to this cultural threat by comparing the development of mass literary culture—of which the "sensation" novel was the latest and most dangerous manifestation—to the progress of an epidemic. The "original germ, the primitive monad" from which the "sensation" novel had grown was the cheap novel catering to the half-educated masses. The immorality, sensationalism, and titillation inseparable from these novels had spread "virus"-like in all directions—"from the penny journal to the shilling magazine, and from the shilling magazine to the thirty shilling volume" or, to use more direct terms, from "the hovel to the mansion."[31] The cultural infection emanating from the lower depths had, thus, succeeded in bringing about an unthinkable union between the reading habits of the "kitchen" and the "drawing room."[32]

The major anxieties that underpin the reviews—infection, the effects of sensational fiction produced for the half-educated masses, the changing relationship between "hovels" and respectable drawing rooms—reappear in Inquiry Commission reports on the sanitary conditions of London slums that were released through the 1830s and '40s. For example, Simon's first *Annual Report* of October 1849 shared with the literary reviews a middle-class horror of life in the lower depths as well as an anxiety about the "moral" contagion that came out of the slums.[33] However, far from joining the literary critics in their effort to sustain an autonomous cultural sphere for the middle class, Simon's whole attempt was to shock the respectable with his horrific accounts of disease-bearing slums that lay in their immediate neighborhood. The sanitary reports did not follow the reviews in constituting the cheap, low-life novels as the virus-like vectors of cultural contamination. On the contrary, some observers at least argued that the sensational urban mysteries—which exemplified, according to *Temple Bar,* the low and contaminating literary entertainment—shared John Simon's commitment to circulating knowledge about the atrocious sanitary conditions that prevailed in London's slums. Looking for precedents from literature that would convey a sense of the "fearful interest of [the] unvarnished disclosures" that Simon's first *Report* was about to make, the *Times* could point only to "the vivid horrors of those fictitious chronicles, *The Mysteries of Paris* and *The Revelations of London.*"[34] The *Times* follows the literary reviews in focusing on the sensational nature of the fiction produced by authors like Eugene Sue. But rather than being a sign of aesthetic degeneration, this sensationalism becomes, for the *Times,* a means of social exposure, corresponding to the equally dramatic "revelations" made by doctors, sanitary officers, and journalists about the existence, in the heart of the world's metropolis, of a primitive disease-bearing "tribe " or "race."

It is possible now to respond, on the one hand, to the differing ways in which the literary critics and sanitary reformers related to mass-produced sensational urban novels and, on the other, to the changes that this difference produced in the way they treated the idea of infection. For the *Times* the best-selling authors of urban mysteries were important, above all, because they had made visible parts of London that did not exist in the map of the middle classes. It is to the dynamics produced by social difference that both the literary critics and sanitary reformers linked the idea of infection. Thus, in the highbrow literary reviews, infection had worked as a metaphor of intrusion, expressing the inevitably contaminating effect that the literature of the "hovel" or the "kitchen" would have on what was read in "drawing rooms." However, moving from the problem of taste to that of sanitary reform, the "vivid horrors" described in the works such as *The Revelations of London* become not potential threats to the aesthetic integrity of the middle-class novel but rather a mode of representation that the sanitary reformers could emulate in their attempt to draw attention to the urgency of reform. This partnership between the sanitary reports and the best-selling urban novels is reinforced even more by the way doctors treated the relationship between urban disparities and infectious disease. For sanitary reformers such as Dr. Ferrier, infection was not an intrusion from the lower depths but the retribution that a society had to suffer for neglecting the poor. Thus, Ferrier argued that although the poor were the first and worst victims of contagion, it was "hardly possible to prevent communication of the disease to the rich" and that the infection reached "the most opulent" by "secret avenues" and "severely revenge[d] the neglect, or insensibility [by the rich] to the wretchedness surrounding them."[35] Ferrier's warning was echoed by several nineteenth-century doctors and journalists. Cholera, the *Times* wrote, "is the best of all sanitary reformers, it overlooks no mistake and pardons no oversight." Similarly Dr. Sutherland declared that cholera was not "a respecter of classes."[36] This representation of infectious disease as something that moved from "those haunts of beggary where it is rife, into the most still and secluded retreat of refinement,"[37] is, in fact, literally enacted in the plot of *Bleak House*.

Bleak House embodies some of the ways that the discourse of sanitary reform supplemented and intermeshed with the syncretic urban novel to shatter that fantasy of an exclusive cultural sphere that is encoded both in the Victorian quarterly's nightmare of cultural contamination and Sir Leicester's determination to protect the "aura" of his wife's portrait. Thus, at one level, *Bleak House* performs precisely the function that the Victorian quarterlies would associate with spreading infection or contamination: it draws on the expressive resources of the "lower" forms such as the city sketches to produce what from the perspective of highbrow literary criticism would be a sensational, urban plot. On the other hand, like Simon's *Report* of 1848, *Bleak House* was written in the aftermath of the cholera epidemic, and its treatment of infectious disease was, as Lauren Goodlad has shown, a self-conscious response to the "the manifest failures of the Public Health Act."[38] The intersection of these two strands, so critical to the making of the novel, is marked in one of the best-known passages in the novel:

> There is not a drop of Tom's corrupted blood, but propagates infection or contagion somewhere. It shall pollute, this very night, the choice stream . . . of a Norman house, and his grace shall not be able to say Nay to the alliance. There is not an atom of Tom's slime, not a cubic inch of pestilential gas in which he lives, not one obscenity or degradation about

him ... but shall work its retribution, through every order of society, up to the proudest of the proud, and to the highest of the high. (573)

This passage has been extensively commented upon, especially in analyses that document the close and sympathetic relation that *Bleak House* shared with the sanitary reform movement. It is significant, however, that the passage articulates powerfully the case *both* for sanitary reform and for the urban aesthetic. The idea at its heart is, of course, literally realized within the narrative when Esther is stricken ill by an infection that Jo contracts at Tom-all-Alone's. But the tension synchronically articulated in the quoted passage also unfolds diachronically in the main plot of *Bleak House,* and it drives Lady Dedlock to the paupers' graveyard. The location that Dickens chooses for Lady Dedlock's death connects her, as well as the urban plot that she sets into motion, in very specific ways to the discourse of sanitary reform:

> With houses looking on, on every side, save where a reeking little tunnel of a court gives access to an iron gate—with every reeking villainy of life in action close on death, and every poisonous element of death in action close on life—here they lower our dear brother down a foot or two: here, to sow him in corruption to be raised in corruption: an avenging ghost at many a sick bedside: a shameful testimony to future ages, how civilization and barbarianism walked this boastful island together. (148)

As several critics have pointed out, Dickens's description of the paupers' graveyard drew a great deal from several sanitary reports exposing the horrors of "city internments."[39] This intertwining of the discourse of sanitary reform and the figure of Lady Dedlock once again draws attention to the resonant image with which Dickens ends the story of her life. Marked by the social extremes of an internally fractured metropolis, embodying the expressive possibilities thrown up by the sort of discursive intermingling that the quarterly press found so repugnant, the figure of Lady Dedlock—lying presumably amidst "excrementious matter" and horribly close to the corpses that have been "stuffed or impracted"[40]—demonstrates finally the ways in which sensational popular fiction supplemented the work of sanitary reformers.

In the final analysis, then, the connotative shifts in the infection metaphor could be related to differences in the ways in which discourses responded to the problem of *contact* between the disparate social groups who are brought together in the giant metropolis. *Bleak House* is full of such contacts: it strives constantly to bring together the contradictions of the city in disconcerting juxtapositions, and its whole urban aesthetic is predicated on incorporating within the economy of the novel form the expressive resources of such "low" modes as the city sketch. In other words, Dickens sees interactions between the socially and culturally diverse individuals and groups who inhabit the city as both inevitable and generative, and if, in *Bleak House,* disease emerges as a negative manifestation of such interaction it is because, as Dickens insists repeatedly, the metropolitan administration neglects sanitary reform. In the literary reviews, on the other hand, the idea of infection is a metaphor to express an elitist revulsion at what one contemporary described as the snapping of "old sanitaire cordons . . . under pressure of the multitudes"[41]—that is, a means of discrediting precisely the sort of cultural interaction that produced a novel like *Bleak House. Bleak House* not only dramatizes, at the level of its content, the untenable nature of the elitist nostalgia for an exclusive cultural sphere but its modes of articulation also demonstrate the multiple expressive possibilities that such popular forms as radical journalism and the city sketches opened up for the novel form as a whole.

CHAPTER 5

Radical Culture, the City, and the Problem of Selfhood

Great Expectations and *Pendennis*

THIS BOOK has focused throughout on the expressive resources that germinated in radical culture and in popular visual representations of the city and on the effect that these expressive resources had on some of the fundamental features of the Dickensian novel: its organization of time and space, its modes of characterization and plot construction, and its representation of the discourses of power, from parliamentary speeches and the unfolding of Chancery procedure to the conversation that circulates in what Mrs. Merdle calls "Society." *Great Expectations* works with resources from both the radical and the urban aesthetic to engage with a process that lay at the very center of the realistic novel: the gradual and extended unfolding of the protagonist's inner life. Thus, *Great Expectations* deploys radical expressive strategies not, as in *Bleak House* or *Little Dorrit,* to demystify the language of power but to articulate its hero's rise to the status of a gentleman in ways that will complicate his sense of himself. Similarly, Dickens works with the dispersive as well as the juxtapositional impulses within the urban aesthetic to, on the one hand, inscribe within Pip's consciousness the experience of "placelessness" that Michel de Certeau associates with the life of the city,[1] and, on the other, to implicate him in a relationship that will block the possibility of his attaining anything like an integrated social identity.

The radical orientation that underlies the articulation of Pip's inner life becomes evident in the details with which Thackeray works to produce his gentlemanly subjects. One example could be the kind of play that the genealogical details of great families are allowed in a novel like *Pendennis*. As in *Vanity Fair,* aristocratic genealogies circulate all the time in the social world of *Pendennis*. The Major's advice to Pen just before the latter is about to visit one of London's great families is typical:

> "Having obtained the *entree* into Lady Agnes Foker's house," he said to Pen with an affectionate solemnity which befitted the importance of the occasion, "it behoves you, my dear boy, to keep it. You must mind and *never* neglect to call in Grosvenor Street when you come to London. I recommend that you read up carefully, in Debrett, the alliances and genealogy of the Earls of Rosherville and, if you can, to make some trifling allusions to the family, something which you, who have a poetic fancy, can do pretty well." (vol. 1, 164)

The Major's obsession with the conventions and the minutiae of genteel society is the subject of a great deal of irony. Unlike *Little Dorrit,* however, in which satirized references to bloodlines merely denote a deferential attitude to lords and ladies, the Major's advice should be understood as part of a more complex engagement with aristocratic life that unfolds in *Pendennis*. Pen may laugh at his uncle, but he also puts his advice to productive use. Indeed, his uncle's advice, together with what Pen learns at such institutions as Oxbridge and at the London club, where he is made a member, form a repertoire of references, words, gestures, and attitudes that Pen will deploy all the time as he goes about finding his feet as a gentleman. Of course, Pen is, on two occasions, in the danger of destabilizing his gentlemanly status by falling in love with socially undesirable women. But these dangers are created only so that they may be overcome, since, as we'll see, the *mésalliance* is never a source of serious expressive possibilities in Thackeray's work. Rather, the incessant interaction between Pen's developing consciousness about gentlemanly social practices and the details of the social spaces across which he moves both circumscribes the action of *Pendennis* and generates its most characteristic effects: its realistic representation of the nuances of social behavior in elite interiors, as well as the gradual unfolding of Pen's own inner life.

Mrs. Pocket in *Great Expectations* shares the Major's interest in aristocratic genealogies, but in Dickens's novel this interest is merely symptomatic of Mrs. Pocket's own "ornamental . . . but perfectly useless" life (189). This bringing together of class consciousness and a genteel but irresponsible and parasitic life is very much a legacy of radical culture. The effects of this legacy are evident, moreover, not just in the way that Mrs. Pocket is characterized but also in the kind of impact that her knowledge of genealogies is allowed to have in *Great Expectations*. In contrast to what occurs in *Pendennis,* Mrs. Pocket's knowledge of aristocratic lineages is allowed only the most limited social play. There is only one person in the novel with whom Mrs. Pocket can sustain a positive conversation about baronetcies, and this is the stupid Bentley Drummle, who "in his limited way . . . recognized Mrs. Pocket as a woman and sister" (192). This reduction of a form of social knowledge that is one of the drivers of Pendennis's career to a conversation confined to two very stupid people points to a larger difference of method between *Pendennis* and *Great Expectations*. One way to throw this shift into clearer relief is by focusing on a more central feature of *Great Expectations:* Dickens's delineation of Pip's rise to the status of a gentleman.

A striking feature of Pip's upwardly mobile career is that it moves across a peculiarly denuded social terrain. Pip has neither family nor clubroom nor university to sustain the process of his socialization. The "genealogical lack," which Catherine Gallagher sees as integral to Pip's condition,[2] is inscribed in his very name. A legally binding precondition to his elevation to the status of a gentleman is his benefactor's instruction that he continue to adhere to the diminutive name Pip and, by implication, to a social identity that proclaims his lack of familial affiliation. Again, the whole social apparatus—made up of Oxbridge, the clubs, and the drawing rooms of London—that produces Pen's gentlemanliness shrinks in *Great Expectations* to the pedagogical activity of a single tutor who is instructed that Pip need only be trained to "'hold my own' with the average of young men in prosperous circumstances" (197). Thus, *Great Expectations* fails to generate precisely those spaces that had sustained Pen's gentlemanliness. It lacks anything like the elaborately constructed social arena—that network of collateral yet subtly differentiated interiors—in relation to whose details Pen's gentlemanly personality gradually develops. Instead, the novelistic maneuver by which Pip is abruptly transformed from a "poor labouring boy" to a "London gentleman" aims at representing "gentlemanliness" as a social abstraction: a consolidated social status that will distinguish Pip from social inferiors.

The shift in the way gentlemanliness is treated from Thackeray to Dickens has implications that are evident from Pip's first encounter with the world of gentlefolk. Instead of unfolding as a gradual and finely calibrated relationship between the aspiring subject and the details that circulate in elite interiors, gentlemanliness in *Great Expectations* reveals itself (in the starkest possible terms) to be embedded in the idea of class difference:

"He calls the knaves, Jacks, this boy!" said Estella with disdain, before our first game was out. "And what coarse hands he has. And what thick boots!"

I had never thought of being ashamed of my hands before; but I began to consider them a very indifferent pair. Her contempt was so strong, that it became infectious, and I caught it. (60)

What Pip suffers here is that experience of social exclusion to which the language of radicalism had been such a powerful political response. However, the radical response to social difference in *Great Expectations* does not take the form of a rhetoric of general opposition to the mystifying public discourses of the elite. Rather, its effects are to be found in Pip's sense of self-division as it unfolds through the rather unusual self-improvement plot of which he is the protagonist.

The self-improvement plot, as it consolidated through the third quarter of the nineteenth century, was above all celebratory in its orientation.[3] It found in the booming economy of the 1850s and '60s the justification to project self-improvement as both desirable and easily attainable. Following this paradigm—articulated in its simplest form in the pamphlets of Samuel Smiles but also in Lord Palmerston's vision of perpetual social and economic advancement by the "steady and energetic exertion" of one's "moral and intellectual faculties"[4] and in Bagehot's idea about removable inequalities—novels like *John Halifax Gentleman* (1856) and even Dickens's own *David Copperfield* (1850) projected upward social mobility as a smooth and easily negotiable process.[5] One way in which they achieved the internal integrity of the improvement plot was by draining the improving hero's past of any potential that it might possess of intruding into and destabilizing his improved status. Dinah Mulock's hero ends his career as country gentleman, and clearly the mixture of apprehension and moral righteousness with which he now views the rural poor is uncomplicated by any sense of his own past poverty.[6] Again Dickens bases the more complex story of David's maturation on a set of self-conscious repressions. For example, the dark, child-laborer phase of David's past, which might have complicated the stable middle-class identity that he attains, is never allowed to resurface once David is adopted by his aunt Betsy Trotwood. The hero of *Great Expectations,* on the other hand, is given no such immunity. When the gentlemanly Pip runs into the equivalent of Mealy Potatoes, he adopts a "serene and unconscious" attitude to attempt exactly the kind of dissociation that Dickens himself had ensured for David. But the result is disaster: "Suddenly the knees of Trabb's boy smote together, his hair uprose, his cap fell off, he trembled violently in every limb, staggered out into the road, and crying to the populace 'Hold me! I'm so frightened!' feigned to be in such a paroxysm of terror and contrition, occasioned by the dignity of my appearance" (245).

This extraordinary scene stages in the gap opened by Dickens's reorganization of the conventional improvement plot, and especially of the relationship posited by this plot between the improving hero and his past, yet another novelistic improvisation with the language of radicalism. More specifically, Trabb's boy, drawing also on the expressive repertoire of the pantomime clown, deploys his body to generate a parodic language that is comparable to the demystifying discursive maneuvers employed by the radical publicists. At one level, indeed, Trabb's boy does to Pip's posturing exactly what Cobbett had done to Malthus's learned prose: he seizes on the connotative, metatextual elements in Pip's behavior—the serene and unconscious air he affects, rips them out of the context within which these operate as signifiers of dignity, and subjects them to a process of hilarious demystification.

Great Expectations draws on a second figure from the humble world of Pip's past both to destabilize Pip's self-improving career and to sustain the radical demystification of the genteel language. With his gentle, pacifist, and somewhat limited personality, Joe may be very far from conforming to our standard idea of the radical publicist. But it is the very simplicity of Joe's personality—his inability to comprehend or respond to elite protocols of social interaction—that becomes the means by which Dickens is able to destabilize these protocols. When Pip first introduces Joe to Miss Havisham, he has an early experience of the disconcerting effect of Joe's very presence on social interactions based on hierarchies:

> "Oh!" said she [Miss Havisham] to Joe, "You are the husband of the sister of this boy?"
>
> I could hardly imagine poor old Joe looking so unlike himself or so like some extraordinary bird; standing as he did, speechless, with his tuft of feathers ruffled, his mouth open as if he wanted a worm. "You are the husband," repeated Miss Havisham, "of the sister of this boy?"
>
> It was very aggravating; but throughout the interview Joe persisted in answering Me instead of Miss Havisham. (100)

Joe's inability to answer Miss Havisham directly is not merely an awestruck response. Rather, it should be understood as a mode of defamiliarizing, as something that wrenches the gentlemanly language out of the ebb and flow of everyday life to self-consciously throw into relief that taken-for-granted instinct toward domination that is encoded in Miss Havisham's very tone. When Joe meets Pip several years after he was introduced to Miss Havisham, his passive yet uncompromising resistance to the hierarchizing conventions of gentlemanly interaction comically disrupts the set of assumptions, gestures, and modes of address around which Pip himself bases his own social personality:

> A ghost-seeing effect in Joe's own countenance informed me that Herbert had entered the room. So, I presented Joe to Herbert, who held out his hand; but Joe backed from it, and held on by the bird's nest.
> "Your servant, Sir," said Joe, "which I hope as you and Pip,"—here his eye fell on the Avenger, who was putting some toast on table, and so plainly denoted an intention to make that young gentleman one of the family, that I frowned it down and confused him more—"I meantersay, you two gentlemen—which I hope get your elths in this close spot? For the present may be a wery good inn, according to London conditions," said Joe confidentially, ". . . but I wouldn't keep a pig in it myself—not in case that I wished him to fatten wholesome and to eat with a meller flavour to him." (220–21)

Working not, of course, as a real-life political activist but from within the make-belief world of the novel and in a manner oriented toward sustaining the comic, sentimental, human appeal of *Great Expectations,* Joe not only exposes and renders nonsensical the arbitrary divisions imposed by the elite in the social domain but also, without intending to, transforms these into *self-divisions* that will play themselves out as Pip's inner life.

Joe precipitates an inevitable inner division within Pip because the latter's exclusionary practices as a gentleman come into direct conflict with his memory of Joe's benign egalitarianism that he had experienced as a child. Joe had been special for Pip because, unlike every other adult who had inhabited the world of his childhood, Joe's relationship with Pip had been based not on power but on solidarity. Thus, Joe and Pip have always been, in Joe's words, "ever the best of friends" and, in Pip's, "equals" (48). After the reversal in his fortunes, on the other hand, Pip needs to internalize the exclusionary practices that will function as essential markers of his new status; to bring to bear on his relationship with Joe the implications of Estella's cold injunction: "what was fit company for you once, would be quite unfit now" (237). Deeply aware of Pip's anxiety about maintaining social distinctions, Joe can respond only by inserting the language of class into the domain of personal relationships:

> "Us two being alone, Sir,"—began Joe.
> "Joe," I interrupted, pettishly, "how can you call me Sir?"
> Joe looked at me at for a single instant with something faintly like reproach. Utterly preposterous as his cravat was, I was conscious of a sort of dignity in the look. (222)

The informal egalitarianism, solidarity, and unconditional affection that has always underlain Joe's relationship with Pip makes Joe's mode of address unthinkable. But Joe's jarring "Sir" also exposes as unacceptable the limits of the personality within which Pip has chosen to circumscribe his sense of himself. More specifically, Joe's faint "reproach" will remain for Pip a troubling reminder that any system of social relations that reduces an individual to a subservient position on the basis of his accent, manners, or a "preposterous . . . cravat" cannot accommodate experiences that Pip knows to be part of himself.[7]

In his representation of Pip's experience of upward mobility, Dickens draws on the expressive resources of not only the language of radicalism but also the urban aesthetic he had absorbed from a range of visual forms. More specifically, the urban energies that had driven the Lady Dedlock plot in *Bleak House*—the incessant circulation of people, objects, discourses; the uprootings; the unexpected intersections that this generates—continue to unfold powerfully in *Great Expectations*. They generate crucial relationships on the basis not of familial or kinship ties, but of random encounters, as well as subjects marked by the experience of rootlessness, mobility, and above all the sense of a contradictory social universe.

In *Great Expectations*, as in *Bleak House*, the urban aesthetic works, at one level, to uproot people and to break down the walls that separate their homes from the restless ebb and flow of the city. The London of *Great Expectations* may be, as Catherine Gallagher has noted, a surprisingly sparse entity compared to the densely detailed metropolis of *Bleak House*,[8] but this process of whittling down does not, in any way, weaken the dispersive dynamic of the urban aesthetic as it affects individual citizens. Jaggers is a well-entrenched London character, but nothing in London—not even his home—offers Jaggers a still point where he might "unbend his brows a little." Rather, like Snagsby's law stationery shop that extends his home into Cursitor Street, Jaggers's Gerrard Street residence is part of a continuous, restless, always mutating field that demands he remain always "guarded and suspicious" (292). Wemmick's sense of belonging to London is predicated on his knowing, as he tells Pip, "the moves of it" (172), and he is propelled by the legal business that he conducts on Jaggers's behalf to incessant movement between the dramatically disparate social locations that make up the city. If, unlike Jaggers, Wemmick does manage successfully to carve out a space that will resist the dispersive impulses of the metropolis, it is precisely because this domestic idyll is self-consciously fortified and located outside the city.

The effects of the dispersive impulse within the urban aesthetic are more far-reaching in Magwitch, and they are articulated especially through his changing relationship with London. Paradoxically, Magwitch himself thinks of his return from Australia to London as the culmination of a sustained effort toward what he sees as his social integration. Just as Wemmick designs his Walworth home as an utopian space that will compensate for the scattering, dispersive effects of the city, Magwitch hopes to find in Pip—"a brought up London gentleman" (321) whom he has produced and who is "more to me than any son" (320)—the means of integrating himself with those very social structures whose exclusionary pressures Magwitch has experienced not only in England but in far-flung Australia as well. Magwitch is irresistibly drawn to London, despite being legally debarred from entering the city, because he has transformed it successfully into the ground on which he might build a stable social and even familial identity.

Yet Magwitch is unable to publicly enjoy his status as the "father" of a "brought up London gentleman" because he is a fugitive, liable to suffer the death penalty if arrested. In this way Magwitch, who thinks of his return to London as a homecoming, is persistently denied a home: he is moved incessantly from Pip's flat near Fleet Street to an obscure riverside location called Mill Pond Bank and then to the pub from where he plans to make his escape. Moreover, the "experience of lacking a place," which Michel de Certeau describes as characteristic of the urban experience generally,[9] is played out not only in Magwitch's own incessant movement from one place to another but also in the ambulatory maneuvers by which Herbert and Pip hope to confuse Magwitch's whereabouts for anyone who might be interested. The two friends demonstrate how the activity of walking might embody the experience of "placelessness": they take routes that lead nowhere or establish themselves as familiar presences in parts of the city with which they have no connection at all. As they draw on the innumerable and random ambulatory possibilities offered by the city to obscure Magwitch's whereabouts, Herbert and Pip articulate the urban experience as a "relation between the place from which [the city walker] proceeds (an origin) and the nowhere it produces."[10]

We could thus say that Magwitch's story, after he arrives in London, sustains in an extreme form the dispersive impulse of the urban aesthetic. This impulse moves him from one random location to another and denies him any point to which he might arrive. Finally, the experience of being "nowhere" in which Magwitch becomes implicated impinges on his identity. Wemmick and Jaggers will talk about him only on the condition that he remain anonymous or, rather, that he be referred to by a set of undifferentiated hypothetical names: "Tom, Jack or Richard—whichever it may be" (372). Of course, it is Magwitch's status as a fugitive that makes Jaggers and Wemmick extracautious. But Wemmick's mode of referring to the ex-convict also locates the urban aesthetic's dispersive impulse within the domain of the subjective. The effects of this displacement are brought into focus more centrally in the delineation of Pip's story after he enters London as a gentleman.

One way to approach the problem of the new urban subjectivity is by comparing the kind of spaces that underpin it in *Great Expectations* and in *Pendennis*. Thus, the London of *Great Expectations* lacks anything like the network of socially contiguous interiors that, in *Pendennis*, connect the country and the city, and whose details provide the parameters for the development of the protagonist's character. Instead, the London interiors that Pip inhabits are sparse, precarious, relatively isolated spaces that are always liable to be subsumed within the undifferentiated immensity of London. Pip's Barnard's Inn flat, for instance, has about it "a gypsy character" (179). Nothing ever settles in it: like the meals that are often brought in from a neighboring coffee house, everything merely moves through. Pip's flat is also isolated—connected not to the drawing rooms, colleges, and clubs across which Pen moves but to something vaster and much less differentiated. What Pip and Herbert have about them as they settle down to enjoy their first (typically makeshift meal) is not the details of a stable social setting but "all London" (179).

The city that presses against Pip's flat, however, differs in many ways from the densely detailed metropolis of *Bleak House*. The London of *Bleak House* had been intricately mapped, enabling Dickens to achieve certain powerful effects by moving his figures across a wide range of dramatically disparate locations. In *Great Expectations*, on the other hand, the internal markers of the metropolis are often erased and the city unfolds as a vast seamless entity that threatens to inundate interiors and obliterate whatever power these have to sustain a sense of belonging in those who inhabit them.

On the day Magwitch returns, for example, Dickens deploys weather conditions and more significantly the darkness of the night to engulf Pip's Temple home in what he had described elsewhere as the "shadow of the immensity of London."[11]

On that night, Pip's flat seems dysfunctional as an interior that might, in conjunction with other interiors, provide the spatial parameters for the unfolding of inner life. Rather, it is rattled by the violent storm, engulfed in darkness, and drawn into the urban nightscape outside by the persistent movement of the narrative across the passages leading out of it. Indeed, Pip feels like he is inside a "storm beaten lighthouse" (313), utterly isolated, of course, but also stranded in a dark, unmarked terrain that offers no point on which he might anchor a memory or a hope.

The "rudimentariness of the social" in *Great Expectations*,[12] then, becomes the condition for the production of a new novelistic "chronotope":[13] the urban nightscape as a site where the dissociation between consciousness and its social moorings can be most effectively articulated. In "Night Walks," an 1860 essay whose very title suggests its enormous relevance for the later chapters of *Great Expectations*, Dickens picks on "the interminable tangle" of empty night streets as the ground on which he can articulate a form of urban subjectivity that he describes as "Houselessness."[14] As with Dickens's persona in "Night Walks," Pip's experience of "houselessness" unfurls across the London nightscape, but *Great Expectations* also draws on the greater range of expressive resources available to the novel form to saturate this condition with other forms of inner experience. The sequence in *Great Expectations* that begins with Estella finally rejecting Pip and ends with Pip spending the night in the Hummums shows exactly how this happens.

Estella's rejection has important implications for Pip. Estella, Pip says, has been inseparable from the way in which he has been constituted, from the sights that surrounded him when young—"the river . . . the sails of the ships . . . the marshes . . . the clouds"—and from "every graceful fancy that my mind has ever become acquainted with" (364). The most devastating consequence of Estella's absolute and irreversible withdrawal from Pip's life, thus, is the impact that it has on those memories and aspirations that sustained his sense of selfhood.

It is precisely this process of inner disintegration that is, in *Great Expectations*, articulated in relation to the urban nightscape. More specifically, Pip's collapsing sense of selfhood is imaged in the long, purposeless walk to London that he undertakes after Estella's rejection. Pip first hides himself "among some lanes and bypaths" of his native village and then, after crossing London Bridge "past midnight" (365), branches off with the vague intention of going to a home to which he is denied access. Pip's aimless walk that is not even allowed a destination is itself symptomatic of an urban experience that Michel de Certeau has described as "the indefinite process of being absent and in search of a proper."[15] Moreover, the interiors that Pip does inhabit in the third part of the book seem like extensions of the streets: they are temporary shelters, mere passages. Indeed, they help to link the disintegration of Pip's sense of selfhood to the dispersive effects of the city and, in this way, to locate the experience of "Houselessness" deep within Pip's subjectivity. For example, the physical and mental exhaustion that Pip experiences after he is denied access to his home by Wemmick's mysterious note finds no relief in the "inhospitable" vaultlike room where he is forced to spend the night. Here, indeed, Wemmick's injunction—"Don't go home"—becomes inseparable from Pip's sense of selfhood. It not only plaits itself into his consciousness "as a bodily pain would have done" but also penetrates into the depths of his mind—invades his sleep and dreams:

> Even when I thought of Estella, and how we parted that day for ever, and when I recalled all the circumstances of our parting, and all her looks and tones, and the action of her fingers while she knitted—even then I was pursuing, here and there and everywhere the caution "Don't go home." When at last I dozed, in sheer exhaustion of mind and body, it became a vast shadowy verb which I had to conjugate. Imperative mood, present tense: Do not thou go home . . . potentially: I may not, cannot go home, and I might not, could not, would not and should not go home; until I felt I was going distracted, and rolled over on the pillow. (367)

Wemmick's note and its effect on Pip, then, exemplify the urban aesthetic's propensity to powerfully articulate the dispersive impulses inseparable from the urban experience. The sense of homelessness that is inscribed into the depths of Pip's consciousness as he lies awake at the Hummums is also the defining condition of his existence in the city. Pip's "lonely home—if it deserved the name" merely provides temporary shelter to heterogeneous people before dispersing them across the vast, undifferentiated city outside. It is constituted as a "tenancy" that Pip plans to further "underlet" (461)—a part of that conglomerate made up of disconnected people of whom Michel de Certeau has written:

> The moving about that the city multiplies and concentrates makes the city itself an immense social experience of lacking a place—an experience that

is, to be sure, broken up into countless tiny deportations (displacements and walks), compensated for by relationships and intersections of these exoduses that intertwine and create an urban fabric, and placed under the sign of what ought to be, ultimately the place, but is only a name, the City. The identity furnished by this place is all the more symbolic (named) because, in spite of the inequality of its citizens' positions and profits, there is only a pullulation of passers-by, a network of residences temporarily appropriated by pedestrian traffic, a shuffling among pretences of the proper, a universe of rented spaces haunted by a nowhere or by dreamed-of places.[16]

This passage from *The Practice of Everyday Life* is important because it registers the dispersive impulses of the city: the "countless tiny deportations" that it seems to affect every day but also the "intersections of these exoduses that intertwine and create an urban fabric." *Bleak House,* as the previous chapter showed, had drawn on the city's numerous impersonal transactions to generate a plot based on unexpected intersections between the most unconnected lives. In *Pendennis,* too, Thackeray speaks of the "curious volume" that may have resulted if some enterprising author decided to track the divergent activities of an unconnected group of people who happen to occupy apartments in the same inner city building: "If we could but get the history of a single day as it passed in any of those four storied houses in the dingy court where our friends Pen and Warrington dwelt, some Temple Asmodeus might furnish us with a queer volume" (vol. 1, 295). Yet, if Thackeray invokes "one of those four storied houses in the dingy courts" of London as a chronotope that might generate intersections between unrelated people who have moved to the city, it is in order to throw into relief the very different principles of organization that underlay his own novel. To be sure, Thackeray does expose his hero to the heterogeneous forms of social life that flourishes in the metropolis. Like the protagonists of *Life in London,* Pen becomes interested in "seeing life" and going into "a hundred queer London haunts" (vol. 1, 303). However, with one important exception (which I will discuss) Pen's encounters with "coal heavers in their taprooms; boxers in their inn parlours; honest citizens disporting in the suburbs or on the river" (vol. 1, 303) are not allowed to generate any significant lines of action within the novel. These lines of action are, on the contrary, aligned far more closely to the Major's ideas about what constitutes proper relationships among gentlefolk. The Major may be the object of relentless authorial irony, but his opposition to *mésalliance*s also embodies the social orientation of a novel which declares, early on, its skepticism about fiction that makes unrealistic plot connections between "a ruffian ... in St. Giles's" and "a young lady from Belgravia."

Jaggers's function in *Great Expectations* is similar to that of the Major in *Pendennis*. Indeed, Jaggers helps to generate the social boundaries within which the action of *Great Expectations* will unfold in an even more direct way than the relatively ineffectual Major. But comparing the effects of Jaggers's intervention with those of the Major uncovers the distinctive way in which the urban aesthetic organizes social space in *Great Expectations*. In *Pendennis* the Major embodies a familial link that connects the genteel yet provincial home where Pen grows up and the varied but essentially gentlemanly world that he will inhabit in London. In this sense, Major Pendennis's presence helps to emphasize the contiguity of the social domains across which Pen moves and to render this movement itself as smooth and easily negotiable, rather than as something that involves any major dislocation. Jaggers, on the other hand, conducts a series of maneuvers that uproots characters from their original habitations and relocates them in radically different social milieus. He transplants the daughter of social outcasts to the weird but elite world that Miss Havisham inhabits, and he facilitates a strange legal transaction by which a poor provincial boy is transformed into a gentleman on the basis of a convict's money. Indeed, if "the genealogical lack" from which so many of the characters of *Great Expectations* suffer aborts the development of action based on the bonds of the family or of social contiguity, Jaggers works with the resources of urban modernity (the newspaper, the legal deed that will legitimize a relationship with no basis in tradition or family) to generate a new social configuration: the fabricated family. It is a newspaper insertion that gives Miss Havisham access to Jaggers and to the possibility that she might become Estella's "Mother by adoption" (304). And the legal document that Magwitch draws up with Jaggers's help not only appoints the latter as Pip's "guardian" but also initiates a strange, new relationship which will culminate in Magwitch's conviction that he is "more than father" to Pip.

Like *Bleak House,* then, *Great Expectations* is propelled by the divergent impulses that the urban aesthetic typically generates: on the one hand, by the impulse that disperses, isolates, and renders homeless and, on the other, by the one that is oriented toward precipitating unexpected intersections. Moreover, just as the urban aesthetic's dispersive impulse is connected with the physical features of the city—with the tangle of empty roads in the night or shelters that are no more than enclosed passages—its propensity to affect unexpected conjunctions, too, reflects the way in which London's buildings are often configured. For example, very soon after he arrives in London, Pip finds himself looking at two buildings that exist in close physical proximity but that bear completely different cultural and social connotations:

> So I came into Smithfield; and the shameful place, being all asmear with filth and fat and blood and foam, seemed to stick to me. So, I rubbed it off with all possible speed by turning into a street where I saw the great black dome of Saint Paul's bulging at me from behind a grim stone building which a bystander said was Newgate Prison (165).

This configuration could be read as another example of the technique that, in *Bleak House,* had precipitated that tense juxtaposition between St. Paul's Cathedral and Jo (and by implication that unreclaimed social domain that he represents). This reading, however, would only be partially accurate. Unlike *Bleak House,* where juxtaposed locations generate lines of action that will ultimately intersect, *Great Expectations* does not work toward literally connecting the radically disparate spaces that make up London. Rather, the absence in *Great Expectations* of any equivalent of the discursive path that, in *Bleak House,* connects Lady Dedlock's town house to the paupers' graveyard, points to some important transformations in both Dickens's representation of the city and the working of the urban aesthetic from the earlier to the later novel. In *Bleak House* London is intricately mapped and the novel achieves its most characteristic effects by plotting intersections between lines of action that originate from its myriad, radically disparate locations. The London of *Great Expectations,* on the other hand, is relatively sparse in terms of topographical details. Nevertheless, these details generate a method that continues to be closely linked to the city but that also suggests the greater degree of abstraction at which the urban aesthetic works in the later novel.

One way to illustrate this transformation is by focusing on that key moment when Pip suddenly feels that Molly, Jaggers's nervous but somehow menacing housekeeper, is Estella's mother. Pip notices "a certain action of her fingers" and recognizes in a flash that he has seen something uncannily similar:

> I looked at those hands, I looked at those eyes, I looked at that flowing hair; and I compared them with other hands, other eyes, and other hair that I knew of and with what those might be after twenty years of a brutal husband and a stormy life. I looked again at those hands and eyes of the housekeeper, and thought of the inexplicable feeling that had come over me when I last walked—not alone—in the ruined garden, and through the

deserted brewery. I thought how the same feeling had come back when I saw a face looking at me, and a hand waving at me, from a stage-coach window; and how it had come back again, and had flashed about me like Lightning, when I had passed in a carriage—not alone—through a sudden glare of light in a dark street. (390)

It is the third moment in the series that Pip re-experiences so vividly that is most important for my argument. A certain image of Estella's fingers is stamped forever on Pip's brain by a process that is very much part of the urban dynamic: a "sudden glare of light" (269) illuminates Estella's hands as she and Pip travel in a coach through a dark London street close to Newgate. Yet this random but, at the same time, significant intersection, so symptomatic of the centripetal trajectory within the urban aesthetic, is abstracted from the city itself. Its implications are articulated in relation not to the disparate urban locations across which the novel could be made to move but to a set of unimaginable relationships that the novel will plot. Put another way, the urban aesthetic in *Great Expectations* works not so much with the details of a densely crowded city as with a more properly literary trope: the *mésalliance,* in Mikhail Bakhtin's sense, as indicative of not just a sexual liaison between two socially disparate people but of any dramatically unexpected and destabilizing conjunction.[17]

I need, at this point, to turn again to *Pendennis* because this novel engages much more self-consciously than *Great Expectations* with the status of the *mésalliance* as a trope of urban literature even as it itself refuses to generate sensational effects by having "a ruffian . . . in St. Giles" visited "constantly by a lady in from Belgravia." Thus, Thackeray's delineation of the Pen–Fanny love affair, the most protracted among the several potential *mésalliances* that the novel depicts, draws self-consciously on the discursive strategies of the city sketches. Pen's chance encounter with Fanny is a direct result of a maneuver by which Pen is moved, after the termination of the London season, from the clubs, drawing rooms, and offices that he normally inhabits to the streets that he begins to scour for their "infinite varieties" (vol. 2, 81). Significantly, however, what Thackeray takes from the city sketches are strategies that work toward containing tensions generated by the city's propensity to bring its socially disparate inhabitants into close contact. Indeed, Thackeray deploys these strategies to abort discursive possibilities that actually interested him—for example, the possibility of exploring realistically those sexual urges that are normally repressed in the more respectable forms of novel writing but that, in fact, facilitate a more complex representation of inner life.[18] Thus, while Thackeray insists in his preface that the attraction Pen experiences toward Fanny is a measure of the psychological complexity with which he has been represented, he does not allow Pen's sexuality enough play to precipitate a *mésalliance* and, in the process, to disrupt the basic expressive orientation of Thackeray's novel: its nuanced representation of life as it unfolds in upper- and middle-class interiors. When Pen's passion for Fanny can no longer be contained within the "satiric humour . . . not deprived of sympathy" (vol. 2, 81) with which Pen usually negotiates the street life of London, Thackeray quite literally purges it: "He laughed at himself as he lay on his pillow, thinking of this second cure which had been effected upon him. He did not care in the least about Fanny now: he wondered how he ever should have cared; and according to his custom made an autopsy of that dead passion, and anatomized his own dead sensation for his poor little nurse" (vol. 2, 145).

Thackeray's intervention not only aborts Pen's passion for Fanny the moment it threatens to become socially destabilizing but also marks an interesting displacement: the redeployment in *Pendennis* of Egan's discursive strategies to contain not the physical dangers that London may pose to those who wish to savor its pleasures but the excesses of Pen's inner life. More specifically, the camera obscura view of London that Pierce Egan had recommended to his readers, and that is embedded in Pen's own "anthropologist's" interest in London's street scenes, is now reactivated in the domain of inner life. As Pen transforms himself into a sophisticated kind of *flâneur*—a sort of anthropologist of the emotions—he can savor, without pain or involvement, the transformations of inner life in the same way as Pierce Egan and his protagonists had learned to savor urban variety.

The simultaneous emphasis on the urban origins of the *mésalliance* trope and the containment of its potential for social destabilization is achieved even more effectively in the way Thackeray represents Fanny's involvement with Pen. Thus, in a typically metatextual operation, Thackeray relates to Fanny's reading habits her propensity to slide into an unviable love affair and, by implication, to push *Pendennis* itself in the direction of those popular novels that its preface had ironically rejected:

> . . . and if we could peep into Fanny's bed (which she shared in a cupboard, along with those two little sisters to whom we have seen Mr. Costigan administering gingerbread and apples), we should find the poor little maid tossing upon her mattress, to the great disturbance of its other two occupants, and thinking over all the delights and events of that delightful, eventful night, and all the words, looks and actions of Arthur, its splendid hero. Many novels had Fanny read, in secret and at home, in three volumes and

in numbers. Periodical literature had not reached the height which it has attained subsequently, and the girls of Fanny's generation were not enabled to purchase sixteen pages of excitement for a penny, rich with histories of crime, murder, oppressed virtue, and the heartless seductions of the aristocracy; but she had had the benefit of the circulating library which, in conjunction with her school and a small brandy ball and millinery business, Miss Minifer kept,—and Arthur appeared to her at once as the type and realization of all the heroes of all those darling greasy volumes which the young girl had devoured. (vol. 2, 96)

Thackeray here subsumes the social resonances that the *mésalliance* is always capable of generating within Fanny's extremely simplistic response. In this way, he reduces the *mésalliance* to its most rudimentary form—to something that belongs to those "darling greasy volumes" which Fanny devours and that works with murders and seductions to generate incessant excitement. Thus, the *mésalliance* toward which Fanny herself moves could be said to express the superficiality of the popular novels and of those who read them. It is exactly by exposing this superficiality in Fanny herself—she is shown to find a new admirer very soon after her breakup with Pen—that Thackeray is able, on the one hand, to eject her without moral complications out of Pen's life and, on the other, to dissociate his novel from the kinds of effects that the central *mésalliance* of *Great Expectations*—between gentlemanliness and crime—is made to sustain.

Thackeray's propensity to probe the *mésalliance* but, at the same time, to abort its most powerful expressive effects and indeed to show these effects to be radically incompatible with the demands of "realism," is evident once again in a strand of *Pendennis* that seems, at first glance, to belong to the class of popular novels that he mocked in his preface. The revelation, late in the novel, that the blackmailing, bigamous, ex-convict Amory is, in fact, the biological father of the sophisticated and aristocratic Blanche is, moreover, particularly relevant for this chapter, because it looks forward uncannily to the relationship between Estella and Magwitch. However, while the disclosure of Magwitch's relationship with both the ladylike Estella and the gentlemanly Pip is central to the novel's meaning, Amory's appearance—and the consequent *mésalliance* in which he implicates Blanche—is part of a paradoxical maneuver. More specifically, Amory's appearance pushes Blanche beyond the pale of respectability and enables Thackeray to reconstitute as socially unthinkable her relationship with Pen, which he had, in any case, shown to be spiritually and emotionally impoverished. Thus, the *mésalliance,* far from precipitating some central effect in *Pendennis,* functions as a sort of discursive threat, the possibility of which will enable Thackeray to pull Pen out of a bad relationship and in this way to restore not only his hero's moral integrity but also the true artistic orientation of the novel he was writing. Warrington, whose point of view often echoes that of Thackeray himself, picks precisely on the *mésalliance* as his means of outlining the social threshold beyond which the action of *Pendennis* cannot be allowed to traverse: "No. Our boy can't meddle with such a wretched intrigue as that. Arthur Pendennis can't marry a convict's daughter; and sit in Parliament as Member for the hulks" (vol. 2, 333).

The *mésalliance* between the criminal and the gentleman that Warrington (and Thackeray) rejects so decisively lies, of course, at the heart of *Great Expectations*. Gentlemanliness and criminality become inextricably coupled the moment Pip supplies Magwitch with food and a file in the second chapter of the novel. Magwitch's gratitude, together with his own need for social compensation, will prompt him to invest his considerable later earnings toward making Pip a gentleman. At the same time, although Pip will not know the identity of his secret benefactor until relatively late in the novel, he will always see himself as complicit in the activities of an escaped convict. The mismatch (between the gentlemanly status that Pip will acquire and the criminality in which this status is always implicated) is, thus, encoded into the very structure of *Great Expectations* in its second chapter and will be made to resurface during several key moments in the novel. I will now focus on some of these moments and especially on the signifiers that produce them, and I will argue that these signifiers are designed (like the broadsheets in *Industry and Idleness* or the newspapers in *Bleak House*) to circulate freely and, in this way, to facilitate those unexpected conjunctions between widely disparate texts, objects, and people that are so characteristic of the urban aesthetic.

One example of how signifiers often function in *Great Expectations* is to be found in the tenth chapter of the novel. Here a stranger invites Pip and Joe for a drink at Three Jolly Bargemen. The stranger then gifts Pip a certain sum of money, but he also silently draws Pip's attention to the file that he uses to stir his drink. The stranger's file in conjunction with the money that he gifts to Pip, thus, work to bring into focus once again the novel's central *mésalliance*. What is more, the file draws attention to its own status as a signifier when it reappears in the nightmare that Pip experiences soon after his meeting with the stranger:

> I had a sadly broken sleep when I got to bed . . . I was haunted by the file too. A dread possessed me that when I least expected it, the file would

reappear. I coaxed myself to sleep by thinking of Miss Havisham's, next Wednesday; and in my sleep I saw the file coming at me out of a door, without seeing who held it, and I screamed myself awake. (79)

Dissociated from any specific location or even person, driven by an energy whose source is invisible, the file becomes a free-floating signifier capable of turning up anywhere. It is this irresistible mobility that the file acquires in Pip's dream that distinguishes it from the way signifiers function in the realistically constructed interiors of a novel like *Pendennis*. In the latter, to adapt the terms of Roland Barthes's classic exposition, the "effect of the real" is created by the surreptitious orchestration of connotations that ensures that the minute, apparently arbitrary bits of information that adhere to signifiers over and above what they denote are brought together in "operations of solidarity." Signifiers, in a realistically constructed scene, therefore, "stick."[19] In contrast, the file in Pip's nightmare refuses the responsibility of being part of a semiotic consensus, of entering into operations of solidarity with an accompanying set of signifiers to project an internally integrated, realistic scene. Rather, it draws its signifying potential from its *mobility:* its ability to disengage itself from the situation that it originally helped to articulate and to turn up anywhere regardless of the requirements of verisimilitude.

The file of Pip's nightmare may be thought of as a characteristic urban signifier because in its unimpeded mobility it is oriented toward registering not the continuities of domestic realism but the unexpected, often unthinkable intersection of images, people, and goods that circulate all the time in the city. This is why it finds in the big city a site where it can proliferate and—through a process of incessant mutation—continue to force on Pip's consciousness the radical disjunction between his acquired status as a London gentleman and his early association with crime. For example, the social category signified by the file in Pip's nightmare takes a more elaborate form in the two convicts, whose bodies are deeply marked by the signs of their status and whom London throws up in an outbound coach as Pip's traveling companions. Anxious to preserve the integrity of his status as gentleman, Pip seeks to displace the convicts to the domain of the social and even biological "other." With their "coarse, mangy, ungainly, outer surfaces," they have for him the appearance of "lower animals." Yet, like the phantom file that comes rushing at Pip, the urban aesthetic that underlies *Great Expectations* as a whole is oriented toward effecting the unthinkable fusion: "It is impossible to express with what acuteness I felt the convict's breathing, not only on the back of my head, but all along my spine. The sensation was like being touched in the marrow with some pungent and searching acid, and it set my very teeth on edge" (228).

Pip will repeatedly be exposed to experiences like these in London. Pip's early association with a convict will now find signifiers not in some single tangible objects such as a file or a leg iron, but in something as diffuse and pervasive as the atmosphere of London itself. If the London of *Bleak House* is enveloped in a fog that is both an attribute of the city's weather conditions and a metaphor for the Chancery's obfuscations, the metropolis in *Great Expectations* is permeated by grit that originates in Newgate but seems to stick everywhere: in the jail official' s mildewed clothes "bought cheap," as Pip believes, "of the executioner" (166); in patches that Jaggers's office gets from "the greasy shoulders" (199) of his clients; and, above all, on Pip's person no matter how far he wants to get away from any suggestion of criminality. As Pip waits for Estella at the coach station, he is deeply conscious of his own status as a gentleman and of Estella's "proud and refined" personality. But he also finds it impossible to escape from the "taint of the prison" (264).

The circulatory impulse that carries the prison dust to Pip's clothes, his breath, and his lungs suggests certain continuities in the unfolding of the urban aesthetic from *Bleak House* to *Great Expectations*. To be sure, *Great Expectations* does not allow the circulatory dynamic of the urban aesthetic the kind of space that is available to it in *Bleak House*. It reduces to a single, extended *mésalliance* the many relationships between socially disparate people and locations that are plotted in *Bleak House*, and the densely detailed metropolis mapped in the earlier novel shrinks, in *Great Expectations*, to a narrow field circumscribed more or less by Newgate, on the one hand, and, on the other, to those spaces of respectability inhabited by Pip, Jaggers, and Wemmick. But this narrowing of field suggests that Dickens was deploying the circulatory dynamic of the urban aesthetic to focus on a single theme: the incessant traffic of people, goods, and money that goes on all the time between respectable London and its criminal "other." The concluding part of this chapter will deal in more detail with this traffic between respectability and criminality that goes on independently of the mismatch inscribed across Pip's career, to explore what it says about the urban aesthetic and especially about its capacity to articulate extra-individualistic, objective social problems.

Great Expectations has, of course, provoked several readings that relate its preoccupation with criminals, prisons, and lawyers to the larger discourses on crime and its management that circulated in nineteenth-century England.[20] The most interesting among these readings is Jeremy Tambling's essay "Prison-bound: Dickens, Foucault and *Great Expectations*" which—according to the title—seems to draw a great deal from the work of Michel Foucault and especially from his *Discipline and Punish*. For Tambling the world of *Great Expectations* represents a full-blown "Panopticon society" where the "sense of being looked at is pervasive."[21] Moreover, drawing on a strand of thought that belongs more to the *History of Sexuality,* volume 1, than to *Discipline and Punish,* Tambling argues that surveillance in *Great Expectations* also deploys technologies of subjection that penetrate into the deepest layers of subjectivity and urge the individual to incessantly engage in the twin processes of introspection and confession. In *Great Expectations* the effects of this technology of subjection are manifest in the relentless guilt that dogs Pip and in the autobiographical, even confessional mode in which his story unfolds.

It would seem, then, that Tambling deploys Foucault's idea of surveillance to explain Pip's guilt and even the autobiographical/confessional mode in which *Great Expectations* is written. Yet Foucault's shifting interest from the institutionally driven operations of power to what he describes as "technologies of the self" has as its focus the problem of sexuality:[22] something that is not really the object of surveillance in *Great Expectations*. Moreover, in *Discipline and Punish* (as indeed in *Great Expectations*) surveillance does not only operate as a technology that makes visible and brings everything, even one's secret thoughts, under the scrutiny of an all-seeing eye. In fact, it is also exercised through procedures hidden in the details of the penal apparatus: procedures that are, as Michel de Certeau has shown, "without discursive legitimacy, techniques foreign to the Enlightenment."[23] Following de Certeau's reading of surveillance as it operates in *Discipline and Punish,* it now becomes necessary to focus on the microprocedures by which the law in *Great Expectations* isolates the criminal milieu, creates differentiations within it, and penetrates and continuously appropriates and deploys its resources. To do this would be to turn again to the circulatory dynamic within the urban aesthetic and to explain why the central *mésalliances* that it helps to plot also articulates a more objective social relationship: that between criminality and everything that derives its social identity in opposition against criminality.

Great Expectations is, of course, self-consciously concerned with how a legally sanctified social domain is constituted by a whole system of signs and representations dissociating it from the everyday processes of society and, more specifically, with how this domain is dependent on the arbitrating operations of a legal machinery always capable of isolating criminality.

The two convicts who travel with Pip during his journey to Kent compel and receive attention not because they have committed heinous offences, but because they are an "Exhibition," "their ironed legs," their "coarse, mangy, ungainly outer surfaces" (226, 227) marking them off socially, culturally, and even biologically from the respectable members of society.

One way to track both the effects and the function of such penal branding is by focusing on the figure of Magwitch. Magwitch's body is, of course, marked through and through with the signs of his criminal status. "The very grain of the man," as Pip puts it, proclaims a "Prisoner, Felon, Bondman, plain as plain could be" (338). Moreover, Magwitch is closely associated with Australia—the "thief colony" whose dystopian cultural connotations have been detailed in Robert Hughes's *The Fatal Shore*. Separated from England by a wall "14,000 miles thick," inhabited by her "excrementious mass," and "spinning forever at the outer rim of the world, in ever worsening moral darkness," Australia was, in the Victorian imagination, "a *chloaca*, invisible, its contents filthy and unnamable."[24] In this sense, quite irrespective of the crimes that he may have actually committed, Magwitch is constituted as somebody in whose being every fantasy about criminality can be contained. It is this status that Magwitch acquires as the absolute "other" of Victorian respectability—as someone capable of committing, as Pip says, "all the crimes in the Calendar" (338)—that points to one of the functions that a figure like him serves for a discourse dedicated to isolating criminality and, in this way, distinguishing it sharply from respectability. By focusing on a figure like Magwitch, holding him up as an "Exhibition," symbolically summing up in his pathologized figure all forms of illegalities, official society in *Great Expectations* can claim to have displaced criminality as a whole to the realm of the degraded "other." In fact, however, it leaves in the shade those illegalities that it wishes to tolerate. Thus, for example, Pip can, for a large part of the novel, claim for himself the status of a respectable gentleman, "genetically" different from the likes of Magwitch even as he tolerates and, indeed, participates in the shady activities of Jaggers and Wemmick.

The interesting thing, of course, is that Magwitch's public status as a criminal capable of committing every offence is discursively *constituted*: it is not, in fact, borne out by the details of his career. These details are supplied by Magwitch himself in his long account of his early life to Pip:

"I was took up, took up, took up, to that extent I reg' larly growed up took up."

> "This was the way it was when I was a ragged little creetur as much to be pitied as I ever see . . . I got the name of being hardened . . ."
>
> "Tramping, begging, thieving, working sometimes, when I could—though that warn't as often as you might think, till you put the question would you ha' been overready to give me work yourselves—a bit of a poacher, a bit of a labourer, a bit of a waggoner, a bit of a haymaker, a bit of a labourer, a bit of a most things that don't pay and lead to trouble, I got to be a man." (346–47)

What is important here is not the seriousness of Magwitch's offences—these, before he falls into the clutches of the gentlemanly Compeyson, do not, in fact, extend beyond the occasional theft—but that Magwitch is the inevitable target of punishment. Born in the lowest stratum of society, exposed constantly to prison terms, and driven consequently into the circuits of delinquency—"Tramping, begging, thieving, working sometimes," Magwitch illustrates how penal techniques in *Great Expectations* aim not at eliminating crime but at encouraging recidivism. Magwitch himself sums up his life in "a mouthful of English": "In jail and out of jail, in jail and out of jail, in jail and out of jail" (346).

Thus, Dickens's account of Magwitch's early life can be read as an indictment of a penal system that is unenlightened and unimaginative. But, as Michel Foucault has argued, the official encouragement of large-scale recidivism is crucial to its management of crime. More specifically, Foucault demonstrates how the legal machinery in France worked consciously to perpetuate "a closed milieu of delinquency" so that it could then pressurize it, place it under surveillance, penetrate it, and constantly use it for its own purposes.[25]

In *Great Expectations* the process by which criminality is legally identified and segregated itself involves the use and the exploitation of the criminal milieu. To be sure, the law is *publicly* constituted as a strictly objective system of arbitration: the accused is given certain rights, she/he is convicted only by trial in court, and arguments are evaluated in court according to whether or not they adhere, in Jaggers's phrase, "to the strict line of fact" (336). Yet in practice Jaggers's own spectacular successes in court depend not only on his ability to manipulate, repress, and confuse facts but even more crucially on his access to Newgate. Newgate is, in Wemmick's phrase, the "next thing" (259) to Jaggers's office and Jaggers himself, as Pip tells Estella, "has the reputation of being more in the secrets of that dismal place than any man in London" (269). It is not merely that Jaggers can make enormous and effective use of "Newgate intelligence" in court. More crucially, it is precisely by penetrating the criminal milieu, by exploiting the precarious situation of the individual delinquent, and alternatively bribing and threatening her/him, that Jaggers can use a whole range of illegalities to fight a case while keeping himself on the right of the law.

Jaggers's methods of fighting a case, his actual success in court, suggest that criminality is far from being a solid, easily identifiable mass of activities that exist outside respectable society. It is, in fact, something that is far more ambiguous—something that constantly circulates through the fine underground channels that connect Newgate to the High Court. In *Great Expectations* the most palpable symbol of this constant traffic between criminality and respectability is the wealth that is generated in the criminal milieu but recycled back into respectable society. Jaggers himself does not even attempt to conceal the criminal origins of his wealth. The starting point of Jaggers's career as a lawyer is his successful defense of a murderer, and the most noticeable objects in Jaggers's office are the villainous-looking casts, made to the likeness of two hardened offenders who have been, in Wemmick's words, "Famous clients of ours that got us a world of credit" (200). In fact, Jaggers's criminal clients fetch him not only credit but also money. Wemmick stops at the individual cells at Newgate not only to gather intelligence or locate appropriate witnesses but also to negotiate "fees." With Wemmick the acquisition of criminal property, especially the property of prisoners condemned to death, has become so routine that it is made to appear as part of his cheery practicality:

> While he was putting up the other cast and coming down from the chair, the thought crossed my mind that all his personal jewelry was derived from like sources. As he had shown no diffidence on the subject, I ventured on the liberty of asking him the question when he stood before me, dusting his hands.
>
> "Oh yes," he returned, "these are all gifts of that kind. One brings another, you see; that's the way of it. I always take 'em. They're curiosities. And they're property. They may not be worth much, but, after all, they're property and portable . . . my guiding star always is, 'Get hold of portable properly.'" (201)

What is important about Dickens's representation of Wemmick's transactions is not their extraordinariness but their ordinariness. The very fowl that Wemmick serves to Pip for dinner may have been acquired from a convict, but the signs of Wemmick's links with the criminal world coexist with, indeed are a constituent part of, the happy, almost idyllic ambience that envelops Wemmick's Walworth home:

> The interval between that time and supper, Wemmick devoted to showing me his collection of curiosities. They were mostly of a felonious character, comprising the pen with which a celebrated forgery had been committed, a distinguished razor or two . . . and several manuscript confessions . . . They were agreeably dispersed among small specimens of China and glass, various neat trifles made by the proprietor of the museum, and some tobacco-stoppers carved by the Aged. (209)

Wemmick's museum renders familiar and everyday what would be normally unmentionable in respectable discourse and, in this process, makes visible the countless ties that, in fact, bind respectable society to its criminalized "other." Indeed, Wemmick's remarkable museum may be seen as a microcosmic representation of not only the great world outside but also of the compositional method by which this world is articulated. Thus, just as murderous razors coexist with lovingly preserved tobacco-stoppers carved by Wemmick's father in Wemmick's museum, Dickens works with the juxtapositional energies of the urban aesthetic to create in *Great Expectations* not the autonomous, internally integrated world of the realistic novel but a textual field capable of registering the movement of money, goods, and people between the dramatically disparate zones that make up the city and, in this way, of cutting across those discursive maneuvers by which the nineteenth-century notion of gentlemanliness sought to preserve its internal integrity.

CHAPTER 6

Working with Fragments

Our Mutual Friend as a
Reflection on the Popular Aesthetic

IN MANY WAYS, *Our Mutual Friend* is the most metatexual of Dickens's novels: it looks back on and continues to develop, in extraordinarily productive ways, the differing tropes, expressive techniques, and ways of seeing that have been associated, through the course of this book, with the urban aesthetic. Thus, *Our Mutual Friend* draws imaginatively on modern capitalism's capacity to "uproot . . . and make mobile that which is grounded, clear . . . away and obliterate that which impedes circulation, and make . . . exchangeable what is singular,"[1] to achieve unprecedented effects with the circulating impulse that have been integral to the urban aesthetic as well. In *Our Mutual Friend* the list of things that can be uprooted and made mobile and exchangeable includes not only shares, commodities, information, or images but also dead bodies, body parts, and simulated fragments of inner life. Thus, *Our Mutual Friend* often separates people from their names or from their bodies and, in this way, takes to a new level a familiar feature of the urban aesthetic: its capacity—already evident in *Great Expectations*—to register the dispersive effects of the city on urban subjects. Finally, in his extraordinary delineation of Bradley Headstone's descent from respectability to the netherworld of violence and crime, Dickens reflects back on—but at the same time transforms—the two terminal tropes across which this book has unfolded the urban aesthetic: on the one hand, the fortified interiors that Hogarth had constituted as safe havens against the chaos and immorality of the streets and, on the other, the urban nightscape as the site most capable of sustaining the experience of urban alienation.

One example of the ways in which *Our Mutual Friend* draws upon but also extends a familiar expressive trajectory of the urban aesthetic is to be found in a late chapter of the novel. In this chapter Dickens brings together the effects of finance capitalism and the random intersections that the metropolis precipitates—"the money mills" and "pavements . . . confused by the tread of a million feet." The "money mills" in *Our Mutual Friend* sustain a feverish and seemingly random circulation of shares and currency and, consequently, the unending series of exchanges so important for some of the novel's central effects. These transactions are, however, inseparable from the giant metropolis and its disparate social spaces—its "gritty streets" and "business lanes and courts" but also its drawing rooms; and the "tread of a million footsteps"[2] suggests the urban aesthetic's capacity to register, from amidst the random conglomeration of people that is the city, the unexpected intersections between unrelated people brought together by the city's innumerable financial transactions.

The connection that the sixteenth chapter of *Our Mutual Friend* makes between the "money mills" and the "tread of a million footsteps" that crisscross the metropolis is important because some of the finest writing on *Our Mutual Friend* has tended to treat the novel's economic activity in isolation from the metropolis in which it is embedded. Thus, for example, Catherine Gallagher draws on political economy's emphasis on the body's centrality to track brilliantly the workings of a "bioeconomics" in *Our Mutual Friend*, in which values move not only between people and things but also between dead and live bodies.[3] Similarly Pam Morris locates, in the domain of the visual, a site that is capable of sustaining unlimited economic activity. Bodies in her account become "exhibition surfaces for commodity display" and the act of looking inseparable from speculation.[4] Gallagher's and Morris's exposition of the range of economic activity is, of course, crucial for a novel driven by a process that makes everything—goods, currency, shares, looks, gestures, the living as well as the dead—mobile and exchangeable. But this process requires the giant metropolis—its diverse locations and the range of resources that these locations make available—as the condition of its realization. Aligned, thus, to the city, the economic exchanges described in *Our Mutual Friend* carry forward a set of issues that have been central to this book throughout: the problems of sociability and individuality in the big city.

The underlying connections between the "bioeconomics" of *Our Mutual Friend*, the internal dynamics of Dickens's representation of London, and problems of urban sociability and individuality are apparent in one of the novel's typically startling business activities. The skeletons and stuffed animals that Venus produces from various bones and body parts exemplify an important assumption of political economy: that value may be accumulated, in Catherine Gallagher's words, by drawing it out of "the organic body and storing it up, suspending it in inorganic forms."[5] But Venus's business is crucially dependent on his access to locations available only in the big city—for example, to hospitals and ports from which he buys his raw materials and to West End outlets to which he sells his products. Moreover, some of Venus's transactions have implications for the ways in which the metropolis impinges on the problem of individuality. For example, the deal that Wegg proposes to Venus points to a link between the city's numerous impersonal transactions and the problem—in a basic physical sense—of personal integrity. What Wegg hopes to buy back from Venus are the skeletal remains of his leg, which has found its way from the hospital where it had been amputated to the taxidermist's shop that Venus runs. Wegg's walk to Venus's shop through London's labyrinthine streets, his offer to buy back a part of his own body, and the strange intimacy that the nature of his project gives to what is a business encounter between two strangers bring together a significant set of topographical, social, and anatomical details. These details, indeed, make the Wegg–Venus transaction paradigmatic of an urban aesthetic that is always oriented toward registering the tension between the scattering effects and the random sociability of the urban experience.

The tension dramatized in the working of Venus's business plays itself out on a more elaborate scale in the larger world of *Our Mutual Friend* as a whole. On the one hand, *Our Mutual Friend* deploys the processes of finance capitalism to intensify the experience of dispersal that had been, all along, an important feature in Dickens's representation of urban existence. That is, the novel registers the many ways in which the operations of an economy based on shares and promissory notes—on values completely detached from any material moorings—disperse individual identities as well. The Veneerings, the Lammles, Georgiana Podsnap, and Twemlow may, unlike Wegg, remain physically integrated but each of these characters must, sooner or later, confront some fragment of her or his identity that has become detached from her or him. On the other hand, the novel's many business activities also promote a second and contradictory trajectory associated with the urban aesthetic: they facilitate unexpected encounters between dispersed Londoners and, in this way, a form of urban sociability very different from the more "organic" ties around which the domestic-realistic novel is built.

We could say, in fact, that the money market in *Our Mutual Friend* works to enhance a fundamental and familiar feature of the urban aesthetic: its propensity to depend, for its most characteristic relationships, on not so much the family or the socially contiguous group as the more impersonal, sometimes random encounters that the big city spawns. In *Our Mutual Friend,* the City, in the sense of both the metropolis and its money market, produces several intersections between the most unrelated of people. One "never knows," as Fascination Fledgeby puts it, "when one gets into the City, what people one may knock up against" (510). What Fledgeby says about London's financial district is true about London as well. Here, too, impersonal social and economic interests are constantly bringing together disconnected individuals. For example, the newly rich Boffins attract the attention of callers so diverse that their cards often read like "A Miscellaneous Lot at an Auction" (187). On the other hand, bereft of the social and kinship ties that characters in a Jane Austen novel inherit as part of their social existence, the Boffins, too, depend on the random connections that only a city can provide in order to realize even the deeply personal experience of the joy of parenthood. Thus, the Boffins advertise their desire to adopt an orphan and thereby set into motion a process by which children are dissociated from their families, set into free circulation, and made capable of becoming part of the family that the Boffins hope to fabricate: "The suddenness of an orphan's rise in the market was not to be paralleled by the maddest records of the Stock Exchange. . . . The market was 'rigged' in various artful ways. Counterfeit stock got into circulation. Parents boldly represented themselves as dead, and brought their orphans with them" (175–76).

The fabricated family that the Boffins attempt to put together is, of course, a characteristic formation in the urban aesthetic, dramatizing the latter's movement away from the more organic ties around which the domestic novel had been organized. Such "families" had generated some of the major lines of action in *Great Expectations*. Unlike the Pip–Magwitch relationship, however, the encounter between the Boffins and the London orphan that they hope to adopt cannot be said to sustain the significant effects of the novel's plot. Rather, the urban aesthetic in *Our Mutual Friend,* drawing as well on the expressive possibilities made available by the operations of finance capitalism, works to extend a second set of preoccupations that had been integral to *Great Expectations*. Thus, the sense of "placelessness" inseparable from Pip's experience of London unfolds in *Our Mutual Friend* as a more radically decorporealizing process. The Boffins, for example, are forced to pin their hopes of parenthood on virtual orphans whose mobile, floating identities have been completely dissociated from their material bodily selves.

The virtualization of selfhood and the consequent emptying out of personal relationships that intertwine to make the fabric of the realistic novel are even more evident in the world of the Veneerings. The Veneerings, Podsnaps, and the rest may, like characters in a Jane Austen novel, inhabit similar social spheres and claim to be on terms of intimacy with each other. Unlike what happens in *Mansfield Park* or *Pride and Prejudice*, however, the interactions between the Veneerings, the Podsnaps, and the rest never facilitate the unfolding of their inner lives. These characters, indeed, are not even constituted in what Bakhtin would call "biographical time"; they remain unmarked, through the course of the entire novel, by the biological or maturational effects of time.[6] Rather than developing as a psychologically complex process across time, interiority, in *Our Mutual Friend,* takes the form of a set of socially deployable signs that refer to the subjective domain but attempt to give to instantly fabricated relationships an affective depth that they don't, in fact, have. Twemlow is amazed at how quickly he and several others become "the most intimate friends Veneering had in the world" (10). The Veneerings are not just adept at forging instant friendships; they also simulate, at short notice, the whole human substructure of a Jane Austen novel out of relationships that are both random and superficial. The wedding party that the Veneerings organize for the Lammles is presented as a "family affair," complete with "family friends" (104) and a foster father who gives the bride away after having met her on precisely two occasions.

The ease with which the Veneerings transform an encounter with a stranger into an intimate relationship must not be taken merely to symptomize their superficiality. Rather, the Veneerings are typical operators in a world where the imperatives of trade and the opportunities offered by the big city sustain the incessant circulation of not only shares and goods but also attributes associated with the subjective domain. What Pam Morris has called the "code of sincerity," for instance, has a definite business value in the world of *Our Mutual Friend:* its deployment as a certain disembodied but "cultivated interiority" offers the Lammles a rare chance of making a financial killing.[7] Having extracted a monetary pledge from Fledgeby in return for arranging a lucrative marriage to Georgiana Podsnap, the Lammles work with "the code of sincerity" to simulate for the young couple the effects of inner life and, thus, implicate them in "a variety of delicate sentiments" that they do not, in fact, experience:

"Alfred, my dear, Mr. Fledgeby very justly says, apropos of the last scene, that true constancy would not require any such stimulant as the stage deems necessary." To which Mr. Lammle would reply, "Ay, Sophronia, my love, but, as Georgiana has observed to me, the lady had no sufficient reason to know the state of the gentleman's affections." To which Mrs. Lammle would rejoin, "Very true, Alfred; but Mr. Fledgeby points out," this. To which Alfred would demur: "Undoubtedly, Sophronia, but Georgiana acutely remarks," that. Through this device the two young people conversed at great length, and committed themselves to a variety of delicate sentiments without having once opened their lips . . . (240)

Fascination Fledgeby may not succeed in taking advantage of the "delicate sentiments" that Lammles stakes on him but he, too, is adept at separating out a discursively constituted identity from the person that it represents. Thus, he takes full advantage of the signs of Riah's Jewish identity to set into circulation a stereotypical image that has nothing in common with what his employee really is. In the process, he harnesses the full force of the anti-Jewish prejudice to transfer to the figure of his employee the most venal aspects of his own moneylending business. For the gentle and benign Riah this means having to cohabit the city with a deeply repugnant version of himself. Thus, he is frequently introduced to strangers as the principal of a firm of grinders:

"But whatever you do, Lammle, don't—don't—don't, I beg of you—ever fall into the hands of Pubsey and Co. in the next room, for they are grinders. Regular flayers and grinders, my dear Lammle," repeated Fledgeby, with a peculiar relish, "and they'll skin you inch by the inch, from the nape of your neck to the sole of your foot, and grind every inch of your skin to tooth-powder. You have seen what Mr. Riah is. Never fall into his hands . . ." (385)

Twemlow is even more disconcerted by the experience of decorporealization and reification that is the inevitable result of his being drawn into the circulatory processes of the city. It is a financially irresponsible friend who transforms Twemlow's "name" to a free-floating scrip in London's money market. This means that Twemlow is forced to follow the dictates of a sign that refers to him but has nothing to do with what he really is. Twemlow's bewilderment, as he rushes about answering the legally enforceable summons from those who possess his "name," suggests precisely a disjunction between what he knows to be his life and the way that it unfolds after it has become "assured" to somebody else (513).

The decorporealizing effects of the city on the self unfolds at a more complex level in Dickens's delineation of John Harmon. Harmon is exposed to the most destabilizing aspects of the urban experience immediately after his arrival in London. More specifically, Dickens deploys the machinations of George Radfoot to complicate the ways in which Harmon experiences time and space after he enters the metropolis. The uncertainty that is, in any case, embedded in Harmon's situation plays out as the spatial disorientation he experiences when he is led by the villainous George Radfoot to an unknown destination on London's riverfront. Harmon loses touch with the markers of objective geography: street names, addresses, the names of localities. He cannot remember "what turns we took, and doubles we made" (332), and the riverfront unfolds before his eyes not as a panorama or a topography but as an incoherent patchwork of disjointed fragments: a church spire, "the wall, the dark doorway, the flight of stairs," and finally, "the river, or a dock or a creek" (332, 333) that borders the room where he is drugged. Moreover, the sick and deranged state into which Harmon falls after Radfoot poisons him distorts Harmon's sense of time as well. He is now unable to register the twenty-four hours that pass between one dark, rainy night to another, or, conversely, he perceives a short period of silence as the "silence of days, weeks, months, years . . ." (333).

Harmon's disoriented state is, of course, abnormally induced, but it also symptomizes the urban aesthetic's propensity to break up spatial and temporal continuities in order to work its fragmenting effects on its figures. Indeed, the crisis that ejects John Harmon from everyday time also destabilizes the minimal material preconditions under which an internally integrated sense of selfhood may be attained.[8] Thus, unlike even Lady Dedlock, who is allowed to retain her physical integrity even as her body is made to sustain the contradictory marks of an internally fractured city, John Harmon finds himself actually separated from what will officially be constituted as his own body:

> Going out that night to walk . . . I found a crowd assembled round a placard posted at Whitehall. It described myself, John Harmon, as found dead and mutilated in the river under circumstances of strong suspicion, described my dress, described the papers in my pockets, and stated where I was lying for recognition. In a wild incautious way I hurried there, and

there—with the horror of the death I had escaped before my eyes in its most appalling shape, added to the inconceivable horror . . . (335)

By separating John Harmon from his "corpse" and even his name, by freeing his figure, that is, from a stable identity and even a fixed body, Dickens is able to disperse it across the length and breadth of the city in ways that are beyond anything that Lady Dedlock and Pip are made to experience. John Harmon's identity is displaced, first of all, on George Radfoot's dead body and transformed into a bizarre commodity that, like the remains of Wegg's leg, can be circulated in the networks of exchange that crisscross the London of the novel. As the means of Gaffer Hexam's livelihood, the "meat and drink" (5) that the river yields to the Hexams, the supposed remains of Harmon will be fished out of the Thames, stripped of the value he continues to possess, and then deposited in a sordid riverside police station.

Harmon's figure is scattered across the city not only by a "bioeconomics" that keeps his supposed body in circulation but also by the discursive systems that the metropolis employs to disseminate and seek information about its citizens. These systems work to appropriate John Harmon's identity, to present to the world (and to him) a version of himself that is separate from him. The public notice that Harmon reads is supplemented by a range of official and unofficial discourses—proclamations, court verdicts, newspapers—that proclaim John Harmon dead, describe the sensational circumstances of his murder, and announce rewards for any information relating to him. Decorporealized and thus freed from anything like a fixed social location, the hero of *Our Mutual Friend* now begins to function as the classic urban signifier: it becomes capable of moving itself and, by implication, of also moving the action and the scenes of the novel across the social extremities that made up nineteenth-century London:

> Thus, like the tides on which it had been borne to the knowledge of men, the Harmon Murder—as it came to be popularly called—went up and down, and ebbed and flowed . . . now among palaces, now among hovels, now among lords and ladies and gentlefolks, now among labourers and hammerers and ballast-heavers, until at last, after a long interval of slack water, it got out to the sea and drifted away. (30)

In *Our Mutual Friend* the most complex effects of the urban aesthetic and especially of its propensity to work with the radically disparate elements that circulate in the city are evident in Dickens's delineation of Bradley Headstone. Thus, *Our Mutual Friend* follows *Bleak House* in using surfaces (such as the different sets of clothing that Bradley Headstone is made to wear) to inscribe on the respectable schoolmaster's figure the contradictory marks of a socially divided city. But, unlike *Bleak House* and even *Great Expectations, Our Mutual Friend* also works with complex subjective states generated, for example, by the repressions that respectability demands or by the proscribed but uncontrollable violence of sexual jealousy. Oriented toward destabilizing Bradley Headstone's improving consciousness, the subversive trajectory within the urban aesthetic continues to develop through disconcerting juxtapositions at levels that had not been available to either *Bleak House* or *Great Expectations*.

Any attempt to think of Bradley Headstone as an urban subject must begin by taking into account that streets are as important to the unfolding of his life as the school to which he is attached. Indeed, from the very beginning, Headstone's life is characterized by the tension between his professed commitments—to his classroom and to the happy domesticity that he might have attained if Lizzie had agreed to marry him—and his propensity to always be pulled out of the network of familial and respectable social relationships that sustains the typical bourgeois subject. Bradley may share a minimal social connection with Lizzie because of the mediating figure of Charlie Hexam who, in his effort to "get up in the world" (205), moves from his father's disreputable riverside hovel to the relative respectability of Headstone's school. But this link is not enough for them to be able to interact in an interior setting socially accessible to both. Thus, although Charlie and Headstone carefully plan the meeting at which the latter might propose to Lizzie, Headstone's actual proposal takes place in the streets, during what Lizzie, at least, perceives as an unexpected encounter:

> As they advanced, she saw them coming, and seemed rather troubled. But she greeted her brother with the usual warmth, and touched the extended hand of Bradley.
> "Why, where are you going, Charley, dear?" she asked him then.
> "Nowhere. We came on purpose to meet you."
> "To meet me, Charley?"
> "Yes. We are going to walk with you. But don't let us take the great leading streets where everyone walks, and we can't hear ourselves speak. Let us go by the quiet backways. Here's a large paved court by the church, and quiet, too. Let us go up there."
> "But it's not the way, Charley."
> "Yes it is," said the boy, petulantly. "It's in my way, and my way is yours." (355)

Charley's determination to lead his sister along a single predetermined path, his choice of the semienclosed court as a means of cordoning off his sister and Headstone from the promiscuous traffic of the streets, prove inadequate defenses against the urban aesthetic's propensity to precipitate unexpected (often tense) encounters between people who occupy very different positions in the city's social world. The urban aesthetic not only finds in streets, doorsteps, and, toward the end, even the river the sites where the unlikely love affair between the pretty but poor and unlettered Lizzie and the gentlemanly Eugene Wrayburn might unfold; what is more, it also pits the tense, self-improving Headstone against the implacable class arrogance of Wrayburn and, thus, creates the conditions for its own most complex unfolding.

The tension, or more accurately, the simmering violence that is inseparable from Headstone's consciousness as he follows Eugene across London's night streets has its origins, paradoxically, in that set of enclosed spaces that had emerged, in Hogarth's original articulation of the urban aesthetic, as the sites of the productive, morally, and socially responsible life. Middle-class interiors may continue to sustain economic and social stability in both *Industry and Idleness* and *Our Mutual Friend,* but in the later work they are also associated with a repressive morality that stretches all the way from Podsnap's proscription on anything that might bring "a blush into the face of the young person" (117) to Miss Peecher's propensity to repress those erotic thoughts that would "astonish the pupils" of her school (305). This repressive morality complicates the whole relationship that Hogarth had plotted between Goodchild's commitment to middle-class interiors and his stable, morally privileged, improving career, on the one hand, and the degradation attendant on Idle's life in the streets on the other. Headstone's self-improving career may continue to be predicated on his commitment to a set of respectable interiors, but in *Our Mutual Friend* Dickens implicates the experience of upward social mobility itself in the repressive morality of the middle class and, by implication, in a whole internal process that will work its contradictory and destructive effects deep within the urban subject's consciousness. *Our Mutual Friend* activates these effects by deploying, in an original way, a maneuver that is very much part of the urban aesthetic. Dickens could be said to follow Pierce Egan, for example, when arranging an encounter on one of London's streets between such diverse urban types as Eugene Wrayburn and Bradley Headstone. But *Our Mutual Friend* stakes far more on this encounter than the comic effects that the city's diversity routinely yields in *Life in London:*

The master and the pupil walked on rapidly and silently. They had nearly crossed the bridge, when a gentleman came coolly sauntering towards them, with a cigar in his mouth, his coat thrown back, and his hands behind him. Something in the careless manner of his person, and in a certain lazily arrogant air with which he approached, holding possession of twice as much pavement as another would have claimed, instantly caught the boy's attention. (207)

The provocative arrogance of Eugene Wrayburn's walk already points to the kind of use that Dickens will make of this encounter between two socially disparate individuals who inhabit the city. But it is during the first quarrel that the schoolmaster and the gentlemanly lawyer have over Lizzie that the corrosive effect that the latter's social and sexual arrogance will have on the former's repressed consciousness is revealed:

"You think me of no more value than the dirt under your feet," said Bradley to Eugene, speaking in a carefully weighed and measured tone, or he could not have spoken at all.

"I assure you, Schoolmaster," replied Eugene, "I don't think about you."

"That's not true," returned the other: "you know better."

"That's coarse," Eugene retorted, "but you *don't* know better." (263)

We can uncover more precisely the kind of pressure that Eugene Wrayburn is shown to exert on Headstone by turning to Norbert Elias's great analysis of the ways socially deprived individuals often negotiate the experience of upward mobility. Elias argues that while the experience of upward mobility enables the individual to access social spaces that had hitherto remained closed to her or him, it makes the individual hypersensitive to the ways in which he or she relates to social superiors. Unsure of his or her relationship to "the colonizing upper class," resentful of but at the same time attempting to emulate those who have already arrived, the self-improving individual is "less balanced" and "more severe," threatened from above and below. Exposed to "the cross fire from all sides," the situation of the self-improving individual reveals "the immense effort which individual social advantage requires."[9]

Elias's work helps present the relationship between Headstone and Wrayburn, and especially of what Rosemarie Bodenheimer has called "the alternating current crackling in their scenes together,"[10] as a tense play of class positions that only the social diversity of a city can sustain. Implicated in a sexual rivalry, Wrayburn's aggressive rhetoric aggravates Headstone's sense of social inferiority, destabilizes the respectable parameters within which this life had been lived, and activates that propensity toward violence that had been encoded within what Dickens describes as Headstone's "nature" (263). Compelled through the day to exercise the watchfulness and repression that had been the condition of his integration into respectable society, Headstone finds in London's night streets the possibility of an alternate mode of life:

> Tied up all day with his disciplined show upon him, subdued to the performance of his routine of educational tricks, encircled by a gabbling crowd, he broke loose at night like an ill-tamed wild animal. Under his daily restraint, it was his compensation, not his trouble, to give a glance towards his state at night, and to the freedom of its being indulged. (491)

This passage recalls and, at the same time, radically transforms the oppositions around which Hogarth had structured *Industry and Idleness*. Thus, the schoolroom that Headstone inhabits during the day is constituted not as a fortification against the dangerous and chaotic life of the streets but rather as a psychological cage whose system of restraints only builds up the pressure that will inexorably drive Headstone to the streets. Again, the London streets that Headstone scours during the night are emptied of the teeming life with which these are associated in the whole tradition of urban representations from Hogarth to Egan and beyond. What Dickens does instead is to follow an expressive strategy that he had first deployed in *Great Expectations*, representing the London of *Our Mutual Friend* as a tangle of empty streets that confronts the nocturnal walker with a sense of his or her own unanchored situation. Headstone's lack of moorings is, indeed, self-consciously dramatized in the series of purposeless walks into which he is drawn by Wrayburn:

> I stroll out after dark, stroll a little way, look in at a window, and furtively look out for the schoolmaster. Sooner or later, I perceive the schoolmaster on the watch; sometimes accompanied by his hopeful pupil; oftener, pupil-less. Having made sure of his watching me, I tempt him on, all over London. One night I go east, another night north, in a few nights I go all round the compass. Sometimes I walk; sometimes I proceed in cabs, draining the pocket of the schoolmaster, who then follows in cabs. I study and get up abstruse No Thoroughfares in the course of the day. With Venetian

mystery I seek those No Thoroughfares at night, glide into them by means of dark courts, tempt the schoolmaster to follow, turn suddenly and catch him before he can retreat. (488–89)

Of course it is Headstone's own jealousy and Wrayburn's cold determination to make him suffer for it that draws Headstone into the ambulatory traps that his rival sets up. But the night streets that offer Headstone no destinations may also be thought to sustain a form of urban subjectivity that is darker and more modern than that found in *Industry and Idleness* or *Life in London*. Unable to live within the constraints of respectable interiors, yet deeply ashamed of his plebeian past; proud of his acquired respectability, yet driven inexorably by a taunting, socially superior sexual rival toward acts of violence that will proscribe him forever from respectable society, Headstone's situation as an urban subject is characterized by a radical inability to belong. "To walk," de Certeau has argued, "is to lack a place,"[11] and it is exactly Headstone's "placelessness" that is imaged in the purposeless walks that he is so relentlessly made to undertake. In *Our Mutual Friend,* indeed, the experience of placelessness invades Headstone's body itself: it separates him from himself, transforms him into a "haggard head suspended in air."

This representation of Headstone as a "haggard head . . . flitt[ing] across the road" (492) inserts his figure into the double trajectory along which the urban subject is typically unfolded in Dickens's later fiction. On the one hand, Dickens's image suggests, in its most extreme form, the experience of having lost one's social moorings, of lacking the most obvious of referents: one's body itself. On the other hand, the image also draws attention to Headstone's situation as a mobile and radically unstable urban subject, separated from his respectable body and made liable by the circulatory processes of the city to be brought into contact with those who would have no place in the respectable social domain that he normally inhabits. Headstone's restless night walks do, in fact, throw him in the path of Rogue Riderhood, the disreputable waterside character already implicated in several semicriminal activities.

The bringing together of Bradley Headstone and Rogue Riderhood in a London night street activates the second trajectory within the urban mode of characterization: its propensity to expose the respectable subject to the city's low life. Thus, Dickens had already produced characters such as Lady Dedlock and Pip out of the play of respectability and its degraded other. With Bradley Headstone, however, this play is achieved not by some extraneous plot connection but from pressures that emanate from within the schoolmaster's respectable personality. Thus, Headstone's figure had been designed, from the very beginning, to sustain simultaneously the connotations of respectability and murderous violence. For example, the "respectable hair guard" (261) that he is made to wear is overlain with connotations of extreme violence—transformed, by a play of language, into a murder instrument that Headstone would like to wind around Eugene's neck and use to strangle him. In this sense, the intersection, affected by the urban aesthetic, between the paths of the respectable schoolteacher and the semicriminal Rogue Riderhood only facilitates the full articulation of a tension that had always been encoded within Dickens's representation of the schoolmaster.

The first encounter between Headstone and Riderhood itself sets up an expressive system oriented toward registering the respectable everyday life of the schoolteacher as well as the unregulated drives that will push him beyond the pale of respectability. Walking with Riderhood across London at the dead of night, Headstone never once relinquishes his respectable social identity. Yet the violent project that obsesses him also binds him to Riderhood, driving him inexorably along the route that the disreputable riverside character takes.

The intertwining of Headstone's path with that of Riderhood enables Riderhood to incessantly track the dual trajectory of the schoolmaster's life and, in this way, to bring together the disparate social worlds that Headstone inhabits into relations of tense simultaneity. Thus, for example, Riderhood chooses to bring his knowledge of the "other" Headstone, the pathologically violent criminal who has just attempted to murder Wrayburn, into the room where he teaches, the very space where the schoolmaster's respectable social identity is most firmly embedded:

> "I ain't a learned character myself," said Riderhood, surveying the class, "but I do admire learning in others. I should dearly like to hear these here young folks read that there name off from the writing."
>
> The arms of the class went up. At the miserable master's nod, the shrill chorus arose: "Bradley Headstone!"
>
> "No!" cried Riderhood, "You don't mean it! Headstone! . . . Hooroar for another turn!"
>
> Another tossing of arms, another nod, and another shrill chorus: "Bradley Headstone!"
>
> "I've got it now!," said Riderhood after attentively listening, and internally repeating: "Bradley. I see. Chris'en name, Bradley, sim'lar to Roger,

which is my own. Eh? Fam'ly name, Headstone, sim'lar to Riderhood, which is my own. Eh?" (714)

Moreover, as the beleaguered schoolmaster's story moves toward its terrible denouement, Dickens creates around it a discursive zone that allows for the free intertwining of Headstone's figure with that of Rogue Riderhood. Thus, even in the passage just quoted, Riderhood makes significant use of the breach he has affected in Headstone's respectable personality: he twines his own name around that of the schoolmaster while seeking to understand, in his mock serious way, that Bradley and Headstone denote the former's first and last names. Similarly, Headstone does not hesitate to blur the boundary that separates his figure from that of Riderhood whenever it suits him to do so. On the day when he assaults Wrayburn, for example, Bradley puts on a set of secondhand bargeman's clothes so similar to what Riderhood habitually wears that the latter describes him as a better looking version of "myself" (569). Headstone will never, in fact, be able to free himself from the social identity that he chooses to superimpose on his own. Headstone may have thrown his bargeman's clothes into the river with the hope of regaining his normal existence as a respectable schoolteacher, but in retrieving Headstone's discarded clothes from the river, Riderhood retrieves not only some crucial evidence against Headstone but also the characteristic signifiers of an expressive mode that finds in the individual figure a site where the internal social fractures of nineteenth-century London may be inscribed. The work of such signifiers is dramatically visible in the image with which Dickens concludes the Bradley Headstone story: "When the two were found lying, under the ooze and scum behind one of the rotting gates, Riderhood's hold had relaxed, probably in falling, and his eyes were staring upward. But, he was girdled still with Bradley's iron ring, and the rivets of the iron ring held tight" (722).

This image where the self-improving Bradley Headstone is physically fused to the semicriminal street character resonates against that decisive maneuver by which Hogarth, in his inaugural exposition of the urban aesthetic, had managed to segregate Goodchild from the chaotic and immoral life of the streets even while articulating the capacity of the popular and often immoral print to break into respectable interiors. This latter dynamic—this intrusive and disruptive strand within the urban aesthetic—unfolded powerfully across Dickens's later novels, sustaining, among several other effects, the disconcerting superimpositions of *Bleak House* or the innumerable connections that *Great Expectations* plots between gentlemanliness and criminality. But it was not until his last complete novel that Dickens deployed the destabilizing possibilities within the urban aesthetic against those very binaries by which Hogarth had so carefully separated the domain of respectability from the chaotic and immoral "other." In this sense, the grotesque image with which Dickens concludes Headstone's story marks, in an unusually vivid manner, the basic orientation of an expressive strategy that drew so strongly on Hogarth's sense of the city's menacing differences that it could end only by wreaking its devastating effects on a figure who had always remained at the center of Hogarth's moral imagination: the respectable, hardworking, upwardly mobile subject.

In *Our Mutual Friend,* more than in any of his other works, Dickens is self-consciously concerned with the artistic decisions that went into the making of his own fiction. For example, *Our Mutual Friend* engages powerfully, if indirectly, with a mode of writing that enjoyed great prestige in nineteenth-century England but whose aesthetic priorities were very different from those of Dickens. One difference between Dickens's method and that which underlay the domestic-realistic novel related to the privileged status that the latter accorded to the everyday life of the middle class. More specifically, Dickens felt that domestic realism's preoccupation with "ordinary domestic relationships" had increasingly begun to produce "a little, finite systematic routine" that he embodied both in the day-to-day lives of the Podsnaps and in the sort of novels that they approve:[12]

> Mr. Podsnap's world was not a very large world, morally; no, not even geographically: seeing that, although his business was sustained upon commerce with other countries, he considered other countries with that important reservation, a mistake, and of their manners and customs would conclusively observe, "Not English!" . . . Elsewise, the world got up at eight, shaved close at a quarter past, breakfasted at nine, went to the City at ten, came home at half-past five, and dined at seven. Mr. Podsnap's notions of the Arts in their integrity might have been stated thus, Literature; large print, respectfully descriptive of getting up at eight, shaving close at a quarter past, breakfasting at nine, going to the City at ten, coming home at half-past five, and dining at seven. Painting and Sculpture; models and portraits representing Professors of getting up at eight, shaving close at quarter past, breakfasting at nine, going to the City at ten, coming home at half-past five, and dining at seven. Music; a respectable performance (without variations) on stringed and wind instruments, sedately expressive of getting up at eight, shaving close at quarter past, breakfasting at nine,

going to the City at ten, coming home at half-past five, and dining at seven. (115–16)

Dickens's hostility to the protocols of domestic realism—a hostility that he expressed not only in *Our Mutual Friend* but also more directly in non-fictional pieces—must be understood as his means of asserting certain differences between his own mode of novel writing and the protocols of domestic realism. Thus, the Dickensian novel did not itself ever remain confined to the social parameters within which the domestic novel worked: to the "quiet domesticity, placid emotions that are developed about the paternal hearth,"[13] as Dickens himself put it. Rather, novels like *Bleak House* and *Our Mutual Friend* are driven by plot connections that bring together dramatically disparate social spaces.

Moreover, Dickens's propensity to produce dramatic social juxtapositions, rather than sustaining the internal integrity of the fictional world that he was describing, points to a second and more fundamental difference between Dickens's methods and those associated with realism. The latter sought to produce, for a predominantly middle-class audience, the seamless *continuity* of its everyday life and, in this way, to achieve the effects of truthfulness and naturalness. The realistic novel, as the *Westminster Review* put it, unrolled incidents "in orderly chronological sequence" and unfolded "character according to those laws which experience teaches us to look for as well in the moral as the material world" and which described "outward circumstances in their inexorable certainty yielding to no magician's wand."[14] Judged by the criterion laid out by the *Westminster Review*, the Dickensian novel would appear—and the quarterly press often pointed this out—irregular, inartistic, and commercial: something which produced a variety of entertaining effects by stitching together fragments of various popular, often subliterary modes.[15] It is the interest that *Our Mutual Friend* has in artistic and cultural products that are fabricated from fragments, or in the relationship between artistic labor and the processes of the market, that suggests the depth of Dickens's metatextual engagement, in his last complete novel, with his own practices as a novelist.

Our Mutual Friend does not celebrate every activity generated by the market-driven, hybridizing process associated, throughout this book, with Dickens's own fiction. For example, Silas Wegg's career, first as vendor and performer of street ballads and then as Boffin's reader, exemplifies how easy it is to abuse the relatively informal and accommodating conditions in which popular entertainment may be produced. Thus, while reading for Boffin, the half-literate Wegg habitually improvises with his material, not in order to generate any particular effect but to glide over some passage that he cannot decipher. In this sense, Wegg reduces to a fraud the whole process of fragmentation and rejoining that underlay Dickens's own novel writing. Wegg's activities can nevertheless be understood as part of *Our Mutual Friend*'s metatextual engagement with the conditions in which Dickens's own novels were produced and disseminated. Indeed, as someone who reads for money, works with fragments, moves up the hierarchy of literary entertainment, and is conscious about the bodily energy expended in order to create literary value, Silas Wegg reproduces but degrades some key features of Dickens's own career as a literary entrepreneur. The positive potential of these features, and especially of improvising with fragments, becomes evident in Jenny Wren—not only at the discursive strategies that go into her making but, more metatextually, at the similarities between her methods of work and those of Dickens himself.

Jenny's figure is never represented as a self-coordinating, organic whole. Rather, it is made up of separate pieces that can be juxtaposed in relations of continuity or contrast to produce unexpected effects. For example, Jenny's facial expressions are often so unnatural that they seem to be creations of a puppeteer manipulating two parts of his puppet simultaneously: "She had an elfin chin that was capable of great expression; and whenever she gave this look, she hitched this chin up. As if her eyes and chin worked together on the same wires" (202).

Similarly, Jenny's cascading hair—the "golden stream [that] fell over herself and over the chair, and flowed down to the ground" (395)—and her crippled, diminutive body are treated as separate entities that are brought together to create a powerful, disconcerting effect. The sight of "the little creature looking down out of a Glory of her long, bright, radiant hair" appears, to even as insensitive a character as Fascination Fledgeby, to be a "vision" (255).

But Jenny is not just a typical embodiment of Dickens's methods; she also deploys these methods in her own creative practices. At the simpler level, Jenny fashions her resplendent dolls' dresses out of the bits and pieces of waste material that she regularly picks up from Fledgeby's establishment. At a deeper level, moreover, the success of Jenny Wren's work is dependent on her ability to extract, from the random traffic of London's streets, a set of details that belong to a social world to which she can have no access. In an important passage that resonates against Dickens's own early situation as a speculative pedestrian, Jenny Wren explains exactly how London's streets offer her indispensable material for her work:

Look here. There's a Drawing-Room, or a grand day in the Park, or a Show, or a Fete, or what you like. Very well. I squeeze among the crowd, and I look about me. When I see a great lady very suitable for my business, I say, "You'll do, my dear!" and I take particular notice of her again, and run home, and cut her out and baste her. Then another day I come scudding back again to try on, and then I take particular notice of her again. Sometimes she plainly seems to say, "How that little creature is staring!" . . . All the time I am only saying to myself, "I must hollow out a bit; I must slope away there"; and I am making a perfect slave of her, with making her try on my doll's dress. Evening parties are severer work for me, because there's only a doorway for a full view, and what with hobbling among the wheels of the carriages and the legs of horses, I fully expect to be run over some night. However, there I have 'em, just the same. When they go bobbing into the hall from the carriage, and catch a glimpse of my little physiognomy poked out from behind a policeman's cape in the rain, I dare say they think I am wondering and admiring with all my eyes and heart, but they little think that they are only working for my dolls! (393)

Jenny here makes exactly the same maneuver that Dickens had made in works such as *Sketches by Boz* and *The Uncommercial Traveller*. As Boz or the Uncommercial Traveller, Dickens had scoured the streets in order to find, as Audrey Jaffe puts it, "capital in what must be, for others incidental." The Uncommercial Traveller, especially, makes explicit the project that can be said to underlie the activities of both Dickens and Jenny Wren: "The idea of 'uncommercial travelling,'" as Audrey Jaffe puts it, in an insight that is as applicable to Dickens as to his persona, "is wonderfully disingenuous, for, while not selling *to* those he encounters in the course of his travels, the narrator's intent is rather to sell what he can make of his interest in them—to sell *them*."[16] It is exactly this possibility of turning observations into marketable, cultural commodities to which Jenny Wren refers when she triumphantly claims that while others can merely see her staring at fine ladies, she is, in fact, making these ladies work for her dolls.

Jenny Wren's work does not, however, end with the extraction from London's streets of the details that she will need for her dolls' dresses. These details are often put through a process of radical refashioning before they can be made suitable for the market. Indeed, as someone who is committed to producing only the "gay events of life" (393) for a clientele made up of young children, Jenny will often need to execute, in an extreme form, that process of fragmentation, uprooting, and reactivation inseparable from the Dickensian aesthetic. Thus, for example, Jenny Wren will transform and redeploy a detail appropriated from the saddest of occasions to project a scene that is utterly different from the one in which the detail had originated:

> "Why, godmother," replied the dressmaker, "you must know that we Professors, who live upon our taste and invention, are obliged to keep our eyes always open. And you know already that I have many extra expenses to meet just now. So, it came into my head, while I was weeping at my poor boy's grave, that something in my way might be done with a clergyman."
>
> "What can be done?" asked the old man.
>
> "Not a funeral, never fear!" returned Miss Jenny, anticipating his objection with a nod. "The public don't like to be made melancholy, I know very well. I am seldom called upon to put my young friends into mourning . . . But a doll clergyman, my dear—glossy black curls and whiskers—uniting two of my young friends in matrimony," said Miss Jenny, shaking her forefinger, "is quite another affair. If you don't see those three at the altar in Bond Street in a jiffy, my name's Jack Robinson!" (661)

Jenny's propensity to move signifiers across widely dispersed domains approximates the discrepancy between the harsh conditions of her own life in a poor area of London and the brilliant aristocratic interiors that she helps to fabricate. Indeed, Dickens often focuses on the squalid and harsh conditions of Jenny's life to throw into relief the splendor of the dresses she designs. Toward the middle of the novel, for example, the aged Riah and the crippled Jenny are made to struggle across a maze of dirty and fog-ridden London streets before they are suddenly brought face to face with a resplendent shop window exhibiting Jenny's art:

> Thus conversing, and having crossed Westminster Bridge, they traversed the ground that Riah had lately traversed, and new ground likewise; for, when they had recrossed the Thames by way of London Bridge, they struck down by the river, and held their still foggier course that way.
>
> But previously, as they were going along, Jenny twisted her venerable friend aside to a brilliantly-lighted toyshop window, and said "Now look at 'em! All my work!"
>
> This referred to a dazzling semicircle of dolls in all the colours of the rainbow, who were dressed for presentation at court, for going to balls, for going out driving, for going out on horseback, for going out walking, for going to get married, for going to help other dolls to get married, for all the gay events of life. (392–93)

This sudden, unexpected intersection between a harsh and bleak exterior and a warm, beautifully arranged interior is, of course, a typical effect of the London aesthetic that matured over so many years in Dickens's novels. But the splendid scene that literally springs out of a fog-swept London might also be seen as Dickens's means of showcasing the outstanding work of a self-taught artist who works with the fragments she has picked up from London's streets. Perhaps Dickens was also celebrating, from the vantage point of what was to be his last complete novel and from within the gloomy atmosphere in which much of it is enveloped, that city-based, hybridizing, improvisational, market-driven labor that had produced his own fiction.

NOTES

Introduction

1. See Peter Ackroyd, *Dickens*, 1045. The Charles Dickens Edition might, as Peter Ackroyd puts it, "be seen as encompassing and defining a lifetime's work. It was truly [Dickens's] memorial. His last edition."
2. John Butt and Kathleen Tillotson, *Dickens at Work*, 14.
3. N. N. Feltes, *Modes of Production of Victorian Novels*, 3.
4. See Richard Altick, *The Presence of the Present: Topics of the Day in the Victorian Novel*, esp. 64–68.
5. Gerard Curtis, "Dickens and the Visual Market," in *Literature in the Marketplace: Nineteenth-Century British Publishing and Reading Practices*, ed. John O. Jordan and Robert L. Patten, 220.
6. Martin Meisel, *Realizations: Narrative, Pictorial, and Theatrical Arts in Nineteenth-Century England*, 4.
7. See Sean Shesgreen, "Headnote" to *The Harlot's Progress*, in *Engravings by Hogarth*, 18.
8. On the reception and the continuing popularity of *Industry and Idleness*, see Ronald Paulson, *Hogarth: High Art and Low*, 290–91.
9. Quoted in J. A. Sutherland, *Victorian Novelists and Their Publishers*, 107.
10. See Meisel, *Realizations*, 277–78. In what is, in my opinion, the best account of the afterlife of Hogarth's prints, Martin Meisel reprints the playbill.
11. Pierce Egan, *Life in London, or, the Day and Night Scenes of Jerry Hawthorn, Esq. and his Elegant Friend Corinthian Tom . . . in their Rambles and Sprees through the Metropolis* (London: Sherwood, Neely and Jones, 1822), 4. All subsequent references to *Life in London* are to this edition, and page numbers appear parenthetically in the text following quotations from it.
12. The following announcement with which Dickens launched the first cheap edition of his novels is fairly typical: "It had been intended that this CHEAP EDITION, now

announced, should not be undertaken until the books were much older, or the Author was dead—To become, in his new guise a permanent inmate of many English homes, where, in his old shape he was only known as a guest, or hardly known at all; to be well thumbed and soiled in a plain suit that will be read a great deal by children, and grown people, at the fireside and on the journey; to be hoarded on the humble shelf where there are a few books, and to lie about in libraries like any familiar piece of household stuff—must obviously be among the hopes of a living author venturing on such an enterprise" (quoted in Sutherland, *Victorian Novelists*, 35).

13. William Makepeace Thackeray, *Ballads and Miscellanies*, vol. 13 of *The Oxford Thackeray*, ed. George Saintsbury, 486.

14. Ibid., 466.

15. Peter L. Shillingsburg, *Pegasus in Harness: Victorian Publishing and W. M. Thackeray*, 26.

16. Gordon N. Ray, ed., *The Letters and Private Papers of William Makepeace Thackeray*, vol. 1, 459.

17. There are numerous occasions where Thackeray makes this complaint. For an extended example, see his letter to Edward Fitzgerald, October 7, 1836, in Ray, *Letters*, vol. 1, 322–23.

18. Quoted in Geoffrey Tillotson and Donald Hawes, eds., *William Makepeace Thackeray: The Critical Heritage*, 128.

19. See Kathryn Chittick, *Dickens and the 1830s*, 67–91.

20. Unsigned, "Boz and his *Nicholas Nickleby*," in *Charles Dickens: The Critical Heritage*, ed. Philip Collins, 70.

21. Thomas Henry Lister, "Review of *Sketches, Pickwick, Nickleby, and Oliver Twist*," in Collins, *Dickens: Critical Heritage*, 71.

22. E. B. Hamley, "Remonstrance with Dickens," in Collins, *Dickens: Critical Heritage*, 360–61.

23. See Collins, *Dickens: Critical Heritage*, 126. The *Edinburgh Review*, for example, wrote that Dickens's "desultory" education was not "likely to train him to habits of grave and solid speculation" and that as a "comic satirist," he had made it his business "to observe society in its irregularities and incongruities, not in the sum and total of its operations."

24. M. M. Bakhtin, *Speech Genres and Other Late Essays*, trans. Vern W. McGee, ed. Caryl Emerson and Michael Holquist, 2.

25. Epstein, *Radical Expression*.

26. See Kevin Gilmartin, *Print Politics: The Press and Radical Opposition in Early Nineteenth-Century England*; James Epstein, *Radical Expression: Political Language, Ritual and Symbol in England, 1790–1850*; Marcus Wood, *Radical Satire and Print Culture, 1790–1822*; Iain McCalman, *Radical Underworld: Prophets, Revolutionaries and Pornographers in London, 1795–1840*; Olivia Smith, *The Politics of Language, 1791–1819*.

27. See Sambudha Sen, "*Bleak House* and *Little Dorrit*: The Radical Heritage," *English Literary History* 65, no. 4 (1996): 945–80.

28. Humphrey House first established this view of Dickens's politics in his extremely influential *The Dickens World*. See also William Myers, "The Radicalism of *Little Dorrit*," in *Literature and Politics in the Nineteenth Century*, ed. John Lucas, 77–105, and George Holoch, "Consciousness and Society in *Little Dorrit*," *Victorian Studies* 21, no. 3 (1978): 335–51.

29. Gareth Stedman Jones uses this phrase in *Languages of Class: Studies in English Working Class History, 1832–1982*.

30. See Epstein, *Radical Expression*.
31. Sally Ledger, *Dickens and the Popular Radical Imagination*, 2, 8.

Chapter 1

1. Quoted in M. H. Spielman, *The History of "Punch,"* 323.
2. Walter Jerrold, *Douglas Jerrold and "Punch,"* 4.
3. William Makepeace Thackeray, "George Cruikshank," in *Ballads, Critical Reviews, Tales*, 287–88.
4. E. P. Thompson, *The Making of the English Working Class*, 810.
5. Thackeray, "George Cruikshank," 288.
6. William Makepeace Thackeray, "Pictures of Life and Character," in *Ballads, Critical Reviews*, 488–89.
7. See Spielman, *History of "Punch,"* 322–24.
8. Ibid., 421.
9. Unsigned, "Modern Novelists: Charles Dickens," *Westminster Review* 26 (October 1864): 417.
10. Ibid., 417.
11. I use "reactivation" in Walter Benjamin's sense. See Walter Benjamin, "The Work of Art in the Age of Mechanical Reproduction," in *Illuminations*, trans. Harry Zohn, ed. Hannah Arendt, esp. 220–21.
12. McCalman, *Radical Underworld*, 173.
13. Raymond Williams, "Radical and/or Respectable," in *The Press We Deserve*, ed. Richard Boston, 21.
14. Quoted in Wood, *Radical Satire*, 269.
15. For instance, Richard Carlile, whose early work as an editor and publisher represented the hard-line, austere, rationalist strand within radical journalism, found himself forced to move, by the 1830s, to the sort of entertainment-oriented proreform political satire that would attract not just the older plebeian audience that had grown around radical newspapers but middle-class readers as well. In fact, in his *Humorous Sketches*—a journal that he ran with some degree of commercial success between 1833 and 1836—Carlile had already begun the process of relocating radical expression within the moral universe of respectability that Dickens was to complete. Remarkably, when Chapman and Hall sought to repeat the commercial success of *Humorous Sketches*, they hired not only Carlile's illustrator Robert Seymour but also a young and relatively unknown Dickens as a junior collaborator. See Louis James, *Fiction for the Working Man, 1830–1850*, 27–29.
16. See, for example, Spielman, *History of "Punch,"* esp. 322–25, 420–22.
17. Roger Chartier, "Texts, Printings, Readings," in *The New Cultural History*, ed. Lynn Hunt, 165.
18. See Richard Altick, *Punch: The Lively Youth of a British Institution, 1841–51*, esp. 94–96.
19. See Ledger, *Dickens*, 114, 142.
20. See Unsigned, "The Royal Rhythmical Alphabets," *Punch*, August 21, 1841: 62.
21. See *Punch*, August 21, 1841: 62, and Altick, *Punch*, 135.
22. See Charles Baudelaire, "Some Foreign Caricaturists," in *Selected Writings on Art and Artists*, trans. E. P. Charvet, 233–34.
23. As I move from Cruikshank to Doyle and Leech, I am indebted to Richard Altick's point about a certain softening of graphic caricature. See Altick, *Punch*, esp. 122–35.

24. As Ledger shows, Dickens contributed squibs to the *Examiner* during the 1840s. See Ledger, *Dickens,* 142.

25. Jones, *Languages of Class,* 104, and Gilmartin, *Print Politics,* 1.

26. Smith, *Politics of Language,* 53.

27. In my opinion, the best account of Hone's trial for blasphemy appears in Ben Wilson, *The Laughter of Triumph: William Hone and the Fight for the Free Press,* 222–59.

28. See *Punch,* August 21, 1841: 102.

29. The comparison between Jerrold and Dickens was, in Philip Collins's words, a "critical commonplace of the period." See Collins, *Dickens: Critical Heritage,* 271. Collins's anthology contains many nineteenth-century essays that make this comparison.

30. Charles Dickens, *Little Dorrit* (Harmondsworth: Penguin, 1976), 294. All subsequent references to *Little Dorrit* are to this edition, and page numbers appear parenthetically in the text following quotations from it.

31. On the fictional "nobody," see Catherine Gallagher, *Nobody's Story: The Vanishing Acts of Women Writers in the Marketplace, 1670–1820,* and Catherine Gallagher and Stephen Greenblatt, *Practicing New Historicism.*

32. On the "stylistic aura," see Bakhtin, *Speech Genres,* esp. 87–88.

33. Epstein, *Radical Expression,* 5.

34. W. T. J. Mitchell, *Iconology: Image, Text, Ideology,* 143.

35. Tom Paine, *The Rights of Man,* in *The Selected Works of Tom Paine,* ed. Howard Fast, 118, 166, 113.

36. Unsigned, "Things that Cannot be Done," *Household Words,* October 8, 1853.

37. E. P. Thompson, *Customs in Common: Studies in Traditional Popular Culture,* 74.

38. For a more extended description of the "enactment, combined with various circumstances which made the real 'news'-papers expensive luxuries" and the consequent rise of "periodicals devoted to dealing with affairs in a humourous fashion [that] did not rank with news journals and so, avoiding taxation, could be sold at a price below that which had to be demanded for taxed papers" see Jerrold, *Douglas Jerrold,* 4.

39. See Jerrold, *Douglas Jerrold,* 8.

40. Quoted in Ben Wilson, *The Laughter of Triumph: William Hone and the Fight for Free Press,* 23.

41. Quoted in James Sambrook, *William Cobbett,* 107–8.

42. Raymond Williams, "Notes on English Prose," in *Writing in Society,* 89.

43. See Bourdieu, *Symbolic Power,* 85.

44. Sidmouth quoted in McCalman, *Radical Underworld,* 176.

45. Jonathan Bate, *Shakespearean Constitutions: Politics, Theatre, Criticism, 1730–1830,* 102.

46. Thompson, *Making of the English Working Class,* 810.

47. William Hone, *The Every-Day Book; or, Everlasting Calendar of Popular Amusements Sports, Past times, Ceremonies, Manners, Customs and Events,* vol. 2, 130.

48. On Romantic theories of art see W. T. J. Mitchell, *Picture Theory,* esp. 116–20

49. Gallagher and Greenblatt, *Practicing New Historicism,* 169.

50. Hone, *The Every-Day Book,* 130

51. Alex Woloch, *The One vs. the Many: Minor Characters and the Space of the Protagonist in the Novel,* 19, 144, 149, 150.

52. Charles Dickens, *Sketches by Boz* (Oxford: Oxford University Press, 1997), 152. All subsequent references to *Sketches by Boz* are to this edition, and page numbers appear parenthetically in the text following quotations from it.

53. Quoted in Wilson, *Laughter of Triumph*, 340.
54. On the "schemata" see E. H. Gombrich, *Art and Illusion: A Study in the Psychology of Pictorial Representation*.
55. Norman Bryson, *Vision and Painting: The Logic of the Gaze*. Bryson uses these phrases in his critical engagement with Gombrich's ideal of the "schemata."
56. Quoted in Ledger, *Dickens*, 49.
57. See Baudelaire, *Selected Writings on Art*, esp. 231.
58. E. H. Gombrich, *Meditations on Hobby Horse and Other Essays on the Theory of Art*, 122.
59. Epstein, *Radical Expression*, 71.
60. Walter Jerrold, *The Essays of Douglas Jerrold*, 156, 159.

Chapter 2

1. William Makepeace Thackeray, "Going to See a Man Hanged," in *A Shabby Genteel Story and Other Writings*, 114.
2. William Makepeace Thackeray, *Vanity Fair* (London: Wordsworth Classics, 1980), 483. All subsequent references to *Vanity Fair* are to this edition, and page numbers appear parenthetically in the text following quotations from it.
3. On the way Paine uses the present tense and the pronoun "we" in order to constitute his readers into a community of participants, see Smith, *Politics of Language*, esp. 53–54. On Cobbett's habitual use of the language of "us" and "them," see Thompson, *Making of the English Working Class*, esp. 820–24, where Thompson makes brilliant stylistic distinctions between the writing of Hazlitt and that of Cobbett.
4. "This typical (generic) expression can be regarded as the word's 'stylistic aura,' but this aura belongs not to the word of the language as such but to that genre in which the given word usually functions. It is an echo of the generic whole that resounds in the word." See M. M. Bakhtin, "The Problem of Speech Genres," in *Speech Genres*, 87–88.
5. See Jürgen Habermas, *The Structural Transformation: An Inquiry into a Category of Bourgeois Society*, trans. Thomas Burger, esp. 61–66.
6. Gilmartin, *Print Politics*, pp. 28–29.
7. Unsigned, "Journalism," *Fraser's Magazine* 34 (December 1846): 632.
8. Smith, *Politics of Language*, 155.
9. William Makepeace Thackeray, *The Newcomes*, vol. 2 (London: J. M. Dent, 1962), 306. All subsequent references to *The Newcomes* are to this edition, and page numbers appear parenthetically in the text following quotations from it.
10. As Trey Philpotts has shown, variations of "How not do it" circulated in many forms of writing, not all of which were satiric or radical. For example, Carlyle in *Past and Present* refers to the "Donothingism" of "the non working aristocracy" and he exhorts them to "Descend, O do nothing Pomp; quit thy down cushion." But Carlyle's style suggests a social location very different from that of Dickens: it suggests the isolation of the prophetic intellectual rather than embedding him among the excluded majority. See Trey Philpotts, *The Companion to Little Dorrit*, 134. Michael Cotsell suggests an extremely interesting contemporary source for Dickens's satire on the Circumlocution Office. This is a satiric piece by Charles Buller entitled "Mr. Mothercountry of the Colonial Office" which appeared in 1840 and was reprinted in 1849. Mr. Mothercountry is modeled on Sir James Stephen, who served as the prototype for Tite Barnacle as well, and he has perfected "a complete art of irrelevant and apparently purposeless correspondence, by which he

manages to spin out an affair until it . . . evaporates into something absolutely insignificant." See Michael Cotsell, "The Stephen Family and Dickens's Circumlocution Office Satire," *Dickens Quarterly* 3, no. 4 (1986): 176–77.

11. Mill's words are quoted in Alan Ryan, "Utilitarianism and the Bureaucracy," in *Studies in the Growth of Nineteenth-Century Government*, ed. Gillian Sutherland, 53.

12. See endnote 3, but also Philpotts, *Companion*, 141–44.

13. Richard Terdiman, *Discourse/Counter Discourse: The Theory and Practice of Symbolic Resistance in Nineteenth Century France*, 152, 153. See also Jon Klancher's description of radical rewriting as "a stormy representation of one social discourse by another" in *The Making of English Reading Audiences, 1790–1832*, 27.

14. See Smith, *Politics of Language*, esp. 242–50. Cobbett's phrase is from the *Political Register*, November 29, 1817.

15. On the emergence of the upper-class "salon" as a major "chronotope" in the nineteenth-century European novel, see Bakhtin, *Dialogical Imagination*, esp. 246–47.

16. Leo Tolstoy, *War and Peace*, vol. 1, trans. Rosemary Edmonds, 16.

17. As is obvious, I am drawing on Barthes's famous analysis of the party thrown at the *de Lanty* mansion. See Roland Barthes, *S/Z*, trans. Richard Miller, esp. 22–23.

18. Cobbett, *Political Register*, January 10, 1807.

19. Smith, *Politics of Language*, vii.

20. Bourdieu, *Symbolic Power*, 66.

21. Ibid.

22. Woloch, *One vs. Many*, 53.

23. See, for example, Walter Bagehot who claimed that while describing the aristocracy, Thackeray's "thoughts were never long away from the close proximate scene," in Walter Bagehot, "Sterne and Thackeray," *National Review* 18 (April 1864): 524.

24. David Mason, "Pendennis and Copperfield: Thackeray and Dickens," in Tillotson and Hawes, *Thackeray: Critical Heritage*, 116.

25. Woloch, *One vs. Many*, 31.

26. Ibid., 194, 196, 197.

27. Charles Dickens, *Great Expectations* (Harmondsworth: Penguin, 1980), 245. All subsequent references to *Great Expectations* are to this edition, and page numbers appear parenthetically in the text following quotations from it.

28. See Wood, 182.

29. Terdiman, *Discourse/Counter Discourse*, 196.

30. See Baudelaire, "Some Foreign Caricaturists."

31. William Makepeace Thackeray, "History of the Next French Revolution," in *Ballads and Contributions to Punch*, 322, 328.

32. D. A. Miller, *The Novel and the Police*, 97.

33. Walter Bagehot, *The English Constitution*, esp. 80–82.

34. Bourdieu, *Symbolic Power*, 15.

35. Charles Dickens, *Bleak House* (London: Collins, 1953), 320, 243, 41, 320. All subsequent references to *Bleak House* are to this edition, and page numbers appear parenthetically in the text following quotations from it.

36. As Henry Maine wrote, "It does not seem to me a fantastic assertion that the ideas of one of the great novelists of the last generation may be traced to Bentham." Humphrey House, who quotes this in what was in 1941 a major revisionary book on Dickens, demonstrates the strong presence of ideas from philosophical radicalism in the content of Dickens's criticism of the state's institutions. See House, *Dickens World*, esp. 36–40.

37. Ray, *Letters*, vol. 2, 772.

38. Thus, the very cover illustration for the monthly parts of *Little Dorrit* featured a

political cartoon that stretched across the top and depicted Britannia in a bath chair, drawn by a set of effete idiots, and followed by a retinue of fools and toadies. This caricatural fragment in conjunction with the extended written text that follows it may be said to implicitly acknowledge the debt that *Little Dorrit* owed to the radical publicists.

39. Unsigned, "The Caricatures of HB," *London and Westminster Review* 55 (1838), 272.

40. In itself, Krook's death cannot be thought of as a serious social intervention. More specifically, it could be argued that the sensational and fantastic nature of Krook's death seriously compromises its effectiveness as an intervention for reform by sublimating whatever popular discontentment there might actually have existed about Chancery practice—providing the means of its release rather than channeling it for direct action. In an influential essay Jonathan Arac has, indeed, asserted that although Krook is "totally consumed he takes nothing with him." What Arac does not take into account is that Krook's death becomes an occasion for the author to step out of the domain of fiction and directly address his audience about the mess that incompetent administrators, arbitrarily catapulted to positions of power, make of England's key institutions. See Jonathan Arac, "Narrative Form and Social Sense in *Bleak House* and *The French Revolution*," *Nineteenth Century Fiction* 32, no. 1 (1977): 69.

41. Julia Kristeva, *Desire in Language: A Semiotic Approach to Literature and Art*, trans. Thomas Gora, Alice Jardine, and Leon Roudiez, 46, 45.

42. Ledger, *Dickens*, 41.

43. Wilson, *Laughter of Triumph*, 240. For an extended description of Hone's trial, see also 223–59.

44. Ibid., 232, 237.

45. Robert Southey, *Essays Moral and Political*, vol. 1, 120–21.

46. See Chittick, *Dickens and the 1930s*.

47. Edwin Whipple, "Hard Times," *Atlantic Monthly* 39 (March 1877): 355.

48. Walter Bagehot, "Charles Dickens," *National Review* 7 (October 1858): 458.

49. Peter Bailey, "'A Mingled Mass of Perfectly Legitimate Pleasures': The Victorian Middle Class and the Problem of Leisure," *Victorian Studies* 21 (Autumn 1977): 13.

50. In his *Life of Sir James Fitzjames Stephen*, Leslie Stephen suggested a personal angle that motivated Fitzjames Stephen's attacks on Dickens's later novels: "The attack on the 'Circumlocution Office' was, I doubt not, especially offensive because 'Barnacle Tite' and the effete aristocrats who are satirized in 'Little Dorrit,' stood for Sir James Stephen and his friends." This personal angle only throws into sharper focus the political and cultural threat that Dickens's fiction posed to social circles inhabited by the Stephens. The passage from Leslie Stephen is quoted in Cotsell, "The Stephen Family."

51. James Fitzjames Stephen, "The Relation of Novels to Life," in *Victorian Criticism of the Novel*, ed. Edwin Eigner and George J. Worth, 94, and James Fitzjames Stephen, "Mr. Dickens as Politician," *Saturday Review* 3 (January 1857): 8.

52. From an unsigned review of the Library edition of Dickens's *Works*, which Philip Collins extracts and attributes "almost certainly" to Stephen. See Collins, *Dickens: Critical Heritage*, 385.

53. On the use that Hone made of Sterne's character Dr. Slop, in his prolonged and innovative engagement with the influential conservative journalist, Dr. John Stoddart, see Wilson, *Laughter of Triumph*, esp. 136–42.

54. Thus, Stephen sought to pin the novel down to the subjectivity of an individual destiny and to those "ordinary domestic relations" within which such subjectivity could be constituted. In these circumstances it is not surprising that Stephen should argue that "using the novel to ventilate opinions" was to step outside its "legitimate province." These

and similar ideas, scattered through the many articles on the novel that Stephen published in the *Saturday* and the *Edinburgh Review*s between 1855 and 1858, suggest that the emphasis on "character" and on familiar domestic experiences that were to become key components of what was later to be designated the "realistic" aesthetic, developed in the course of the polemics that the quarterlies spearheaded against not only "idealism" and "sensationalism," but also against the radical heritage of the popular Dickensian novel. The phrases quoted from Stephen appear in "Relation of Novels," 95, "License of Modern Novelists," 125, and "Relation of Novels," 113.

55. Unsigned, "Modern Novelists," 416.

Chapter 3

1. Jonathan Crary, *Techniques of the Observer: On Vision and Modernity in the Nineteenth Century*, 39.
2. John Wright, *Mornings at Bow Street*, 49, 51.
3. Shelly Rice, *Parisian Views*, 18.
4. Michel de Certeau, *The Practice of Everyday Life*, 117.
5. See Shesgreen, "Headnote;" William Gaunt, *The World of William Hogarth*, 14–24, 61–64; F. D. Klingender, *Hogarth and English Caricature*, iii–viii; Robert S. Cowley, *Marriage-A-La-Mode: A Review of Hogarth's Narrative Art*, 4–5.
6. On the reception and the continuing popularity of *Industry and Idleness*, see Paulson, *Hogarth*, 290–91.
7. The political ramifications of the crowd have, of course, been extensively and insightfully discussed. What I am looking at is the significance of the crowd in popular representations of the city. On the politics of the "Tyburn crowd" see Peter Linebaugh, *The London Hanged: Crime and Civil Society in the Eighteenth Century*.
8. Donald J. Gray, "Views and Sketches of London in the Nineteenth Century," in *Victorian Artists and the City: A Collection of Essays*, ed. Ira Bruce Nadel and F. S. Schwarzbach, 43.
9. In one of his early works on Hogarth, Ronald Paulson locates the source of this paradox in the artist's subjectivity. Hogarth, Paulson argues, "gave Goodchild his successful career (and, originally, his own name)—and Idle his face and probably his secret proclivities." See Ronald Paulson, *Popular and Polite Art in the Age of Hogarth and Fielding*, 21.
10. In the second volume of his biography of Hogarth Paulson demonstrates that the tension between Hogarth's fascination with the life on the streets and his moral condemnation of it was very much in evidence in the reception of *Industry and Idleness* as well. See Paulson, *Hogarth*, 290–91.
11. Linebaugh, *London Hanged*, 89, 90. See also Michel Foucault, *Discipline and Punish: The Birth of the Prison*, esp. 65–67.
12. De Certeau, *Practice of Everyday Life*, 96.
13. David Henkin, *City Reading: Written Words and Public Spaces in Antebellum New York*, 12. As will be quickly evident to anyone who has read Henkin's fine book, I am here merely redeploying a distinction that he first made.
14. Ibid., 1.
15. Ibid., 102.
16. See Meisel, *Realizations*, esp. 24–25, 116–22, 268–72.
17. Quoted in Walter Benjamin, *Charles Baudelaire: A Lyric Poet in the Era of High Capitalism*, 47.

18. John Marriott, introduction to *Unknown London: Early Modernist Visions of the Metropolis, 1815–45*, vol. 1, xvii.
19. Ibid., xxiii.
20. W. T. Moncrieff, *Tom and Jerry Or, Life in London: An Operatic Extravaganza*, in Marriott, *Unknown London*, vol. 1, 259.
21. Cf. "technology has subjected the human sensorium to a complex kind of training," Walter Benjamin, quoted in Crary, *Techniques of the Observer*, 112.
22. Stephan Oettermann, *The Panorama: History of a Mass Medium*, 134.
23. Quoted in ibid., 137.
24. Gillen D'Arcy Wood, *The Shock of the Real: Romanticism and Visual Culture, 1760–1860*, 100.
25. See ibid., 100–3, 132–36.
26. Oettermann, *Panorama*, 137.
27. Crary, *Techniques of the Observer*, 10.
28. George Cruikshank, *The Worship of Bacchus. A Critique by John Stewart; a Descriptive Lecture by George Cruikshank; and Opinions of the Press*, 10, 12.
29. Roland Barthes, "Semiology and Urbanism," in *The Semiotic Challenge*, 195.
30. Sharon Marcus, *Apartment Stories: City and Home in Nineteenth-Century Paris and London*, 104.
31. Charles Dickens, "The Last Words of the Old Year," *Household Words*, January 4, 1851.
32. Henry Mayhew and J. Binny, *Criminal Prisons of London*, 8.
33. Graham Storey and K. J. Fielding, *The Letters of Charles Dickens. Volume 5: 1847–49*, 19.
34. Nancy West, "Fantasy, Photography and the Marketplace: Oliver Wendell Holmes and the Stereoscope," *Nineteenth Century Contexts* 19, no. 3 (1996): 244.
35. Quoted in ibid., 251.
36. Crary, *Techniques of the Observer*, 128.
37. Anonymous, "Photography," *Household Words*, October 10, 1857: 352.
38. Crary, *Techniques of the Observer*, 125.
39. Marcus, *Apartment Stories*, 37. As Kate Flint has shown, Dickens was familiar with the figure of Asmodeus. See Kate Flint, *Dickens*, 71.
40. See Deborah Epstein Nord, *Walking the Victorian Streets: Women, Representation and the City*, 65–67.
41. Audrey Jaffe, *Vanishing Points: Dickens, Narrative, and the Subject of Omniscience*, 26.
42. Ibid., 26.
43. De Certeau, *Practice of Everyday Life*, 97.
44. Ibid., 115. As de Certeau argues, "Every story is a travel story—a spatial *practice*."
45. Ibid., 115.
46. William Makepeace Thackeray, "De Juventute," *The Roundabout Papers*, 434.
47. William Makepeace Thackeray, "Travels in London," in *Miscellaneous Papers*, 181.

Chapter 4

1. See, for example, D. A. Miller, "Discipline in Different Voices: Bureaucracy, Police, Family, and *Bleak House*," in *Novel and Police*, 33–58, and Nord, *Walking the Victorian Streets*, esp. 99–111.

2. Quoted in Benjamin, *Baudelaire*, 69.
3. Gray, "Views and Sketches," 43.
4. See Geoffrey Best, *Mid-Victorian Britain, 1815-1875*; Gareth Stedman Jones, *Outcast London: A Study of the Relationship between the Classes in Victorian England*; Anthony Wohl, *The Eternal Slum: Housing and Social Policy in Victorian London*; and Gertrude Himmelfarb, *The Idea of Poverty: England in the Early Industrial Age*.
5. Quoted in John Forster, *The Life of Charles Dickens*, 525-26. According to the editors of the Pilgrim edition of Dickens's *Letters*, a large part of what Forster passes off as a letter to him was, in fact, a review of "The Drunkard's Children: A Sequel to the Bottle" that Dickens wrote for the *Examiner* (July 8, 1848). See Storey and Fielding, *Letters of Charles Dickens*, vol. 5, 156.
6. On panoramas, see Meisel, *Realizations*; Crary, *Techniques of the Observer*, esp. 112-13; Rice, *Parisian Views*; Oettermann, *Panorama*.
7. Charles Dickens, "The American Panorama," *Examiner*, December 16, 1848: 806.
8. For the reception of Mayhew's *London Labour*, see Himmelfarb, *Idea of Poverty*, esp. 307-62.
9. Stephen, "License of Modern Novelists," 125.
10. Raymond Williams, *The Country and the City*, 191.
11. Bagehot, "Charles Dickens,"
12. Terdiman, *Discourse/Counter Discourse*, 122, 121.
13. Ibid., 125.
14. See Benjamin, *Baudelaire*, esp. 36-37.
15. See also Jean Sudrann's extremely interesting, "'The Philosopher's Property': Thackeray and the Use of Time," *Victorian Studies* 10, no. 10 (1967): 374.
16. M. M. Bakhtin, *Problems of Dostoyevsky's Poetics*, ed. and trans. Caryl Emerson, 169.
17. An important exception is Michael Denning, *Mechanic Accents: Dime Novels and Working Class Culture in America*. As will become quickly evident, Denning's work has influenced my own reading of Lady Dedlock.
18. Henry James, "Our Mutual Friend," *The Nation*, December 21, 1865: 787.
19. The privileging of the psychologically authentic character had begun in the pages of the great Victorian quarterlies themselves and it was Lewes himself who, in an article devoted significantly to Thackeray, made the distinction that was to remain normative at least for the next hundred and twenty years, between artists who drew their characters from "Life" and those who found their inspiration in "the phantasmagoria of the stage and circulating library." About twenty years later, the young Henry James was articulating the assumptions of what was now a fairly well-developed critical tradition when, while launching a full-blown realistic critique against Dickens, he repeated Lewes's distinction in his own terms. For James, since what Dickens offered was not human beings at all but "a community of eccentrics," it would be appropriate to speak of him as a writer who produced not characters, but "simply figures." The phrases from Lewes's writing appear in G. H. Lewes, "Recent Novels: French and English," *Fraser's Magazine* 36 (December 1847): 687, and G. H. Lewes, Untitled, *Morning Chronicle*, March 6, 1848: 440.
20. Woloch, *One vs. Many*, 13.
21. Ibid., 150.
22. Ibid., 151.
23. G. H. Lewes, "Realism in Art: Recent German Fiction," *Westminster Review* 70 (October 1858): 493.
24. Quoted in Blanchard Jerrold, *The Life of George Cruikshank in Two Epochs*, 39.
25. *Letters*, vol. 4, 612-13.

26. Quoted in J. C. Reid, *Bucks and Bruisers: Pierce and Regency England*, 210.
27. M. M. Bakhtin, *Rabelais and His World*, trans. Helene Iswolsky, 321, and *Dostoyevsky's Poetics*, 104.
28. On the nineteenth-century market for portraits of beautiful, titled women, see Curtis, "Dickens in the Visual Market," 232–35.
29. Benjamin, "The Work of Art," 221.
30. Unsigned, "Our Novels: The Sensation School," *Temple Bar* 29 (April 1870): 421.
31. H. L. Mansel, "Sensation Novels," *Quarterly Review* 114 (April 1863): 505–6; quoted in Winifred Hughes, *The Maniac in the Cellar*, 41; Charles Knight, *Passages of a Working Life*, vol. 3, 180.
32. Anonymous, "Sensation Novelists: Miss Braddon," *North British Review* 44 (September 1865).
33. See Christopher Hamlin, *Public Health and Social Justice in the Age of Chadwick*, 22–24.
34. Quoted in Royston Lambert, *Sir John Simon and English Social Administration*, 135.
35. Quoted in Hamlin, *Public Health and Social Justice*, 70.
36. *Times*, September 5, 1848, and quoted in Asa Briggs, "Cholera and Society in the Nineteenth Century," *Past and Present* 19 (April 1961): 84.
37. Quoted in Deborah Epstein Nord, "The City as Theatre: From Georgian to Early Victorian London," *Victorian Studies* 31, no. 2 (1988): 102.
38. Lauren M. E. Goodlad, *Victorian Literature and the Victorian State: Character and Governance in a Liberal Society*, 87.
39. See, for example, Trevor Blount, "The Graveyard Satire of *Bleak House*," *Review of English Studies* 14, no. 56 (1963): 370–79. On the tussle between the General Board of Health (under Chadwick and Shaftsbury) and the Treasury Office over the Internments Act, see Philpotts, *Companion to Little Dorrit*, 135.
40. *Times*, September 18, 1848, and "Report from the Select Committee of Improvement of Health of Towns: On the Effect of Internments of Bodies in Towns," *Parliamentary Papers* (1842), 160–62.
41. Matthew Brown, *Views and Opinions*, 280.

Chapter 5

1. De Certeau, *Practice of Everyday Life*, 103.
2. Gallagher and Greenblatt, *Practicing New Historicism*, 185.
3. On the proliferation of self-improvement literature after the late 1840s, see Kenneth Fielden, "Samuel Smiles and Self Help," *Victorian Studies* 12, no. 2 (1968): 156–77, and J. F. C. Harrison, "The Victorian Gospel of Success," *Victorian Studies* 1, no. 2 (1957): 155–64.
4. Quoted in Best, *Mid-Victorian Britain*, 233.
5. For detailed accounts of this celebratory discourse as it unfolded during the late 1850s and '60s, see Fielden, "Samuel Smiles," and Harrison, "Victorian Gospel."
6. On the conclusion of *John Halifax Gentleman*, see Patrick Brantlinger, *The Spirit of Reform: British Literature and Politics, 1832–67*, 123.
7. I am aware, of course, that the articulation of social difference in *Great Expectations*—as in *Little Dorrit*—is ultimately contained within the work-oriented, self-improving ideology of the entrepreneurial middle class. This is, moreover, consistent with the long tradition of scholarship that, following the seminal work of Humphrey House, embeds the

"radicalism" that informs Dickens's fiction as a whole to the ideological universe of the middle class. Thus the story of Pip's improvement—his recognition of gentlemanliness as both emotionally impoverishing and economically parasitic—is consistent with the ideological impulse that produced a whole line of Dickensian heroes: David Copperfield, George Rouncewell, Daniel Doyce. However, like *Little Dorrit,* whose political orientation unfolds across two registers—on the one hand, as the entrepreneurial Daniel Doyce's deeply critical but patient and reasonable response to the workings of an aristocracy-dominated bureaucracy and, on the other, as the more strident, fundamentally oppositional language of radicalism reactivated in the authorial comments on the Circumlocution Office—*Great Expectations* sustains a radical articulation of class divisions even as it seeks, through a range of discursive maneuvers, to reconcile Pip to Joe and to complete the story of the former's growth into a humane, hardworking, productive, and reasonable member of official society. Joe may help to facilitate Pip's rehabilitation but his function, through most of the novel, is to expose the limits of Pip's gentlemanly personality. For an account of *Great Expectations* along the lines outlined above see Robin Gilmour, *The Idea of the Gentleman in the Victorian Novel*; on *Little Dorrit* see William Myers "The Radicalism of *Little Dorrit*" in *Literature and Politics in the Nineteenth Century,* ed. John Lucas, pp. 75–105.

8. As Gallagher puts it, "Pip's metropolitan environment not only fails to resemble the realized societies of Balzac's Paris or Eliot's Middlemarch, but also bears little likeness to Dickens's normal London. Sparsely populated, with a higher-than-usual proportion of eccentrics, this is a milieu of the margins . . . ." See Gallagher and Greenblatt, *Practicing New Historicism,* 180.

9. De Certeau, *Practice of Everyday Life,* 103.

10. Ibid., 103.

11. Charles Dickens, "Night Walks" (1860), in *Selected Journalism,* 75.

12. Gallagher and Greenblatt, *Practicing New Historicism,* 178.

13. On the chronotope, see Bakhtin, *Dialogical Imagination,* 84.

14. Dickens, "Night Walks," 74.

15. De Certeau, *Practice of Everyday Life,* 103.

16. Ibid., 103.

17. On the significance of the *mésalliance* as an expressive resource within the novel, see Bakhtin, *Problems of Dostoyevsky's Poetics,* esp. 123–24.

18. As James Wheatly suggests, "Thackeray is at his best making this period of adjustment not only dramatically believable but very nearly the proper response to the life presented in the novel. A brief infatuation with the lower-class Fanny is presented as being in part an unconscious revulsion from so passionless a life . . . ." See James H. Wheatly, *Patterns in Thackeray's Fiction,* 111. See also Anna Monsarrat, *An Uneasy Victorian: Thackeray the Man,* 233.

19. Barthes, *S/Z,* 22.

20. See Philip Collins, *Dickens and Crime*; Ankhi Mukherjee, "Missed Encounters: Repetition, Rewriting, and Contemporary Returns to Charles Dickens's Great Expectations," *Contemporary Literature* 46, no. 1 (2005): 108–33.

21. Jeremy Tambling, *Dickens, Violence and Society: Dreams of the Scaffold,* 31.

22. In an essay entitled significantly "Sexuality and Solitude" where he declares his intention to move from his study of "asylums, prisons and so on" to that of power relations as they unfold in the domain of subjectivity, Foucault is explicit in linking "technologies of the self" to sexuality. See Michel Foucault, in *On Signs: A Semiotic Reader,* ed. Marshall Blonsky, 367.

23. De Certeau, *Practice of Everyday Life,* 63.

24. Robert Hughes, *The Filial Shore,* 1, 2, 385.

25. Michel Foucault, *Discipline and Punish*, 272. As will be quickly evident, I have drawn heavily on Foucault's work for my analysis of criminality in *Great Expectations*.

Chapter 6

1. Crary, *Techniques of the Observer*, 10.
2. Charles Dickens, *Our Mutual Friend* (Hertfordshire: Wordsworth Editions, 1997), 542. All subsequent references to *Our Mutual Friend* are to this edition, and page numbers appear parenthetically in the text following quotations from it.
3. See Catherine Gallagher, *The Body Economic: Life, Death and Sensation in Political Economy and the Victorian Novel*, esp. 86–118.
4. See Pam Morris, *Imagining Inclusive Society in Nineteenth Century Novels: The Code of Sincerity in the Public Sphere*, 202.
5. Gallagher, *Body Economic*, 96.
6. See Bakhtin, *Dialogical Imagination*, esp. 89–91.
7. Morris, *Imagining Inclusive Society*, 209, 201.
8. For an important discussion on Harmon's attempt to "recover his identity by reconstructing sequence" and the "problem of realism," see Elizabeth Deeds Ermarth, *Realism and Consensus in the English Novel: Time, Space and Narrative*, esp. 198–99.
9. Norbert Elias, *State Formation and Civilization*, trans. Edmund Jephcott, 297, 312.
10. Rosemarie Bodenheimer, "Dickens Fascinated," *Victorian Studies* 48, no. 2 (2006): 274.
11. De Certeau, *Practice of Everyday Life*, 103.
12. Stephen, "License of Modern Novelists," 125, and quoted in Forster, *Life*, 123.
13. Unsigned, "The Sensational Williams," *All The Year Round*, February 13, 1864.
14. Unsigned, "The Progress of Fiction," *Westminster Review* 60 (October 1853).
15. For a fuller discussion see my introduction.
16. Jaffe, *Vanishing Points*, 26, 27.

BIBLIOGRAPHY

Ackroyd, Peter. *Dickens*. London: Minerva, 1990.
Altick, Richard. *The Presence of the Present: Topics of the Day in the Victorian Novel*. Columbus: The Ohio State University Press, 1991.
———. *Punch: The Lively Youth of a British Institution, 1841–51*. Columbus: The Ohio State University Press, 1997.
Anonymous. "Photography." *Household Words*, October 10, 1857.
Anonymous. "The Progress of Fiction." *Westminster Review* 60 (October 1853).
Anonymous. "Sensation Novelists: Miss Braddon." *North British Review* 44 (September 1865): 180–204.
Arac, Jonathan. "Narrative Form and Social Sense in *Bleak House* and *The French Revolution*." *Nineteenth Century Fiction* 32, no. 1 (1977): 54–72.
Bagehot, Walter. "Charles Dickens." *National Review* 7 (October 1858): 458–86.
———. *The English Constitution*. Glasgow: Fontana, 1978.
———. "Sterne and Thackeray." *National Review* 18 (April 1864).
Bailey, Peter. "'A Mingled Mass of Perfectly Legitimate Pleasures': The Victorian Middle Class and the Problem of Leisure." *Victorian Studies* 21 (Autumn 1977): 7–28.
Bakhtin, M. M. "Forms of Time and Chronotope in the Novel." In *The Dialogical Imagination*, translated by Michael Holquist, edited by Caryl Emerson and Michael Holquist, 84–259. Austin: University of Texas Press, 1981.
———. "The Problem of Speech Genres." In *Speech Genres and Other Late Essays*, translated by Vern W. McGee, edited by Caryl Emerson and Michael Holquist, 60–102. Austin: University of Texas Press, 1986.
———. *Problems of Dostoyevsky's Poetics*. Edited and translated by Caryl Emerson. Manchester: Manchester University Press, 1984.
———. *Rabelais and His World*. Translated by Helene Iswolsky. Bloomington: Indiana University Press, 1984.
———. *Speech Genres and Other Late Essays*. Translated by Vern W. McGee. Edited by Caryl Emerson and Michael Holquist. Austin: University of Texas Press, 1986.

Barthes, Roland. "Semiology and Urbanism." In *The Semiotic Challenge*, 155–57. Oxford: Basil Blackwell, 1988.
———. *S/Z*. Translated by Richard Miller. New York: Wang and Hill, 1974.
Bate, Jonathan. *Shakespearean Constitutions: Politics, Theatre, Criticism, 1730–1830*. Oxford: Clarendon Press, 1989.
Baudelaire, Charles. "Some Foreign Caricaturists." In *Selected Writings on Art and Artists*, translated by E. P. Charvet. Cambridge: Cambridge University Press, 1972.
Benjamin, Walter. *Charles Baudelaire: A Lyric Poet in the Era of High Capitalism*. London: Verso, 1973.
———. "The Work of Art in the Age of Mechanical Reproduction." In *Illuminations*, translated by Harry Zohn, edited by Hannah Arendt, 217–51. New York: Schocken Books, 1968.
Best, Geoffrey. *Mid-Victorian Britain, 1815–1875*. London: Weidenfield and Nicolson, 1971.
Blount, Trevor. "The Graveyard Satire of *Bleak House*." *Review of English Studies* 14, no. 56 (1963): 370–79.
Bodenheimer, Rosemarie. "Dickens Fascinated." *Victorian Studies* 48, no. 2 (2006): 268–76.
Bourdieu, Pierre. *Language and Symbolic Power*. Translated by Raymond and Mathew Adamson. Cambridge: Polity Press, 1991.
Brantlinger, Patrick. *The Spirit of Reform: British Literature and Politics, 1832–67*. Cambridge, MA: Harvard University Press, 1977.
Briggs, Asa. "Cholera and Society in the Nineteenth Century." *Past and Present* 19 (April 1961): 76–96.
Brown, Matthew. *Views and Opinions*. London: Strahan, 1866.
Bryson, Norman. *Vision and Painting: The Logic of the Gaze*. London: Palgrave, 1984.
Butt, John and Kathleen Tillotson. *Dickens at Work*. London: Methuen, 1957.
Chartier, Roger. "Texts, Printings, Readings." In *The New Cultural History*, edited by Lynn Hunt, 154–76. Berkeley: University of California Press, 1989.
Chittick, Kathryn. *Dickens and the 1830s*. Cambridge: Cambridge University Press, 1990.
Cobbett, William. "Untitled." *Political Register*, January 10, 1807.
———. "Untitled." *Political Register*, November 29, 1817.
Collins, Philip. *Dickens and Crime*. London: St. Martin's Press, 1994.
———, ed. *Dickens: The Critical Heritage*. London: Routledge 1986.
Cotsell, Michael. "The Stephen Family and Dickens's Circumlocution Office Satire." *Dickens Quarterly* 3, no. 4 (1986): 175–78.
Cowley, Robert S. *Marriage-A-La-Mode: A Review of Hogarth's Narrative Art*. Manchester: Manchester University Press, 1984.
Crary, Jonathan. *Techniques of the Observer: On Vision and Modernity in the Nineteenth Century*. Cambridge, Massachusetts: MIT Press, 1999.
Cruikshank, George. *The Worship of Bacchus. A Critique by John Stewart; a Descriptive Lecture by George Cruikshank; and Opinions of the Press*. London: William Tweedie and Son, 1862.
Curtis, Gerard. "Dickens in the Visual Market." In *Literature in the Marketplace: Nineteenth-Century British Publishing and Reading Practices*, edited by John O. Jordon and Robert L. Patten, 213–50. Cambridge: Cambridge University Press, 1995.
De Certeau, Michel. *The Practice of Everyday Life*. Berkeley: University of California Press, 1988.
Denning, Michael. *Mechanic Accents: Dime Novels and Working Class Culture in America*. London: Verso, 1987.

Dickens, Charles. "The American Panorama." *Examiner*, December 16, 1848.
——. *Bleak House*. London: Collins, 1953. Originally published in 1853 by Bradbury and Evans
——. *Great Expectations*. Harmondsworth: Penguin, 1980. Originally published in 1861 by Chapman and Hall
——. "The Last Words of the Old Year." *Household Words*, January 4, 1851: 337–39.
——. *Little Dorrit*. Harmondsworth: Penguin, 1976. Originally published in 1857 by Bradbury and Evans
——. "Night Walks." In *Selected Journalism*, 73–81. London: Penguin, 1990. Originally published in *The Uncommercial Traveller* in 1860 by Chapman and Hall
——. *Our Mutual Friend*. Hertfordshire: Wordsworth Classics, 1997. Originally published in 1865 by Chapman and Hall
——. Review of "The Drunkard's Children: A Sequel to the Bottle." *Examiner*, July 8, 1848.
——. *Sketches by Boz*. Oxford: Oxford University Press, 1997. Originally published in 1836 by Chapman and Hall
Egan, Pierce. *Life in London or, the Day and Night Scenes of Jerry Hawthorn Esq, and his Elegant Friend Corinthian Tom, Accompanied by Bob Logic, the Oxonian, in their Rambles and Sprees through the Metropolis*. London: Sherwood, Neely and Jones, 1822.
Elias, Norbert. *State Formation and Civilization*. Translated by Edmund Jephcott. Oxford: Basil Blackwell, 1982.
Epstein, James. *Radical Expression: Political Language, Ritual and Symbol in England, 1790–1850*. Oxford: Oxford University Press, 1994.
Ermarth, Elizabeth Deeds. *Realism and Consensus in the English Novel: Time, Space and Narrative*. Edinburgh: Edinburgh University Press, 1998.
Feltes, N. N. *Modes of Production of Victorian Novels*. Chicago: University of Chicago Press, 1986.
Fielden, Kenneth. "Samuel Smiles and Self Help." *Victorian Studies* 12, no. 2 (1968): 156–77.
Flint, Kate. *Dickens*. Brighton: Harvester Press, 1986.
Forster, John. *The Life of Charles Dickens*. London: Hazell, Watson and Viney Ltd., 1868.
Foucault, Michel. *Discipline and Punish: The Birth of the Prison*. London: Peregrine, 1978.
——."Sexuality and Solitude." In *On Signs: A Semiotic Reader*, edited by Marshall Blonsky, 363–65. Oxford: Basil Blackwell, 1985.
Gallagher, Catherine. *The Body Economic: Life, Death and Sensation in Political Economy and the Victorian Novel*. Princeton, NJ: Princeton University Press, 2006.
——. *Nobody's Story: The Vanishing Acts of Women Writers in the Marketplace, 1670–1820*. Berkeley: University of California Press, 1994.
—— and Stephen Greenblatt, *Practicing New Historicism*. Chicago: University of Chicago Press, 2000.
Gaunt, William. *The World of William Hogarth*. London: Jonathan Cape, 1978.
George, Dorothy. *English Political Caricature: A Study of Opinion and Propaganda*. Oxford: Oxford University Press, 1959.
Gilmour, Robin. *The Idea of the Gentleman in the Victorian Novel*. London: Allen and Unwin, 1981.
Gilmartin, Kevin. *Print Politics: The Press and Radical Opposition in Early Nineteenth-Century England*. Cambridge: Cambridge University Press, 1996.
Gombrich, E. H. *Art and Illusion: A Study in the Psychology of Pictorial Representation*. London: Phaidon Press, 1960.

———. *Meditations on Hobby Horse and Other Essays on the Theory of Art*. London: Phaidon Press, 1963.

Goodlad, Lauren M. E. *Victorian Literature and the Victorian State: Character and Governance in a Liberal Society*. Baltimore, MD, and London: Johns Hopkins University Press, 2003.

Gray, Donald J. "Views and Sketches of London in the Nineteenth Century." In *Victorian Artists and the City: A Collection of Essays*, edited by Ira Bruce Nadel and F. S. Schwarzbach, 43–59. New York: Pergamon Press, 1980.

Habermas, Jürgen. *The Structural Transformation of the Public Sphere: An Inquiry into a Category of Bourgeois Society*. Translated by Thomas Burger. Cambridge: Polity Press, 1992.

Hamley, E. B. "Remonstrance with Dickens." (1857) Reprinted in *Charles Dickens: The Critical Heritage*, edited by Philip Collins, Routledge, 1986.

Hamlin, Christopher. *Public Health and Social Justice in the Age of Chadwick*. Cambridge: Cambridge University Press, 1998.

Harrison, J. F. C. "The Victorian Gospel of Success." *Victorian Studies* 1, no. 2 (1957): 155–64.

Henkin, David. *City Reading: Written Words and Public Spaces in Antebellum New York*. New York: Columbia University Press, 1998.

Himmelfarb, Gertrude. *The Idea of Poverty: England in the Early Industrial Age*. London: Faber, 1984.

Holoch, George. "Consciousness and Society in *Little Dorrit*." *Victorian Studies* 21, no. 3 (1978): 335–51.

Hone, William. *The Every-Day Book; or, Everlasting Calendar of Popular Amusements Sports, Past times, Ceremonies, Manners, Customs and Events*. Vol. 2. London: Hunt and Clarke, 1827.

House, Humphrey. *The Dickens World*. Oxford: Oxford University Press, 1942.

Hughes, Robert. *The Fatal Shore*. London: Collins Harvill, 1987.

Hughes, Winifred. *The Maniac in the Cellar*. Princeton, NJ: Princeton University Press, 1980.

Jaffe, Audrey. *Vanishing Points: Dickens, Narrative, and the Subject of Omniscience*. Berkeley: University of California Press, 1991.

James, Henry. "Our Mutual Friend." *The Nation*, December 21, 1865: 786–87.

James, Louis. *Fiction for the Working Man, 1830–1850*. Harmondsworth: Penguin, 1963.

Jameson, Fredrick. *The Political Unconscious: Narrative as a Socially Symbolic Act*. London: Methuen, 1981.

Jerrold, Blanchard. *The Life of George Cruikshank in Two Epochs*. London: Chatto and Windus, 1898.

Jerrold, Walter. *Douglas Jerrold and "Punch."* London: Macmillan and Co., 1910.

———. *The Essays of Douglas Jerrold*. London: J. M. Dent, 1903.

Jones, Gareth Stedman. *Languages of Class: Studies in English Working Class History, 1832–1982*. Cambridge: Cambridge University Press, 1983.

———. *Outcast London: A Study of the Relationship between the Classes in Victorian England*. London: Oxford University Press, 1971.

Klancher, Jon. *The Making of English Reading Audiences, 1790–1832*. Madison: University of Wisconsin Press, 1987.

Klingender, F. D. *Hogarth and English Caricature*. London: Transatlantic Arts, 1944.

Knight, Charles. *Passages of a Working Life*. Vol. 3. London: Sampson Low, 1865.

Kristeva, Julia. *Desire in Language: A Semiotic Approach to Literature and Art*. Translated by Thomas Gora, Alice Jardine, and Leon Roudiez. Oxford: Basil Blackwell, 1981.

Lambert, Royston. *Sir John Simon and English Social Administration*. London: Macgibbon and Kee, 1965.
Ledger, Sally. *Dickens and the Popular Radical Imagination*. Cambridge: Cambridge University Press, 2007.
Lewes, G. H. "Realism in Art: Recent German Fiction." *Westminster Review* 70 (October 1858): 488–518.
———. "Recent Novels: French and English." *Fraser's Magazine* 36 (December 1847).
———. Untitled. *Morning Chronicle*, March 6, 1848.
Linebaugh, Peter. *The London Hanged: Crime and Civil Society in the Eighteenth Century*. London: Penguin, 1991.
Lister, Thomas Henry. "Review of *Sketches, Pickwick, Nickleby, and Oliver Twist*." (1838) Reprinted in *Charles Dickens: The Critical Heritage*.
Mansel, H. L. "Sensation Novels." *Quarterly Review* 114 (April 1863): 481–514.
Marcus, Sharon. *Apartment Stories: City and Home in Nineteenth-Century Paris and London*. Berkeley: University of California Press, 1999.
Marriott, John, ed. *Unknown London: Early Modernist Visions of the Metropolis, 1815–45*. Vol. 1. London: Pickering and Chatto, 2000.
Mason, David. "Pendennis and Copperfield: Thackeray and Dickens." (1851) Reprinted in *William Makepeace Thackeray: The Critical Heritage*, edited by Geoffrey Tillotson and Donald Hawes. London: Routledge, 1968.
Mayhew, Henry and J. Binny. *Criminal Prisons of London*. London: Frank Cass, 1968.
McCalman, Iain. *Radical Underworld: Prophets, Revolutionaries and Pornographers in London, 1795–1840*. Cambridge: Cambridge University Press, 1988.
Meisel, Martin. *Realizations: Narrative, Pictorial, and Theatrical Arts in Nineteenth-Century England*. Princeton, NJ: Princeton University Press, 1983.
Miller, Andrew. *Novels Behind Glass: Commodity Culture and Victorian Narrative*. Cambridge: Cambridge University Press, 1995.
Miller, D. A. "Discipline in Different Voices: Bureaucracy, Police, Family, and *Bleak House*." In *The Novel and the Police*, 59–89. Berkeley: University of California Press, 1988.
———. *The Novel and the Police*. Berkeley: University of California Press, 1988.
Mitchell, W. T. J. *Iconology: Image, Text, Ideology*. Chicago: Chicago University Press, 1986.
———. *Picture Theory*. Chicago: Chicago University Press, 1994.
Moncrieff, W. T. *Tom and Jerry Or, Life in London: An Operatic Extravaganza*. (1821) Reprinted in *Unknown London: Early Modernist Visions of the Metropolis, 1815–45*, vol. 1, edited by John Marriott, 255–80. London: Pickering and Chatto, 2000.
Monsarrat, Anna. *An Uneasy Victorian: Thackeray the Man*. London: Cassell, 1980.
Morris, Pam. *Imagining Inclusive Society in Nineteenth Century Novels: The Code of Sincerity in the Public Sphere*. Baltimore, MD: Johns Hopkins University Press, 2004.
Mukherjee, Ankhi. "Missed Encounters: Repetition, Rewriting, and Contemporary Returns to Charles Dickens's Great Expectations." *Contemporary Literature* 46, no. 1 (2005): 108–33.
Myers, William. "The Radicalism of *Little Dorrit*." In *Literature and Politics in the Nineteenth Century*, edited by John Lucas, 77–105. London: Methuen, 1970.
Nord, Deborah Epstein. "The City as Theatre: From Georgian to Early Victorian London." *Victorian Studies* 31, no. 2 (1988): 159–88.
———. *Walking the Victorian Streets: Women, Representation and the City*. Ithaca: Cornell University Press, 1995.
Oettermann, Stephan. *The Panorama: History of a Mass Medium*. New York: Zone Books, 1997.

Paine, Tom. *The Rights of Man.* (1791) Reprinted in *The Selected Works of Tom Paine,* edited by Howard Fast. New York: Random House, 1945.
Paulson, Ronald. *Hogarth: High Art and Low.* Piscataway, NJ: Rutgers University Press, 1992.
———. *Popular and Polite Art in the Age of Hogarth and Fielding.* London: University of Notre Dame Press, 1973.
Philpotts, Trey. *The Companion to Little Dorrit.* Robertsbridge: Helm Information, 2003.
Ray, Gordon N., ed. *The Letters and Private Papers of William Makepeace Thackeray.* Vol. 1. Oxford: Oxford University Press, 1945.
Reid, J. C. *Bucks and Bruisers: Pierce and Regency England.* London: Routledge and Kegan Paul, 1971.
"Report from the Select Committee of Improvement of Health of Towns: On the Effect of Internments of Bodies in Towns." *Parliamentary Papers* (1842).
Rice, Shelly. *Parisian Views.* Cambridge, MA: MIT Press, 1997.
Ryan, Alan. "Utilitarianism and the Bureaucracy." In *Studies in the Growth of Nineteenth-Century Government,* edited by Gillian Sutherland, 33–63. London: Routledge and Kegan Paul, 1972.
Sambrook, James. *William Cobbett.* London: Routledge, 1973.
Sen, Sambudha. "*Bleak House* and *Little Dorrit:* The Radical Heritage." *English Literary History* 65, no. 4 (1996): 945–80.
Shesgreen, Sean. "Headnote" to *The Harlot's Progress.* In *Engravings by Hogarth,* 18. New York: Dover Publications, 1973.
Shillingsburg, Peter L. *Pegasus in Harness: Victorian Publishing and W. M. Thackeray.* Charlottesville: University of Virginia Press, 1992.
Smith, Olivia. *The Politics of Language, 1791–1819.* Oxford: Oxford University Press, 1984.
Southey, Robert. *Essays Moral and Political.* Vol. 1. London: John Murray, 1832.
Spielman, M. H. *The History of "Punch."* New York: Cassell, 1895.
Stephen, James Fitzjames. "The License of Modern Novelists." *Edinburgh Review* 106 (July 1857)
———. "Mr. Dickens as Politician." *Saturday Review* 3 (January 1857).
———. "The Relation of Novels to Life." (1855) Reprinted in *Victorian Criticism of the Novel,* edited by Edwin Eigner and George J. Worth, 93–119. Cambridge: Cambridge University Press, 1985.
Stephen, Leslie. *Life of Sir James Fitzjames Stephen.* London: Smith Elder, 1895.
Storey, Graham and K. J. Fielding, eds. *The Letters of Charles Dickens. Volume 5: 1847–49.* Oxford: Clarendon Press, 1981.
Sudrann, Jean. "'The Philosopher's Property': Thackeray and the Use of Time." *Victorian Studies* 10, no. 10 (1967): 359–88.
Sutherland, J. A. *Victorian Novelists and Their Publishers.* Chicago: University of Chicago Press, 1976.
Tambling, Jeremy. *Dickens, Violence and Society: Dreams of the Scaffold.* New York: Macmillan, 1995.
Terdiman, Richard. *Discourse/Counter Discourse: The Theory and Practice of Symbolic Resistance in Nineteenth Century France.* Ithaca, NY: Cornell University Press, 1985.
Thackeray, William Makepeace. *Ballads and Miscellanies.* Vol. 13 of *The Oxford Thackeray.* Edited by George Saintsbury. London: Oxford University Press, 1908.
———. "De Juventute." In *The Roundabout Papers.* London: Smith Elder, 1907.
———. "George Cruikshank." In *Ballads, Critical Reviews, Tales.* London: Smith Elder, 1907.

———. "Going to See a Man Hanged." *Fraser's Magazine* 22 (1840). Reprinted in *A Shabby Genteel Story and Other Writings*, 110–26. London: J. M. Dent, 1993.

———. "Travels in London." In *Miscellaneous Papers*. London: Smith Elder, 1907.

———. *Vanity Fair*. Hertfordshire: Wordsworth Classics, 1980. Originally published by Bradbury and Evans in 1848.

Thompson, E. P. *Customs in Common: Studies in Traditional Popular Culture*. New York: New Press, 1993.

———. *The Making of the English Working Class*. Harmondsworth: Penguin, 1963.

Tillotson, Geoffrey and Donald Hawes, eds. *William Makepeace Thackeray: The Critical Heritage*. London: Routledge, 1968.

Tolstoy, Leo. *War and Peace*. Vol. 1. (1869) Translated by Rosemary Edmonds. Harmondsworth: Penguin, 1968.

Unsigned. "Boz and his *Nicholas Nickleby*." (1838) Reprinted in *Charles Dickens: The Critical Heritage*,

Unsigned. "The Caricatures of HB." *London and Westminster Review* 55 (1838).

Unsigned. "Journalism." *Fraser's Magazine* 34 (December 1846).

Unsigned. "Modern Novelists: Charles Dickens." *Westminster Review* 26 (October 1864).

Unsigned. "Our Novels: The Sensation School." *Temple Bar* 29 (April 1870): 410–24.

Unsigned. "The Royal Rhythmical Alphabets." *Punch*, August 21, 1841.

Unsigned. "The Sensational Williams." *All The Year Round,* February 13, 1864: 14–17.

Unsigned. "Things that Cannot be Done." *Household Words*, October 8, 1853.

West, Nancy. "Fantasy, Photography and the Marketplace: Oliver Wendell Holmes and the Stereoscope." *Nineteenth-Century Contexts* 19, no. 3 (1996): 231–58.

Wheatly, James H. *Patterns in Thackeray's Fiction*. Cambridge, MA: Harvard University Press, 1969.

Whipple, Edwin. "Hard Times." *Atlantic Monthly* 39 (March 1877): 353–58.

Williams, Raymond. *The Country and the City*. London: Granada, 1975.

———. "Notes on English Prose." In *Writing in Society*, 67–121. London: Verso, 1983.

———. "Radical and/or Respectable." In *The Press We Deserve*, edited by Richard Boston, 14–26. London: Routledge and Kegan Paul, 1970.

Wilson, Ben. *The Laughter of Triumph: William Hone and the Fight for the Free Press*. London: Faber and Faber, 2005.

Wohl, Anthony. *The Eternal Slum: Housing and Social Policy in Victorian London*. London: Edward Arnold, 1977.

Woloch, Alex. *The One vs. the Many: Minor Characters and the Space of the Protagonist in the Novel*. Princeton, NJ: Princeton University Press, 2003.

Wood, Gillen D'Arcy. *The Shock of the Real: Romanticism and Visual Culture, 1760–1860*. New York: Palgrave, 2001.

Wood, Marcus. *Radical Satire and Print Culture, 1790–1822*. Oxford: Oxford University Press, 1994.

Wright, John. *Mornings at Bow Street*. London: Charles Baldwyn, 1825.

INDEX

A Harlot's Progress (Hogarth), 67
advertisements, 2, 3
Altick, Richard, 2
All the World Going to See the Great Exhibition of 1851 (Cruikshank), 85
Art of Novels, 7, 12, 25, 53
Austen, Jane, 144, 145

Bagehot, Walter, 53, 62, 100, 101, 102, 119
Bailey, Peter, 62
Bakhtin, Mikhail, 8, 106, 109, 130, 167n4
Balzac, 79
Banvard's Geographical Panorama of the Mississippi and Missouri Rivers, 96
Barthes, Roland, 86, 134
Bate, Jonathan, 27
Baudelaire, 19, 34, 51, 95
Benjamin, Walter, 102
Bentham, Jeremy, 54
Blackwood's Magazine, 8
Bleak House (Dickens), 2, 21, 35, 36, 52, 53–58, 61, 62, 75, 83, 87, 90, 94, 95, 95–96, 98–99, 100–101, 102, 102–3, 104, 105–6, 107, 109–10, 113–15, 116, 122, 124, 127, 128, 129, 133, 135, 148, 149, 155, 157; Lady Dedlock, 99, 101, 103, 104, 106, 109, 110–11, 114, 122, 129, 147, 148, 153. *See also* Bagehot; Dickens; *The Novel and the Police*
Bodenheimer, Rosemarie, 151
Bourdieu, Pierre, 26, 45
Burke, 22

caricature, 4, 12, 13, 14, 16, 17, 19, 27, 30, 32, 33, 34, 35, 41, 46, 47, 48, 50. *See also* Cruikshank; Dickens; Hone; Thackeray
Carlile, 16, 27, 165n15
Chartier, Robert, 18
city, 3, 4, 10–11, 31, 38, 65, 66, 67, 71, 75, 76, 78, 79, 81, 82, 83, 85, 86, 88, 90, 92, 94, 95, 96, 99, 100, 101, 102, 107, 108, 113, 115, 116, 122, 123, 124, 129, 130, 142, 144, 147, 148, 150, 151, 152, 153, 156. *See also* Dickens; Cruikshank; London; panorama; Pierce Egan; stereoscope; Thackeray
characterization, 3, 10, 11, 31, 90, 105, 106, 107, 108, 109, 116, 153, 172n19. *See also* Alex Wolloch; Dickens; Thackeray

Cobbett, William, 8, 9, 18, 21, 24–25, 26, 27, 38, 41, 42–43, 44, 45, 58, 60, 61, 62, 63, 120. See also *Political Register*
Coriolanus Addressing the Plebeians (Cruikshank), 27–30
Crary, Jonathan, 66, 85, 88–89
Cribb, 4,
Cruikshank, George, 4, 8, 14–15, 16, 17, 19, 27–30, 32–33, 46, 51, 54, 79, 85–86, 96, 107–8; figures, 28–29. See also *All the World Going to See the Great Exhibition of 1851; Coriolanus Addressing the Plebeians; Everlasting Calendar of Popular Entertainments; The Dispersion of the Works of All Nations from the Great Exhibition of 1851; The Drunkard's Children; The Political House that Jack Built; The Worship of Bacchus;* Dickens; Hone; satire; Thackeray
Curtis, Gerard, 2

David Copperfield (Dickens), 119; David, 119, 120
Davidson, 16
de Certeau, Michel, 67, 91, 92, 116, 126, 126–27, 136, 153. See also *The Practice of Everyday Life;* Dickens
Dickens, 1, 2, 6, 7, 9, 10, 11, 15–16, 16, 18, 19, 21, 22, 24, 25, 26, 30, 31, 38, 40, 44–46, 48, 53–60, 65, 67, 83, 87, 90, 91, 92, 93, 94, 94–95, 96, 96–98, 98, 102, 105, 106, 108, 109, 114, 115, 116, 119, 120, 141, 143, 147–61, 163n12; on market, 1; on part issue, 2; on public pronouncements, 6, 9; criticism/response by press, 7–8, 61, 62, 99–100; on journalistic tradition, 8; as a novelist, 9, 64, 157; on characterization, 31–34, 49–51, 83, 90,95, 107, 109; on parliamentary debates, 38, 40–41, 46. See also *Bleak House; David Copperfield; Great Expectations; Household Words; Little Dorrit; Nicholas Nickleby; Oliver Twist; Our Mutual Friend; Pickwick Papers; Sketches by Boz; The Uncommercial Traveller;* Alex Wolloch; characterization; Dickensian aesthetic; language of radicalism; *Punch;* urban aesthetic
Dickensian aesthetic, 2, 10, 12, 16, 35, 43, 46; aesthetic, 7, 11, 19, 25, 26, 42, 54, 58, 60, 61, 62, 64, 92, 93, 100. See also Dickens; urban aesthetic
Dickens and the Popular Radical Imagination (Ledger), 9, 22, 58–59
Discipline and Punishment (Foucault), 136
Dobbin, William, 98
Doyle, Richard, 19
Dr. Ferrier, 113
Dr. Sutherland, 113
Duke of Wellington, 19, 20

Edinburgh Review, 8, 111
Egan, Pierce, 4, 65–66, 75, 78, 79–83, 90, 92, 109, 131, 150, 152. See also Dickens; *Life in London*
Elias Norbert, 151
English Literary History, 9
Epstein, James, 8, 13, 22. See also radical expression
Everlasting Calendar of Popular Entertainments (Cruikshank), 30

Feltes, N. N., 2
Fielding, 4
Fitzgerald, Edward, 14
Foucault, Michel, 136, 138. See also *Discipline and Punishment; History of Sexuality Volume I*
Fraser's Magazine, 39

Gallagher, Catherine, 30, 118, 122, 142, 143
Gillray, James, 15, 26
Gilmartin, Kevin, 19, 38
Gin Lane (Hogarth), 96, 97
Goldsmith, 4,
Goodlad, Lauren, 113
Gray, Donald, 73
Great Exhibition, 55, 85, 86
Great Expectations (Dickens), 116, 117–26, 128–30, 132, 133–40, 141, 144,

149, 152, 155, 173n7; Pip, 32, 49–50, 116, 117, 118–26, 128–30, 132, 133–35, 137, 138, 139, 144, 148, 153; Mrs. Pocket, 117–18; Joe, 120–22; Magwitch, 123–24, 125, 128, 132, 133, 137–38, 144

Harrison, Ainsworth, 4
Henkin, David, 75
History of Sexuality Volume I (Foucault), 136
Hogarth, William, 3–4, 10, 65, 67–78, 79, 83, 94, 94–95, 96, 141, 150, 152, 155, 156; figures, 69, 70, 72, 77, 97. See also *A Harlot's Progress*; *Gin Lane*; *Industry and Idleness*
Hone, William, 4, 8, 9, 14, 16, 17, 18, 19, 21, 24, 27–30, 33, 51, 54, 58, 60, 61, 62, 64; on journalistic tradition, 8; trial, 20, 58, 59–60; *Coriolanus*, 27–30. See also *The Political House that Jack Built*; Cruikshank
Horner, Thomas, 83–84, 90, 91. See also panorama
Household Words (Dickens), 86, 88
Hughes, Robert, 137. See also *The Fatal Shore*
Hunt, 27
hybridizing, 2, 3, 4, 94, 157, 161

Industry and Idleness, 3, 10, 67–78, 91, 94, 102, 133, 150, 152, 153. See also Hogarth

Jaffe, Audrey, 90–91, 159
Jack Shepherd, 3, 4
James, Henry, 107
Jerrold, Douglas, 13, 15, 18, 19, 20–21, 23–24, 25, 34, 34–35, 37, 52, 54, 55
John Halifax Gentleman, 119
Jones, Gareth Stedman, 19
Jules Janin, 89

Kathryn Chittick, 7
Krauss, Rosalind, 88
Kristeva, Julia, 57

language of radicalism, 9, 10, 19, 21, 27, 40, 58, 60, 64, 120, 122. See also Gareth Stedman Jones; Dickens; radical, satire; Thackeray
Leech, John, 15
Le Diable boiteux (Lesage), 89
Lewes, George Henry, 106
Life in London (Egan), 4, 65–66, 75, 78, 79–83, 90, 127, 150, 153
Linebaugh, Peter, 74–75
Little Dorrit (Dickens), 8, 21, 36, 38, 40, 41, 45–46, 51, 58, 116, 117
London, 3, 10, 66, 68, 71, 75, 76, 78, 79, 81, 82, 83, 84, 85, 86, 87, 90, 91, 92, 94, 98, 99, 100, 101, 107, 109, 112, 117, 118, 122, 123, 124, 125, 127, 128, 129, 135, 142, 144, 147, 148, 150, 152, 153, 158, 159, 160, 161. See also Dickens; city; Thackeray
Lord Chamberlain, 36
Lord Chancellor, 19, 35, 54, 56
Lord Eldon, 51
Lord Ellenborough, 21, 59
Lord Palmerston, 119

Malthus, 24–25, 41, 120
Mansfield Park (Austen), 145
Marcus, Stephen, 89
market, 2, 4, 8, 16, 17, 144, 157, 161; book market, 1; print market, 3, 4, 6, 17, 21, 30, 74, 110; circulation, 32, 33, 75, 83, 84, 85, 95, 100, 110, 111, 122, 141, 142, 144, 145, 146, 148. See also city; Dickens; Thackeray
Marriot, John, 79, 81
Mayhew, Henry, 86, 98
McCalman, Iain, 16
Meisel, Martin, 2–3
Mill, John Stuart, 40–41
Miller, D. A., 53, 94. See also *The Novel and the Police*
Mitchell, W. T. J., 22, 27
Morning Post, 102
Mornings at Bow Street (Wright), 66
Morris, Pam, 142
Mulock, Dinah, 119

National Review, 62

Nicholas Nickleby (Dickens), 8
"Night Walks," 125
Nord, Deborah Epstein, 90, 94
Northern Star, 16
nursery rhyme, 4, 16, 18

Oliver Twist (Dickens), 7, 8
On Liberty, 16
Our Mutual Friend (Dickens), 83, 90, 141–61
Osborne, George, 95, 98
Ottermann, 85

Paine, Thomas, 8, 15, 16, 19–20, 21, 25, 26, 38, 54; on journalistic tradition, 8
Pall Mall Gazette, 36
panorama, 10, 65, 78, 83, 84, 85, 86, 87, 88, 90, 91, 94, 96, 98. *See also* city; Thomas Horner; Cruikshank; Dickens; urban aesthetic
parliament, 9, 19; parliamentary, 32, 38, 39, 40, 46
Peterloo massacre, 16, 27
Pendennis (Thackeray), 11, 36–37, 39, 39–40, 51, 54, 116, 117, 118, 124, 127–28, 130–33; Pen, 117, 127, 128, 130–31, 132, 134
Pickwick Papers (Dickens), 1, 2, 8; Pickwick, 32
Political Register (Cobbett), 42
political journalism, 4
Pride and Prejudice (Austen), 145
Punch, 6, 13, 15, 16, 17, 18–19, 19, 20, 23, 25, 37, 46, 52, 92. *See also* Dickens; Thackeray

Quarterly Review, 24, 59, 61

radical: expression, 8–9, 9, 10, 13, 17, 18, 36, 46, 57, 65; journalism, 8, 15, 16, 17, 23, 54, 63, 64, 115; style, 19–20, 21, 24, 40; language, 21, 22, 24, 34, 42, 64; response in press, 60–61. *See also* Dickens; Epstein; satire
Reform Bill (1832), 13
Rowlandson, 51

satire, 8, 9; graphic and visual, 4, 8, 9, 26–27, 31, 33, 34–35, 46–48, 50, 51, 55, 56; political, 9, 13; radical, 9, 15, 17, 19, 34. *See also* Cruikshank; Dickens; Hone; Thackeray
Saturday Review, 61
Seymour, 51
Shakespeare, 108, 109
Shelley, Rice, 66
Shillingsburg, Peter, 6
Simon, John, 109, 112; *Annual Report,* 112, 113
Sketches by Boz (Dickens), 31–32, 33–34, 90, 91–92, 159; Boz, 62, 90, 91, 92, 159
Smiles, Samuel, 119
Smith, Olivia, 20, 39, 42
Smollet, 4,
Southey, Robert, 61, 62, 63
Spectator, 7–8
Stephen, James Fitzjames, 24, 62–64, 169n54
stereoscope, 10, 65, 78, 88, 89, 90, 94, 98, 99
Sterne, Lawrence, 4, 63, 64
Swift, 63

Tambling, Jeremy, 135–36
Temple Bar, 111, 112
Terdiman, Richard, 41, 100
Thackeray, William Mackepeace, 4–7, 10, 11, 13–15, 18, 25, 30–31, 32–33, 36–38, 39–40, 43–44, 46–48, 51–52, 54, 65, 92–93, 95, 98, 99, 103–4, 116, 118, 127, 130–33, 164n13, 164n17; magazine work, 4, 6; on Art of Novels, 7, 12, 25–26; on Dickens, 7; on realism and Nature, 7, 12, 26; on journalistic tradition, 8, 13–15; on radical expression, 10, 13, 15, 36–38, 39–40; on *Punch,* 6, 13, 15, 25, 37, 92; on Cruikshank, 14–15; characterization, 31, 32–33, 34; on graphic satire, 46–48. *See also Pendennis; The Newcomes; Vanity Fair;* caricature; city; characterization; language of radicalism; urban aesthetic
The Book of Snobs, 19
The Circumlocution Office, 8, 40, 41

The Dispersion of the Works of All Nations from the Great Exhibition of 1851 (Cruikshank), 85
The Drunkard's Children (Cruikshank), 96
The Fatal Shore (Hughes), 137
The Political House that Jack Built (Hone), 4, 9, 16–17, 47. *See also* Hone
The Political Showman (Cruikshank), 19
The Practice of Everyday Life (de Certeau), 67, 127
The Mysteries of Paris, 112
The Newcomes (Thackeray), 11, 39, 46–47, 47–48
The Novel and the Police (Miller), 53
The One vs. The Many (Wolloch), 106–7
The Revelations of London, 112
The Rights of Man (Paine), 22, 23–24
The Uncommercial Traveller (Dickens), 159
The Worship of Bacchus (Cruikshank), 85
Thompson, E. P., 22–23
Tillotson, Kathleen and John Butt, 1–2
Times, 102, 112, 113
Tolstoy, Leo, 42–43

urban aesthetic, 11, 65, 75, 78, 79–81, 82, 87, 88, 90, 95, 96, 99, 102, 108, 114, 115, 122, 128, 134, 135, 140, 141–42, 143, 144, 147, 150, 156; aesthetic, 112, 112–13, 116, 123, 128. *See also* Dickens; Thackeray; panorama

Vanity Fair (Thackeray), 11, 30–31, 36, 37–38, 42, 44, 47, 48, 51–52, 54, 94, 95, 96, 98, 102, 103–4, 104–5, 105, 117; Becky, 47, 98, 102, 103–4, 109

War and Peace (Tolstoy), 42–43
Westminster Review, 15–16, 57, 59, 61, 64, 157
Whipple, Edwin, 62
Williams, Raymond, 25, 99
Wilson, Ben, 60

www.ingramcontent.com/pod-product-compliance
Lightning Source LLC
Chambersburg PA
CBHW020947230426
43666CB00005B/215